DEBT PROBLEMS OF EASTERN EUROPE

T0328489

SOVIET AND EAST EUROPEAN STUDIES

Editorial Board

JULIAN COOPER, RON HILL, MICHAEL KASER, PAUL LEWIS,
MARTIN McCAULEY, FRED SINGLETON, STEPHEN WHITE

The National Association for Soviet and East European Studies exists for the purpose of promoting study and research on the social sciences as they relate to the Soviet Union and the countries of Eastern Europe. The Monograph Series is intended to promote the publication of works presenting substantial and original research in the economics, politics, sociology and modern history of the USSR and Eastern Europe.

SOVIET AND EAST EUROPEAN STUDIES

DEBT PROBLEMS OF EASTERN EUROPE

ILIANA ZLOCH-CHRISTY

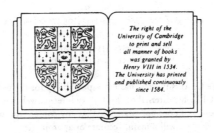

The right of the
University of Cambridge
to print and sell
all manner of books
was granted by
Henry VIII in 1534.
The University has printed
and published continuously
since 1584.

CAMBRIDGE UNIVERSITY PRESS

CAMBRIDGE

NEW YORK NEW ROCHELLE MELBOURNE SYDNEY

CAMBRIDGE UNIVERSITY PRESS
Cambridge, New York, Melbourne, Madrid, Cape Town, Singapore,
São Paulo, Delhi, Dubai, Tokyo, Mexico City

Cambridge University Press
The Edinburgh Building, Cambridge CB2 8RU, UK

Published in the United States of America by Cambridge University Press, New York

www.cambridge.org
Information on this title: www.cambridge.org/9780521169318

First published 1987
First paperback edition 2011

A catalogue record for this publication is available from the British Library

Library of Congress Cataloguing in Publication data
Zloch-Christy, Iliana, 1953–
Debt problems of Eastern Europe.
(Soviet and East European studies)
Bibliography: p.
1. Debts, External – Europe, Eastern.   2. Foreign
exchange problem – Europe, Eastern.   1. Title.
11. Series.
HJ8615.Z57   1988   336.3′435′0947   87–11634

ISBN 978-0-521-33542-3 Hardback
ISBN 978-0-521-16931-8 Paperback

To
DANIELA,
FRANK HOLZMAN,
and
ALEXANDER VAN DER BELLEN

Contents

Figures and tables

Figures

Tables*

Text

* Minor discrepancies between constituent figures and totals in the tables and the charts are due to rounding.

Appendix

Preface

Over the past few years much concern has been expressed over the convertible-currency debt problems of Eastern Europe.* The Soviet Union and its allies contracted massive debts to the West during the 1970s. Gross convertible-currency debt increased from $8.3 billion in 1970 to $77.1 billion in 1979 and peaked at $92.8 billion in 1981. Poland and Romania suspended payments to Western creditors in 1981. Hungary and the GDR experienced a serious liquidity crisis in early 1982. The Eastern European debt problem marked the beginning of the international debt crisis that by the end of 1982 had engulfed many other countries, especially in Latin America.

Purpose

The purpose of this book is to analyze the post-1970s development of the Eastern European convertible-currency debt. Five key questions are addressed:

1. What are the main external and internal origins of the indebtedness?
2. Were (and are) convertible-currency debt difficulties inherent in the economic development of Eastern Europe during the 1970s and the 1980s?
3. How has CMEA adjustment to external disturbances affected the national economies?

* The terms "Eastern Europe," "CMEA," "Comecon," and "centrally planned economies" are used as synonyms. Eastern Europe refers to the Soviet Union and the six smaller European members of CMEA, also called the Eastern European Six, i.e., Bulgaria, Czechoslovakia, German Democratic Republic (GDR), Hungary, Poland, and Romania.

4. What policies have Western commercial banks, governments, and international financial institutions taken toward resolving Eastern European debt problems?
5. What is the outlook for convertible-currency debt in the late 1980s?

Structure

After a brief discussion of illiquidity, insolvency, and debt repudiation (see "Note on state creditworthiness"), the book divides naturally into eight chapters. Chapter 1 explores the systemic roots of convertible-currency debt problems in centrally planned economies. It focuses on the problems of the economic system, development strategies, foreign trade behavior, and the balance-of-payments experience in centrally planned economies, the impact of external disturbances on their macroeconomic policy, and the correlation between international borrowing and investment activity.

The following chapters turn specifically to the analysis of Eastern European debt in the seventies and the eighties. Chapter 2 examines debt trends, asking three main questions:

1. Were the debt difficulties ones of insolvency or of illiquidity?
2. What were the internal and the external origins of the debt?
3. How did macroeconomic policy adjust to the balance-of-payments disequilibrium and how will that effect economic development in Eastern Europe until the end of 1980s?

Chapter 3 concerns the Polish and Romanian debt reschedulings, whereas Chapter 4 discusses the role of international financial institutions – the International Monetary Fund, the Bank for International Settlements, and the World Bank – in resolving the debt problems of Hungary, Poland, and Romania. Chapter 5 examines the policy strategies of the CMEA borrowers and their Western creditors. Methodologies for assessing risk in lending to Eastern Europe are considered in Chapter 6. Chapter 7 analyses the prospects of CMEA debt in the late 1980s, collectively and by country, using a computer model. The analysis focuses on this fundamental question: Are the Eastern European debt problems manageable in the medium term? Finally, Chapter 8 discusses the financing of East–West trade and summarizes the main findings of the study.

Acknowledgments

In preparing this study I received help and encouragement from many sources. The volume could never have been written without the intellectual support of the Russian Research Center at Harvard and the External Debt Division of the World Bank. For financial aid during the earlier stages of my work, I thank the Austrian Federal Ministry of Science and Research, the Oesterreichische Postsparkasse, the Austrian Federal Chamber of Commerce, the Oesterreichische Kontrollbank, and the Wilson International Center for Scholars in Washington, D.C.

Most of the ideas presented here were first developed in discussions and seminars with my colleagues and teachers at Harvard. Detailed advice and comments from Frank Holzman, Joe Berliner, Abram Bergson, Marshall Goldman, Janos Kornai, and Kent Osband are gratefully acknowledged.

I am very grateful to Nicholas Hope for his generous patience in reviewing drafts of the study and for valuable discussions. I would like to thank, also Mark Allen, Timothy King, Lee Kjelleren, Bela Loederer, Paul Marer, Martin Schrenk, Jozef M. van Brabant, and two anonymous readers for carefully reviewing an earlier draft and for making numerous suggestions for improvement. Daniel Bond, Ed Hewett, Klaus Schroeder, Jan Vanous, and Thomas Wolf provided helpful advice and criticism. Ibrahim Levent assisted me with the computer programming. I am, of course, responsible for any remaining errors.

None has influenced my thinking and my work more than, or provided as much support and inspiration over so long a period as, Frank Holzman and my former dissertation advisor, Alexander Van der Bellen. My debt to them can never be repaid, but I hope that they know how much their efforts have been appreciated. My daughter Daniela also was an important source of inspiration in completing my work. To her and to my teachers I have dedicated this book.

Washington, DC

Note on state creditworthiness

State creditworthiness depends on the ability of an economy to generate sufficient resources to maintain service payments on outstanding external debt and on continued access to routine refinancing of normal levels of short- and long-term external debt. It must be judged mainly by analyzing the balance of payments, since domestic resources have to be transformed into foreign exchange earnings. Such an analysis provides the answer to the question of whether a debtor nation is able to generate enough of a transferable surplus and earn sufficient foreign exchange to service its debt within a prescribed period of time (Holzman 1981, p. 166). The willingness of the borrowing country to service its debt has to be considered as well. Three types of creditworthiness risk are involved in loans to sovereign states: *illiquidity, insolvency,* and *repudiation.* Each results in a default on a contractual obligation: the first two from an inability to service, the third from an unwillingness to service. These key terms are explained below, in order to provide the background for a more formal approach to the indebtedness of the Eastern European countries.*

Illiquidity

Analyses of corporate debt typically distinguish between a firm that has a positive net worth but cannot meet its present bills and one that has a negative net worth and faces bankruptcy. The first is called "illiquid," the second "insolvent." If a firm is merely illiquid

* Normal lending risks in the market economies are project risk, unless and until the whole nation experiences an economic management and external payments crisis. The risk to lenders to the centrally planned economies in Eastern Europe is always a country risk problem rather than a project risk problem (see discussion Chapter 6). Because all projects are contracted with state organizations, the Eastern European country will meet its debt obligations even if the specific projects fail.

additional lending is appropriate to tide it over short-term debt difficulties.

The same concept can be applied to sovereign states. If the debt problems of a country can be solved over the short term, it has only illiquidity difficulties (Clausen 1983, p. 5). That means the debtor country can service its debt comfortably over the medium to long term but not in the short term. To analyze whether the debtor country is illiquid or has more difficult problems, it is necessary to examine the prospective path of the balance of payments over the medium term. The operational concept here is the potential or *ex ante* balance of payments, given minimally acceptable growth rates. If the prospective deficits show an improving trend, then the appropriate diagnosis of a country's debt problem is one of illiquidity (Cline 1984, p. 40).

Insolvency

When the state is unable to fulfill its financial obligations to its creditors over an extended period it is essentially insolvent. Response to state insolvency can take various forms. The state can reduce the rates of interest paid or postpone payments for some period, or it can reduce principal obligations, by postponing repayments, by transforming the obligation into a different type, or by reducing the capital amount of its debt. As in the case of state illiquidity, to analyze whether the debtor country is insolvent, it is necessary to examine the prospective path of its balance of payments. If the *ex ante* balance of payments, given minimally acceptable growth rates, shows such a large external deficit that there is no viable way it can be financed over the medium term (taking into account the restricted borrowing possibilities on the international financial markets), then the country's debt problem can be defined as one of insolvency. The basic approach of such a quantitative analysis is to determine whether underlying trends are leading toward improvement or deterioration of the external payments situation.

Repudiation

"Repudiation" can be defined as a complete cessation of payments, usually with an express declaration by the debtor country that it refuses to admit the binding character of an obligation. It may be expected to occur mainly when a country's authorities themselves feel that their country is essentially insolvent, so that the policies required to service the debt are too economically or politically costly for the country to bear. A repudiation may extend to the debt as a whole, to some part of it, or to its contractual terms. Repudiations have often followed revolutions, when the new government has repudiated obligations contracted by a previous de jure or de facto government, alleging that the prior government had no authority to bind the nation.

In today's international community, where interdependence is ever-deepening, the risk of outright debt repudiation by a debtor country has seemingly lessened, irrespective of the politicoeconomic bloc to which that country belongs. Debt repudiation could mean that the debtor country will be politically and economically isolated for a very long time.

It is obvious that state illiquidity, insolvency, and repudiation in international financial relations differ from the international laws applying to private illiquidity, insolvency, or repudiation from which they have taken their names. Under private law, insolvency is established by easily determinable facts or events, and results either in a compromise with creditors or in judicial proceeding, culminating in a decree that authorizes the creditors to liquidate the assets of the bankrupt firm and recover their assets so far as possible. In state illiquidity, insolvency, or repudiation, there is no judicial proceeding resulting in a decree. The debtor country is subject to no judicial forums, and cannot be compelled to pay, except through its need for renewed access to credit or through diplomatic or other political pressure to change its domestic policies in order to service its external debt. It has to be stressed, however, that, in contrast with a bankrupt firm, changes in an apparently insolvent country's policies, as well as in external political and economic circumstances, can lead to a restoration of creditworthiness. For economic, political, or moral reasons, an illiquid, insolvent, or repudiating sovereign state usually endeavors to effect a compromise with its creditors to ensure that its credit standing and reputation do not suffer too greatly.

Abbreviations and symbols

Abbreviations

BIS	Bank for International Settlements
CMEA	Council for Mutual Economic Assistance
CPE	centrally planned economies
DME	developed market economies
ECE	Economic Commission for Europe
EEC	European Economic Community
EIB	European Investment Bank
IBEC	International Bank for Economic Cooperation
IBRD	International Bank for Reconstruction and Development
IIB	International Investment Bank
GATT	General Agreement on Tariffs and Trade
GDP	gross domestic product
GNP	gross national product
IMF	International Monetary Fund
LDC	less developed country
LIBOR	London interbank offered rate
NIC	newly industrialized country
NMP	net material product
OECD	Organization for Economic Cooperation and Development
OPEC	Organization of Petroleum Exporting Countries
SDR	special drawing rights
UN	United Nations
UNCTAD	United Nations Conference on Trade and Development
WEFA	Wharton Econometric Forecasting Associates

Symbols

n.a.	not available
—	nil or negligible

1

Economic growth, external disturbances, and macroeconomic adjustment in Eastern Europe

The current debt problems of the Eastern European countries have deep systemic roots. This chapter discusses from a theoretical standpoint problems of economic growth and investment policy in centrally planned economies, the influence of external disturbances and of adjustment policies, and the correlation between borrowing in the international financial markets and investment ("the debt cycle"). The main question addressed is as follows: What are the systemic factors that cause convertible-currency debt difficulties to be inherent in the economic development of Eastern Europe at present?

Economic system, policies, and the convertible-currency trade balance

There is no single comprehensive theory of the functioning of communist centrally planned economies. In its stead are hundreds of books and thousands of articles that discuss certain regularities of the Eastern European economies.[1] The theoretical approach to economic growth, investment activity, foreign trade performance, and balance-of-payments problems in Eastern Europe, as discussed in this chapter, is based primarily on the works of Kornai, Holzman, Portes, and Kalecki.

---

[1] Brus (1973); Goldmann and Kouba (1969); Gregory (1981); Holzman (1974, 1979); Kalecki (1969); Kornai (1959, 1972, 1980, 1982); Lange (1961); Nove (1977); Wiles (1962); and many others.

Kornai (1984) distinguishes four phases in the development of the centrally planned economies:

1. the *heroic-enthusiastic phase* (rapid nationalization, confiscation, and radical redistribution of private wealth);
2. the *bureaucratic-hierarchical command economy*;
3. reform processes, evolving in the direction of *less centralized market socialism*; and
4. *mature market socialism*.

Ignoring the significant differences among the Eastern European countries due to differences in historical background, culture, size, national economic and foreign policy, and so on, the current stage of their economic development most nearly fits the second of the above-mentioned types: the bureaucratic-hierarchical command economy.

The main features of the bureaucratic-hierarchical centrally planned economy are the following:

state ownership of the means of production;

detailed central plans for enterprise inputs, outputs, and foreign trade;

financial plans that mirror the physical flows embodied in the quantitative plans;

information flows and bargaining over plans and actual access to resources, which occur mainly in a bureaucratic rather than a market setting;

rigid prices set by the central authorities to facilitate quantitative planning and evaluation;

plan fulfillment, rather than profit, as the main evaluative criterion for enterprises;

a relatively free labor market, but regulated wages from the center;

a monolithic state banking system with no fractional reserve banking; and

a dichotomized money supply in which household and enterprise money stocks are strictly separated.

Hungary is the only Eastern European centrally planned economy that could be considered as having "less centralized market socialism" (Kornai) or a "modified planned economy" (Wolf), especially if the recent economic reforms (1982, 1985) are successfully implemented in the years to come. According to Wolf

(1985a, pp. 115-23), the "modified planned economy" has the following features:

Detailed inputs and outputs are no longer developed in close consultation with the central authorities.

Enterprise profitability is meant to supplant plan fulfillment.

Information flows and bargaining over plans occur significantly in a market setting, and encouragement is given to the market as an allocator of resources.

The system of wage regulation gives the enterprises much greater leeway in determining the distribution and growth of wages among their employees.

Price controls are reduced in scope.

More direct export-oriented linkages are encouraged between domestic enterprises and foreign markets.

Domestic and foreign currency prices for a wide range of products are linked.

Bank credits and enterprise self-financing become much more important in financing of domestic investment.

The "privatization" of economic activity, particularly in the handicraft, service, and other sectors, is increased.

Kornai (1980) describes the centrally planned economies in Eastern Europe as "economies of shortage." Shortage,[2] in Kornai's analysis, is a summary description of a large group of phenomena, including chronic excess demand and forced adjustment (forced substitution and saving, rationing, queuing, etc.). Shortage is a basic form of persistent imbalance in the centrally planned economies, and Kornai (1984, pp. 14-16) classifies the main shortages as being in:

investment (characterized by a lack of investment resources and by investment "hunger" at all levels of bureaucratic hierarchy in the CMEA-planned economies),
labor (Kornai 1980, pp. 252-4),
imported goods,
convertible foreign currency,
foreign credit,

---

[2] What Kornai calls "shortage" is called by other economists "overall excess demand," "repressed inflation," "persistent overheating," "sellers' market," etc.

household consumer goods (in groups of commodities or in the
    assortment of supply),
household services (telephone, repair, public transport, retail trade,
    health and education, cultural services, etc.), and
private production activities (machines, spare parts, equipment,
    building materials, etc.).

All of these shortages are linked. The policymakers in the centrally planned economies have a certain freeedom to "reallocate" shortages (i.e., lacks of goods and services), since they are able to reassign the availability of goods and services. For example, machine shortages can be eased or even eliminated by imports, which in turn increases the chronic shortage of (convertible) foreign currency. As Kornai has said (1980, p. 39), shortage in the centrally planned economies breeds shortage. The forced reallocation of shortages may multiply and spill over to the whole economy.

The shortage phenomenon is closely associated with surpluses. Excess demand and excess supply at the aggregate level are not mutually exclusive. The seller's market creates surpluses of unwanted goods and services. Usually the products in Eastern Europe are "distributed" via the plan rather than "sold" (Holzman 1979, p. 300).

Shortages are closely associated with another characteristic of surplus in the centrally planned economies: hoarding of excessively large stocks of inputs on the user's (buyer's) side, prompted by unpredictability of deliveries, resulting mainly from inadequate inventory control on the side of the suppliers, who tend to hold small stocks of goods not always well-adapted to the needs of the buyer. Another linkage between shortage and surplus can develop from bottlenecks for some inputs, which lead to underutilization of some complementary inputs that are available at the time.

Economic growth model

The way in which shortages impact on the economies of Eastern Europe has important implication for their growth. Pursuit of rapid growth tends to intensify shortages, especially of investment goods. To see why, consider the Kalecki economic growth model, which appears at first sight to differ only slightly from the Harrod–Domar-type models known in the West, and expresses the correlations of individual growth factors with the increment in the national income. National income comprises the following components:

productive investment, that is, investment in equipment for the production of goods, machinery, and buildings;

increases in inventories, meaning the value of the increment in capital and stocks;

nonproductive investment, those "which do not contribute to the production of goods" (Kalecki, 1972, p. 3) – residential buildings, hotels, hospitals, and so on;

collective consumption, which includes noninvestment goods consumed by central and local government, and enterprises producing services not included in the national income (education, administration, etc.);

individual consumption; and

exports less imports (Kalecki 1972, p. 4).

Kalecki calls the sum of productive investment and increases in inventories "productive accumulation," and the sum of nonproductive investment and consumption "consumption in the broad sense." This concept of the national income differs from the Western concept in its exclusion of services (transportation, internal trade, etc.).[3] This approach was officially adopted in the Soviet Union after the period of "new economic policy" in the late 1920s and is now used by all of the Eastern European countries.[4]

In Kalecki's theory[5] the growth r of the national income in a given year is

$$r = \frac{1}{m} \frac{I}{Y} - a + u,$$

where

I = productive investment,
Y = national income,
m = capital-output ratio,

[3] Kalecki writes that, for the study of economic dynamics, the treatment of national income as production of goods offers advantages (Kalecki 1972, p. 2.).
[4] For an analysis of the national income accounts of centrally planned economies see, e.g., Bergson and Heymann (1954) and Bergson (1961).
[5] Because of space limitation, I do not describe here all the definitions and assumptions of the Kalecki model; see Kalecki (1972, pp. 1–10).

a = coefficient for amortizaton ("parameter of depreciation"), and

u = coefficient representing improvements in the production process leading with existing equipment to higher output (a "technological progress" factor).

This equation conveys the essential part of Kalecki's growth model of the socialist economy. (Inventory accumulation is disregarded for simplicity.) It determines the growth rate as a function of productive investment, the incremental capital–output ratio, amortization, and improvements in such areas of the production process as the organization of labor, the economical use of raw materials, and so on. Kalecki stresses in his analysis of the rate of economic growth the importance of the share of productive accumulation, and especially of productive investment in the national income. Increased growth requires that investment grow more rapidly than national income (Kalecki 1972, pp. 105–6).[6]

Some aspects of the economic growth patterns in the centrally planned economies, which are closely correlated with the disequilibrium of their balance of trade and balance of payments and, in turn, with their debt problems, are discussed in the sections that follow. The discussion focuses on the problems of forced growth, investment "hunger," and investment cycles.

Forced growth and investment "hunger"

In the centrally planned economies high increments in production are planned. The growth patterns are characterized by the following main trends:

The medium-term growth rate of productive accumulation is maximized rather than the long-term growth rate of consumption.

Productive investment is given priority over nonproductive investment.

Manufacturing, especially heavy industry, is given priority over all other sectors of the economy.

Large enterprises are given priority over medium or smaller units,

---

[6] The usual formulation of the objective of the centrally planned economies in Eastern Europe is "maximizing the growth rates," which may be a constant growth rate rather than an ever-increasing one. Major policy goals of the CPEs typically have included maximizing the growth rate of the capital stock.

even in areas where the medium or small size would be certainly more efficient.

Kornai calls the above-mentioned growth pattern *"forced growth"* or *"rush growth"* (1980, p. 42). The economic development strategy of the Eastern European countries has been oriented primarily toward creating domestic industries, with national or intra-CMEA considerations guiding the development targets since the beginning of the 1950s. This strategy does not focus on an industrial base that is competitive by world market standards. It aims mainly at import substitution in consumer, intermediate, and capital goods production.

The roots of this development strategy in the Eastern European Six lie in transplanting to these countries the highly centralized Soviet system of planning and management that evolved in the early 1950s, the period that saw the creation of the political and economic community of the Soviet bloc. A policy of rapid industrialization was applied to countries that differ from the Soviet Union in their size, culture, natural and human resources, and historical traditions. In the 1950s and the 1960s, the Eastern European Six and the Soviet Union relied on domestic savings and intrabloc bilateral credits to finance ambitious industrial investment targets. In the 1970s, they relied also on hard-currency credits from abroad, as discussed in Chapter 2. Foreign trade was diverted after 1950 to the intrabloc market, and the traditional links of Eastern European Six with the world economy were cut. The Soviet Union became the main supplier of raw materials and capital investment goods. All CMEA countries aimed at creating an industrial base and reducing import dependence on the West. By pursuing this development strategy in the individual countries, not only world market considerations but even considerations about the intra-CMEA economic relations very often took second place. The results of this economic growth policy have led to currently similar industrial bases, with a duplication of productive capacity, a product mix comprising predominantly "soft" goods (which could not be sold easily and profitably on the Western markets, by contrast with "hard" goods), and a concentration on "soft" goods in intra-CMEA trade.

The policy of increasing investment in industrial production for domestic absorption has characterized the development strategies

not only of Eastern Europe but also of many developing countries
since the end of World War II. Although there are significant differences in the political and economic structure of the Eastern
European communist countries and the developing countries
(many of which themselves differ considerably in size, political
regime, growth rates, etc.), for simplicity compare the experience of
the group of the newly industrialized countries (NICs) in Latin
America and East Asia. The NICs in Latin America (e.g., Brazil,
Mexico, and Argentina) pursued mainly inward-oriented development policies focused on import substitution and the creation of an
industrial base to satisfy domestic markets; the NICs of East Asia
(e.g., Korea, Taiwan, Singapore, Hong Kong), on the other hand,
aimed at outward-oriented strategies of export promotion and the
creation of an industrial base that is competitive by world market standards.

Eastern Europe's development strategies are closer to those of the
Latin American NICs; the development policy of Eastern Europe as
a region might be considered as inward-oriented. It has to be
stressed, however, that this generalization refers to the development strategies of the six individual CMEA countries as well; for the
Soviet Union, however, the comparator is less clear.

The emphasis on growth

To "maximize the growth rate" of national income, the fulfillment
of certain requirements for balanced and harmonious growth is disregarded in the CMEA countries. The established proportions of
different sectors of the economy change extremely slowly. Occasional corrections are made, but those are usually only marginal.
The enterprises are given "taut" targets by the central planning
authorities, but these are too high to be achieved, given the available resources (Holzman 1979, p. 299).

Investment "hunger." The investment policy in Eastern Europe is
characterized by expansion drive and investment "hunger." These
can be observed in all levels of the bureaucratic hierarchy – government agencies, nonprofit organizations, political institutions in
charge of economic affairs, and so on. The political leadership in
the CMEA countries gives very high priority to the growth objectives, but the middle levels of the hierarchy may have even stronger

incentives to invest, even when, for some reason (e.g., external disturbances), the top leadership favors less investment (Kornai 1984, p. 28).

Investment tension. On the whole the centrally planned economy is characterized by a tension in the investment sphere, stemming from the almost limitless claims for resources from all levels of the hierarchy. That is one side of the problem of investment policy in Eastern Europe. An important and closely correlated feature of investment is that decisionmakers are not concerned about the financial risk of their investments (Korani 1982, p. 51). The chronic shortages ensure that virtually all products will be sold sooner or later.

The lack of self-imposed restraint on the demand for investment resources and the absence of personal responsibility are two of the main characteristics of the investment policy in the centrally planned economies. At a microeconomic level, the investment decision-makers are not concerned about the financial state of the firm, its present and future profits and earnings, the condition of the state budget, or the anticipated constraints on sales and price signals (Kornai 1982, p. 53). This leads to overambitious investment decisions, and frequently no consideration is given to the availability of resources and the conditions in the world economy. A comparative analysis (Komai 1982, p. 138) of the annual rates of investment in four CMEA countries (Bulgaira, GDR, Hungary, and Poland) and seven industrialized Western countries (Austria, Denmark, Finland, Greece, Ireland, Italy, and Spain) in the period 1968-72 and 1973-77 shows that the Western countries slowed down considerably their growth rates of investment in the second period, whereas some of the Eastern European countries increased theirs (Bulgaria, Hungary) and others (GDR, Poland) slightly decreased them. Pessimistic expectations about future sales prospects (among many other factors) may have influenced investment policy in the Western countries; but the CMEA countries did not seriously consider the adverse impact that the global economic developments of 1973-7 (the oil shock and its aftermath) would have on their economies.

Ex ante estimates. A systemic bias in *ex ante* estimates of investment costs is also characteristic of investment planning in Eastern Europe. In most cases, a modest proposal from the enterprises is better accepted by the authorities; therefore, very often the full costs of individual investment projects are consciously understated while returns are overestimated. Once accepted by the authorities, however, it is difficult to stop the proposed investment at a later stage. If financial losses are suffered after the implementation of the investment project (e.g., excessive investment or operating costs, lower-than-anticipated selling prices), the deficit will be covered by the state budget. This "softness" of the budget (and project) constraint[7] in the centrally planned economies appears not so much in current expenditures as in investment activities. The lack of personal responsibility by the investment decisionmakers contributes to that. Because a large group of people is involved in making decisions, when an investment project fails, all members of the decision group in the bureaucratic hierarchy have an incentive to disguise the failure by "softening" the enterprise's budget constraint.

Investment cycles

Growth cycles. Another important aspect of investment activity in Eastern Europe is its cyclical character. In the centrally planned economies a succession of "stop-go" policies may be observed. Accelerated economic growth and investment are followed by decelerations, or sometimes by contractions. This means that the phenomenon of *cyclical fluctuations,* widely regarded as a phenomenon of market economies, does exist in the CMEA countries. Since the mid-1960s, Eastern European economists have detected fluctuations in their economies. The so-called growth cycles or quasicycles have attracted considerable attention, and several scholars in both the East and West[8] have attempted to provide a theoretical explanation for their existence.

The theories of growth cycles can be classified mainly in the following groups:

---

[7] Kornai writes that the state in Eastern Europe acts as a "general insurance company" (1984, p. 32).
[8] It is not my goal to analyze the theoretical attempts of scholars in both the East and West regarding the problem of investment cycles in the centrally planned economies. Some of the interesting publications on this issue: Bauer (1978); Goldmann and Kouba (1969); Kornai (1980); Kyn, Schrettl, and Slama (1979); and Marrese (1981).

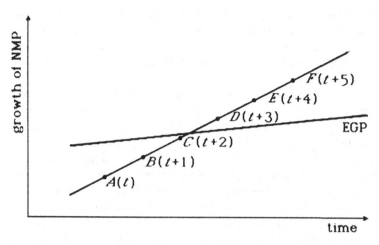

Figure 1.1. Economic growth path.

1. theories of planning cycles, which stress the importance of the behavior of the planners; and
2. theories of investment cycles, which stress the crucial role of investment levels in the economy's fluctuations.

The adherents of both groups of theories stress the overreaction or the wrong reaction of the planner as one of the causes for growth fluctuations in the centrally planned economies. According to Kyn, Schrettl, and Slama (1979, p. 113), the planners persistently repeat their errors and overstrain the economy because (among other factors) they do not know what is its "equilibrium" growth path (EGP). Their overambitious "taut" plans, which annually increase the target rates of growth, push the economy beyond its efficient limits. This can be illustrated as shown in Figure 1.1.

Beginning from national income A in the period t, which increases in the period $t + 1$ to B, the planners, having the impression that the economy has a lot of additional capacity, impose a plan, which is based on the same rate of growth. This can be feasible for some time, and the economy reaches point C in its growth path in time $t + 2$. If the planners, driven by their "vital instinct" for high investments, impose again the same "moderate" rate of growth on the economy in times $t + 3$, $t + 4$, and $t + 5$, they will push it beyond its capacity, reaching points D, E, and F. The consequence is "overheating" of the economy. Plans can be neither fulfulled nor balanced, shortages begin to grow, and the ratio of actual to potential output begins to decline. The typical reaction of the planner is an attempt to reallocate the shortages in the economy, as described at the beginning of this chapter.

According to Goldmann and Kouba (1969), investment fluctuations result from the lag between investment decisions or investment expenditures and the completion of the investment projects. The Polish economist Oscar Lange (1961) attributed the cycle mostly to reinvestment activities. He demonstrated mathematically that a concentration of large-scale investment projects in short time periods creates an "echo-effect" in reinvestment, which determines the growth fluctuations. These fluctuations, however, can be smoothed by the central planner because the life of capital goods is not firmly fixed, allowing for the phased replacement of obsolete capital. The "echo-effect" in reinvestment is about fifteen years, which corresponds to a classical cycle in the market economy. There is, however, one significant difference: Reinvestments in the market economies, which tend to have less than full employment, increase aggregate demand and stimulate economic growth. In the centrally planned economies, the large-scale obsolescence of the capital stock could cause a fall in economic capacity, and consequently of the output.

Goldmann is one of the scholars who put emphasis in their cycle theories on the length of the gestation period of investment goods. He stresses that planners' efforts to push the economy beyond its capacity limits lead to situations in which the economy (and especially the construction industry) cannot absorb growing investments. The result is that the fulfillment of investment projects is delayed, plans cannot be implemented, and investments are cut back. This wavelike behavior of investment activity reappears with a time lag of eight to ten years, which is determined by the gestation period of the large investment projects (cited by Kyn et al. 1979, p. 116). He further argues that the investment cycle in the centrally planned economies might be reinforced by sudden increases of completed productive capacities, which release the tension in the economy and help to accelerate a new wave of investments.[9]

[9] Kyn et al. (1979) show in their analysis considerably shorter investment lags of approximately one year. This indicates that the response to investment decisions in the centrally planned economies is much quicker than is indicated by the works of

Foreign trade performance and the balance of payments

Another problem area for the Eastern European economies lies in their foreign trade performance.[10] As mentioned earlier, one of the "shortages" in the centrally planned economies is the shortage of imported goods. This leads to an "import hunger," which is the driving force behind foreign trade (Kornai 1984, p. 36). This phenomenon parallels investment "hunger." All levels of the bureaucracy are eager to obtain large import quotas and licenses. The largest claims are for high-quality machinery, equipment, and intermediate goods, primarily from the Western countries.[11] This is a result mainly of the inward-oriented development strategy of Eastern Europe since the 1950s; this, as discussed, led to similar patterns of industrial production in the individual countries and to an intrabloc trade structure of predominantly "soft" goods.

The "tension" in the investment sphere breeds the "tension" in the import sector. The import decisionmakers are not concerned about the financial risk of their activities; thus there are no self-imposed restrictions on their import claims. Their responsiveness to prices, costs, and exchange rates is almost nil.

The drive for imports is not supported by an endogenous drive for exports, a logical consequence of which is (among other factors) the almost chronic deficit in the hard-currency balance of trade and balance of payments that emerges whenever imports from Western countries are liberalized. (It must be stressed, however, that the liberalization of hard-currency imports is determined mainly by political considerations, stemming from relations with the Western countries.) Exports are regarded by CMEA planners and enterprises as a "necessary evil" (Holzman 1979, p. 313) to acquire currency for imports.

Apart from exceptional situations, at a micro level producers have little self-imposed motivation to search for export markets in

Kornai, Lange, and others. However, Kyn et al. underline that the responses are within the same upswing or downswing (1979, p. 123).

[10] On the foreign trade behavior of centrally planned economies see, e.g., Holzman (1974, 1978, 1979, 1981); Neuberger and Tyson, (1980); Portes (1980a,b); and van Brabant (1977, 1980).

[11] Although excess demand for Western products increased rapidly in the past fifteen years, it certainly existed during the 1950s and the 1960s; however, it was small compared with the more recent period. Two main factors were responsible for the pre-1970 period: (1) Western controls on exports to the Eastern bloc, and (2) the political pressure within the Comecon countries to foster intrabloc trade.

the West, because such markets would require higher-quality products, prompt delivery, and so on, leading to tension in their production plans. These firms therefore prefer to supply the domestic market or another Eastern Europen country, which, as a "shortage economy," will be a less selective buyer.

The CMEA countries have a reduced ability to sell manufactured goods in competitive Western markets because of their comparative disadvantages in innovation, technological change, and marketing. They tend to be in a constant disequilibrium with the Western economies (Holzman 1979, p. 301). The efforts to modernize the economy, to shift the composition of investment toward more sophisticated branches such as electronics and electrical industry, and to achieve faster growth with increased imports of Western technology, as an alternative to major economic reform of the incentive structure of production in the 1970s, showed clearly that the assimilative capacity of CMEA industries depends heavily on the quality of complementary inputs from domestic sources. Shortcomings in the technological infrastructure and the socioeconomic system of CMEA countries present an obstacle both to rapid and efficient assimilation of Western technology and to the development of exports of competitive manufactured goods to the markets of the industrialized countries. Assimilation of imported technologies has been slow and inefficient in Eastern Europe compared with the experience of the developed market economies. The main systemic factors in the centrally planned economies in CMEA contributing to the inefficient use of Western technology are the following (Gomulka and Nove 1984, pp. 35–7):

excessive duration of the decision-making process in regard to new productive capacity;

insufficient interest in innovation on the part of management in all levels of the bureaucracy;

slow retirement of obsolete machinery;

shortage of domestic specialized production of spare parts, components, tools, instruments, and so on;

absence of competition and price inflexibility in the domestic markets; and

deficiency of the material supply system, which has an adverse effect on machinery infrastructure and also on the functioning of the installed equipment (e.g., difficulties in getting steel of the correct specification).

The imbalances in foreign trade in CMEA countries breed a shortage of convertible currency and a shortage of foreign credits to finance the deficits in the balance of payments. The credits have to be provided mainly by Western commercial banks and government agencies, because of the limited possibilities for borrowing convertible currency funds from the CMEA international banks (International Investment Bank and the International Bank for Economic Cooperation) and the inability to use intrabloc credits provided in inconvertible domestic CMEA currencies or in transferable rubles (the CMEA international currency) to finance balance-of-payments deficits with the West. However, the shortage of convertible currency inevitably leads to forms of export promotion, the main instrument of which is the mandatory export target, which often involves detailed instructions as to what to produce, for which market, and so on; but these plans are often not fulfilled because of the "saleability illusion" (Holzman 1979, pp. 304-6) of the decisionmakers, who overestimate the exports they can sell each year in the West.

The pressure on the medium and lower levels of the bureaucracy to export to market economies results in a drive to export at a lower selling price, by any means and at any cost – thus neglecting real domestic costs. As mentioned, the export decisionmakers are not concerned about the financial risk of their activities: If there are deficits, they will be compensated from the state budget. The budget constraints in foreign trade are a combination of "hard" and "soft" constraints. The convertible currency constraint is "hard" at the national level, but "soft" at the micro level. The budget constraint of the foreign trade firm in domestic currency is "soft" because of many kinds of tax exemptions, subsidies, and so on. This discourages voluntary efforts by the foreign trade enterprises in Eastern Europe to improve the efficiency of their activities.

The imbalances in convertible trade widen with any acceleration of the rate of economic growth that depends on a policy of liberalization of imports from the West. Kalecki was one of the first scholars to show that the difficulties connected with the acceleration of the rate of economic growth in Eastern Europe are related above all to foreign trade (1969, chap. 6). Most of the countries (the only exception being the Soviet Union) are strongly dependent on imports of investment goods and raw materials. The acceleration of economic growth implies the necessity to increase imports and – for balanced foreign trade – exports. The difficulty in balancing foreign trade (particulary with the West) in the centrally planned economies increases because the higher the rate of economic growth, the more rapidly must exports increase and the more difficult it is to find markets for them, in view of the limited demand in Western markets for CMEA goods. A higher rate of growth requires, *ceteris paribus,* a greater effort to push exports or to restrict imports.

An alternative way to sustain high rates of economic growth and investment is to borrow in the Western capital markets. Assuming that the Western capital market is willing to provide credits to the CMEA, borrowing from the West is determined by political considerations in the individual CMEA countries and (for the whole CMEA region) on the overall relations between East and West. In the 1950s and the 1960s, for example, the credit relations were limited because of the political decision to enforce intrabloc trade and credit relations. In the 1970s, the period of détente between East and West, the Eastern European countries decided to activate their credit relations with the West. The willingness to borrow, however, depends on the internal policy choices of the individual countries. For example, some countries (Poland, Romania, Hungary, GDR, Soviet Union) borrowed heavily; but Czechoslovakia has been more cautious, as the debt experience of the 1970s has shown.

Foreign capital plays an important role in filling domestic savings/investment and trade gaps; that is, it helps to alleviate both the foreign exchange constraint upon the growth of the economy and the strain on national savings. Financing of development through external loans is not a new phenomenon exclusive to the LDCs and Eastern Europe: Some of the developed countries continue to depend on external borrowing for major investment projects. What is detrimental for many LDCs (particularly LDCs in Africa and the NICs in Latin America, e.g., Mexico, Brazil, Argentina) and some Eastern European countries (Poland, Romania) at present is the inability to meet their current financial obligations. External (hard-currency) debt problems arise in Eastern Europe from the inability (determined mainly by systemic factors and enhanced by external shocks) to increase the efficiency of investments and (hard-currency) exports at a time when (hard-currency) imports, principal repayments, and interest payments are increasing. Consequently, an Eastern European country is compelled to borrow more, even at higher interest rates, mainly for general balance-of-payments purposes and to maintain a constant flow of net imports.

The accumulation of debt, and consequently debt-servicing difficulties, may be accelerated by mistakes or omissions in macroeconomic policy in the individual countries as well. The macro policy mistakes are not determined primarily by the economic system and development strategy of the centrally planned economies in Eastern Europe. Thus, these mistakes might be considered as country-specific internal factors adversely affecting its international competitiveness and overall foreign payments situation. Two main internal factors may exacerbate the debt problem. On the one hand, aggregate demand management may stimulate excessive spending (gross investment, aggregate consumption, government spending); on the other, relative price movements may stimulate nontradable goods supply and tradable goods demand, leading to a loss in international competitiveness. For example, agricultural wage and price policies in Poland during the 1970s were one of the important factors causing the balance-of-payments crisis. (Encouraging the inefficient state agricultural sector to produce foodstuffs while tying up the dominant private agricultural sector, and rapidly increasing wages while keeping prices unchanged, led to expansion of domestic demand that outpaced the domestic supply potential and consequently spilled over into huge agricultural imports.)

All of this indicates that growth-cum-debt policies, which mean driving economic development in the CMEA centrally planned economies with hard-currency capital imports, lead to debt repayment difficulties that are frequently insuperable. The interest paid on the imported capital ("tax on GDP" to be paid abroad) will burden the future balance of payments, which leads to both loss of resources and a risk of balance-of-payments difficulties. The latter can be mitigated by external windfalls or exacerbated by external shocks.

External disturbances and macroeconomic adjustment

How the centrally planned economies adjust to external disturbances has steadily attracted the attention of Western scholars.[12] Until
the 1970s, the general view was that the individual Eastern European countries and the CMEA as a region were relatively isolated
from the events in the world economy and their centrally planned
economic systems were capable of protecting them from external
shocks. The balance-of-payments problems of Bulgaria in the late
1970s, and of Poland, Romania, the GDR, and Hungary at the
beginning of the 1980s, showed clearly that the CMEA has been
vulnerable to international economic disturbances. Recently the
problems of the alternative policy responses to external disequilibrium have been discussed also in Eastern Europe (Stoilov 1984, pp.
105–18).

In centrally planned economies, disturbances can arise like those
in Western market economies: in factor, commodity, or asset (financial) markets, or in some combination of these. Their origins can be
real or nominal, and their manifestations can be nominal, real, or
joint (Tyson and Kenen 1980, p. 35). The main external factors
negatively affecting the current account of the balance of payments
are a deterioration in the terms of trade, reduced demand for Eastern European exportables, and increases in international interest
rates. Other external disturbances affecting the balance of payments
are changes in the general levels of world prices, changes in the
price level of particular commodities or services, and reductions in
the availability of foreign financing to fund a given deficit on the
current account. The influence of these changes in the international
market on the national economy and the options for policy responses and adjustment depend not only on the source and the type
of disturbance, but also on the intensity of economic links between
the Eastern European country and the international market.

Regardless of what combination of domestic and external factors
has caused the external disequilibrium, adjustment policies in
market economies that are applied with different intensity and in
different ways by the different countries, typically focus on two sets
of policies: expenditure-reduction and expenditure-switching policies. The first set is designed to control aggregate demand – such as

[12] For theoretical discussion see, e.g., Allen (1982); Holzman (1974, 1981); Neuberger and Tyson (1980); Portes (1980a,b, 1983); and Wolf (1980, 1985a,b).

fiscal, monetary, and income policies – whereas the second set affects the relative price of internationally tradable goods and includes the exchange rate, tariffs, and export-promotion policies. These two sets of policies may be accompanied by supply-oriented growth policies aimed at facilitating switching and at expanding the level of domestic output, and may include monetary, fiscal, and other complementary measures.

Expenditure-reduction policies can be used to achieve external balance by reducing utilization or absorption of resources. By absorption reduction, demand for exportables and import substitutes will fall, leading to an improvement of the balance of trade by simultaneously cutting outlays on imports and tradable goods for exports. Expenditure-switching policies, on the other hand, can be used to increase the relative prices of tradable goods relative to those of the nontradable goods, and to reallocate or "switch" resources from the nontradable goods sector, where there is excess supply, to the tradable goods sector, where they can produce for export or import substitutes. Expenditure reduction and expenditure switching can occur in the short run; switching domestic output, although it also may occur over the short run, requires investment and complementary policy measures designed to reallocate productive resources.

CMEA direct controls. The question arises: What policy instruments can planners in Eastern Europe use for the adjustment of their economies to external disequilibrium? The above-mentioned policy responses in the market economies – monetary, fiscal, income, and exchange rate policies – and instruments such as interest rates, money supply, taxes, prices, wages, and exchange rates have different economic effects in the centrally planned economies.[13] I will discuss briefly only the following general characteristics of some of them.[14]

Domestic prices have little economic relevance and play a relatively ineffective and inefficient role in resource allocation. They are

---

[13] For theoretical background see, e.g., Holzman (1974, 1979, 1981, 1983); van Brabant (1974, 1980, 1985); and Wolf (1985a,b).
[14] The following discussion does not refer fully to Hungary, which is attempting to implement market-oriented economic reform. For more details see, e.g., Adam (1985) and Hewett (1983d).

fixed in most Eastern European countries for long periods of time, and changes in demand are not usually reflected in changes in prices.

Domestic price levels tend to be *insulated from foreign prices.* The centralized foreign trade system usually does not permit trade flows to respond to changes in relative prices. In intra-CMEA trade, so-called contract prices, expressed in transferable rubles, are applied. These contract prices are not based on domestic prices in the CMEA countries, but are "adjusted" world market prices. The transferable ruble is an "artificial," intrabloc currency that does not really serve the traditional functions of money: medium of exchange, real unit of account, and store of value. It is only a unit of account in intra-CMEA trade.[15] The trade of centrally planned economies with Western countries is conducted at world market prices, expressed in terms of the world's major currencies: the U.S. dollar, the Deutsche mark, the French Franc, the Italian lira, the British pound, and so on.

Exchange rates[16] are set largely without reference to market forces and have little economic impact. Devaluation/appreciation of the CMEA national currencies or the transferable ruble (which are commodity and financially inconvertible) do not appreciably influence trade, capital flows, or monetary assets held by households and firms. Devaluation is simulated on the export side by reducing prices below world prices; a similar operation on the import side is not feasible. Holzman stresses that the inability to make active use of exchange rate policy is a "substantial handicap" in the adjustment to balance-of-payments deficit in CPEs (Holzman 1979, p. 308). (This applies also to Hungary, which can hardly be considered a free market economy at present because a few large monopolistic and oligopolistic firms dominate.)

Wage changes do not affect prices (at least in the short or medium term). Changes in the demand for goods do not have an immediate influence on the labor market.

---

[15] For the role of contract prices and the transferable ruble in intra-Comecon economic relations see, e.g., Holzman (1983) and van Brabant (1977).
[16] For more detailed discussion see Holzman (1974, 1983); van Brabant (1977, 1985); and Wolf (1984, 1985b).

Tax and interest rate changes have little economic impact on aggregate domestic demand.

These peculiarities of the main economic tools in the centrally planned economies indicate that the adjustment of these economies to external disturbances should be expected to differ markedly from those of the market economies. The incentives to domestic firms and consumers in Eastern Europe are insulated from world market conditions. Adverse external shocks do not have an "automatic" effect on the national economy, as they do to a large extent in the market economies of the Western countries and in the LDCs.

What are the policy options of the CMEA planner in reacting to external disturbances? Eastern European economists generally consider two possibilities (Stoilov 1984):

1. a shift in the allocation of output toward exports, reduction of imports, and the use of the national foreign exchange reserves; and
2. structural changes, such as enlargement and diversification of the export sector, modernization of the export-oriented productions, reduction of the use of imported goods in output through substitution with domestic products, and so on.

The first policy alternative has short-term effects on the balance of payments. In the centrally planned economies, as in the market economies of less developed countries, the three principal components of the current account – exports, imports, and interest payments – are determined largely by external factors in the short run; but the quantum of imports is closely related to domestic spending. Short-term adjustment is based consequently on import-reduction policies. The second policy choice is oriented toward output switching, a long and difficult process.

Stoilov writes that, during the 1980s, the CMEA countries will have to adjust to balance-of-payments deficits by expanding exports and restricting imports (1984, p. 114). Under such a policy, the investment sector will be hit since it relies on imported machinery and equipment. Cutting investment is the typical response in Eastern Europe. Kornai writes that if economic policy leaders feel that something is wrong with the foreign exchange situation, their first action will be to restrain investment (1980, p. 212). In this way they prevent short-term unemployment at the expense of long-run growth. It has to be stressed, however, that in the centrally planned economies in Eastern Europe the most important constraint on long-term growth is the efficiency of investment use. In some countries (Poland, Romania), the share of investment in GNP had been pushed to such high levels that it contributed negatively to growth because of such factors as unfinished investment projects and absorption of resources that could be allocated to exports.

The policy responses to external disequilibrium typically involve "direct controls" (Holzman 1981; Portes 1980a, 1983); planners have the ability to act directly on the components of absorption (expenditures). The direct controls include:

changes in the allocation of resources among investment, government expenditures, and exports;
controls on the volume of imports; and
controls on the supply of goods to households for consumption.

Portes argues that the planners' policy instruments are the real wage, real exports, and government spending. According to Wolf (1985a), real money balances rather than the real wages should be regarded as an important target of the planners' wage and price policies. He stresses that the reestablishment of internal and external equilibrium in CPEs inevitably requires cutbacks in demand for intermediate goods, possibly combined with wage and price restraints (p. 111).

Increasing borrowing. Another policy option to external disturbances in addition to the "direct planning controls" is to step up borrowing abroad, especially in the West, if there is willingness of foreign banks to meet the CMEA borrowing requirements. As in the market economies of many developed and developing countries, continued foreign borrowing will finance the balance-of-payments deficits and help to overcome the bottlenecks in the economy. Borrowing abroad has been typical of the Eastern European countries' policy response to external shocks in the past decade.

Intrabloc trade. The Eastern European countries have one other policy alternative for adjustment to external disequilibrium in trade with the West: a shift in market shares from the Western countries to intrabloc trade. This policy response can be regarded as "quasi-direct control" because of the nature of Eastern European economic integration based on planned trade bilateralism.[17] In the past decade, the CMEA countries have increased their intrabloc trade in "hard" goods – oil, gas, livestock, and meat products, which can be sold for convertible currencies (Fink 1984; Richter 1980) – as a policy alternative to financing balance-of-payments deficits with the market economies.[18] An increase of exports of "soft" goods to the CMEA countries does not have the same effect because inconvertible CMEA currencies cannot be used for servicing the hard-currency debt. However, expanding "soft" goods exports is constrained (except for the GDR and Czechoslovakia) by the lower demand in the other CMEA countries. In the case of the Eastern European Six, an increase of "soft" goods imports from the Soviet market will lead to further widening of the accumulated large deficit with the Soviet Union and burden their national economies additionally with ruble debt. As far as the Soviet Union is concerned, it cannot use trade surpluses with CMEA countries to cover deficits with the West. A shift in imports toward the CMEA market is also constrained by the intrabloc "soft" goods trade structure. The main problem with the expansion of imports from Eastern Europe is that certain goods (spare parts, components, and special materials or machines) can only be obtained from the West. All of these factors mean that reorientation to the CMEA market is difficult in the short to medium term.

The following example illustrates the adjustment alternatives of the Eastern European countries to external disturbances. Suppose that a CMEA country's hard-currency import prices rise 30% while the export prices remain unchanged. If the level of real imports is to remain unchanged, there are three alternatives: (1) The real hard-currency exports have to rise 30%; (2) net borrowing has to rise; or (3) the country's foreign exchange reserves have to be drawn down. The latter two possibilities are only short-term solutions and will fail if the deterioration of terms of trade is not transitory. The adjustment eventually will be some combination of directly imposed import reductions and export expansion.

---

[17] For theoretical background see, e.g., Holzman (1974) and van Brabant (1977, 1980).
[18] The significance of this adjustment policy to external shocks, however, should not be overstated because of the limited resources of "hard-currency goods" in the most of the Comecon countries (without the Soviet Union).

An analysis of options

In Western economic terms, what are the macroeconomic consequences of policies of direct control? What will be the changes in
the allocation of resources? For simplicity of the analysis let us consider the national income equation:

$$\text{GNP} = C + I + G + (X - M),$$

where:

GNP = gross national product,
 C = aggregate consumption,
 I = gross investment,
 G = government spending,
 X = exports,
 M = imports, and
$X - M$ = net exports.

For a given level of GNP, a combination of an expansion of
exports and a reduction of imports must mean a drop in the sum of
consumption, investment, and government spending. In the market economies this process occurs generally through a combination
of price adjustment (rising prices) and government policy adjustment (cutting the government expenditures in response to falling
tax receipts, and policies to influence private demand). Adjustment
cannot be conducted similarly in the centrally planned economies,
because their prices, taxes, interest rates, and so on have different
economic effects than in the market economies. The policy alternatives are generally two:

1. Given the level of the GNP, the GNP must shift from domestic
   use $(C + I + G)$ to net exports $(X - M)$.
2. Reduce the GNP and thereby cut imports by the amount that
   can be financed by the net exports.

If the deterioration of the terms of trade with the West occurs
simultaneously with a deterioration in intrabloc terms of trade,
then, given that the country is locked heavily into trade with its
CMEA partners, the adjustment policies will be pursued more
rigorously, because both CMEA and the outside world create problems that increase the "tax on GNP" to be paid abroad.

The first policy alternative means a difficult transformation in the
composition of the GNP. It requires deep structural changes in the

economy (enlargement of the export sector, modernization of production and increased efficiency, etc.) and, if savings have to be increased over investment, then consumption does not increase in line with GNP and the result is a welfare loss. The following problem arises: Even if domestic absorption ($C + I + G$) falls, there is no guarantee that exports will rise. The reasons are (1) the inherent inability of the economy to produce goods for export[19] and (2) insufficient foreign demand.

The second policy alternative means altering the economy's growth rates in order to adjust to the external disequilibrium resulting from a deterioration of the terms of trade. It requires cuts in domestic absorption to accommodate the "foreign exhange constraint." The cutting of domestic absorption could affect any or all of its components: consumption, investment, or government expenditures.

What will be the consequences of such an adjustment? As stated above, the first reaction of the planners is to cut investment. (However, if there is a possibility to borrow from the West and the planners consider the external shock to be transitory, then borrowing may rise, with only a slight decrease or even an increase in investment in the short run. The decision will vary among the CMEA countries depending on their internal political choices.) The long-run consequences of cutting investment are a reduced capacity to produce and a drop in GNP growth rates, with the associated welfare loss. Cuts in consumption mean that the population must "pay" the price of adjustment immediately, and such a policy may prove too difficult to sustain politically. Cuts in government expenditures can have as a consequence the reduction of social services (health, education, etc.) and lower defense expenditures; placing the burden of adjustment in this latter direction may also prove difficult to sustain politically over the short term.

To sum up: Adverse external shocks do not have the "automatic" self-correcting effect on the centrally planned economies in Eastern Europe that they have on the market economies of the West and the LDCs. Adjustment in the CMEA relies on the instruments of direct planning control and borrowing abroad. The former means that the

---

[19] As was discussed, CPEs have comparative disadvantages in developing and in selling technology, which makes it difficult for them to compete in the Western markets. The same refers to many other Comecon goods (nonmanufactured, agricultural, etc.).

planners have consciously to decide where the burden will fall, which involves extremely difficult political choices.

The "debt cycle"

One of the main characteristics of economic growth in the centrally planned economies is the cyclical nature of investment. The "stop–go" policy in the investment activity is highly influenced by external disturbances, and, as the previous section discussed, the first reaction of the planners facing this situation is to cut investments. The disturbance in the balance of trade and in the balance of payments creates the "external tension" (Lacko 1980, p. 361) in the investment process that is characterized by excess demand and "hunger" for imports primarily for Western technology and equipment. One of the adjustment alternatives to external shocks is continued foreign borrowing (if the Western banks and governments allow it), which enables the planners to overcome the bottlenecks in investment activity.

The following questions arise: Is there a correlation between the investment cycle and borrowing abroad? Does foreign borrowing follow investment's cyclical fluctuations? The answers to these may allow us to predict the direction in which the Eastern European country could be expected to move, as well as give us an impression of its alternative developments.

As noted earlier in the chapter ("Investment cycles"), planners in the CMEA countries are not certain of the equilibrium growth path of their economies, leading them to tend to push the economy beyond its capacity limits. A relatively high rate of growth achieved in previous years leads to a higher planned rate of growth in coming years. Relative improvement in the balance of trade and the possibility to borrow on Western financial markets also seriously influence the annual plan. The policy toward "intensive economic growth" associated with raising the share of investments using imported capital, and the shift in the composition of investments in favor of more sophisticated goods (e.g., electronics) during the 1970s, showed a clear association between investment upswings and external deficits. High investment therefore has generated increasing financing needs.

Overambitious plans, in the sense of using target rates of growth for all components of the GNP ($I, C, G, X - M$), lead to an overstrained economy, which begins to destabilize. The "shortages" in the economy become chronic, which leads to cuts in plan targets, generates a slowdown in investment activity, and requires a downswing in the investment cycle.

Assume for simplicity that there have been no external shocks to the economy, so foreign borrowing is primarily oriented to increasing the productive capacity of the overstrained economy. What will be, in such a situation, the consequences of the slowdown of the investment activity and the "tension" in the balance of trade on the borrowing abroad?

When there are large deficits in the balance of trade, the now-familiar first reaction of the planners is to cut investment, which diminishes the need for imported machinery and equipment and capital inflows through foreign borrowing. In addition to that, accumulated debt (principal and interest) from the period of upswing in the investment cycles creates additional "tension," and the adjustment efforts are in the direction of certain restrictions in borrowing abroad.

This oversimplified model of interaction between investment activity and borrowing shows that the borrowing abroad follows the fluctuations in the investment activity with a certain lag. The external debt has a different development than it would were investment either constant or noncyclically fluctuating.[20]

A new question emerges: What will be the reaction of the planners if external disturbances (deterioration of terms of trade, etc.) occur.[21] There are two possibilities: To sustain the growth rate of investments by actively borrowing abroad or to cut it and avoid foreign borrowing. The first alternative implies, of course, the willingness of the Western banks and governments to provide loans to the Eastern European countries. In this case, obviously, the rate of increased borrowing abroad will be greater than in a situation without external shocks. However, such an investment policy in the shortage-ridden and inefficient centrally planned economies could

---

[20] An interesting undertaking would be an extensive empirical evaluation of this hypothesis drawing on the experience of the Eastern European countries in the 1970s and early 1980s.

[21] I will not discuss the case in which foreign borrowing is primarily oriented for consumption rather than investment. The debt problem in Eastern Europe in the late 1970s, however, is highly influenced in some countries (Poland, Soviet Union) by borrowing for consumption purposes.

deepen the external disequilibrium[22] and require stronger adjustment efforts (see the previous section). The logical consequence will be an eventual restriction of foreign borrowing.

Of course, all this discussion gives only a very simplified description of the correlation between the investment cycle and foreign borrowing in centrally planned economies, and undoubtedly raises as many questions as it answers. One limitation is that it omits an analysis of the effects of borrowing among CMEA countries. At the same time, it establishes a basis for better understanding the direction in which economic development in Eastern European countries can be expected to move.

[22] Eastern European economists' estimates set tolerable disequilibrium in Comecon countries' foreign trade between 25% and 40% of the GNP (Stoilov 1984, p. 107).

2

Eastern European debt crisis

The debt problems of LDCs and Eastern European countries really hit the headlines in mid-1982. On August 13, 1982, Mexico's Finance Minister Jesus Silva Herzog announced the inability of his country to meet foreign payment obligations. Soon both Argentina and Brazil, the other two largest debtor developing countries, were forced to disrupt normal debt servicing. The debt of Latin American countries doubled from $162 billion in 1978 to $330 billion in 1982 (World Bank, *World Debt Tables,* March 1986, p. 250). The total indebtedness of nonoil developing countries reached $654 billion. Reschedulings of official and commercial bank debt increased from $478 million in 1975 to an estimated $28 billion in 1982. Defaults or prolonged payment difficulties by major debtors have threatened the stability of the international financial system.

Actually the "hot time" for the Western banks and governments began one year earlier. On March 27, 1981, in London, the chief borrowing official of Poland's Bank Handlowy had met with some forty representatives of the more than five hundred banks that had lent money to Poland and had announced Poland's inability to meet payments obligations. Romania followed Poland in suspending payments a few months later in July 1981. The Eastern European debt crisis had begun. How it was created and what has been the adjustment policy in Eastern Europe are the subjects of this chapter.

Debt trends

Was the debt crisis in the Eastern European countries an insolvency or an illiquidity crisis? An analysis of the debt situation of the Soviet Union and the six CMEA countries is required to answer this question.[1] The analysis in this section concentrates on the following problems:

What has happened to the balance of trade and the current account?
How have flows of debt capital and terms of borrowing changed?
How have the main indicators of the debt burden changed?

Since the beginning of the 1970s the Eastern European countries have rapidly increased their hard-currency trade and current account deficits, as well as their debt to the West. There were two main periods in the development of their debt situation: that up to the end of the 1970s and that beginning in the 1980s.[2]

Growing indebtedness during the 1970s

Trade deficits. The CMEA countries ran large trade deficits from 1971 to 1979 (Tables 2.1 and 2.2). From an average of $27 million in 1971–3, the total deficit soared to $9.4 billion in 1975, and was still $5.1 billion in 1978. The smaller Eastern European countries ran higher trade deficits than did the Soviet Union: Together, their total deficit increased from an average of $356 million in 1971–3 to $5.8 billion in 1975, and to $6.6 billion and $5.1 billion in 1978 and 1979, respectively. Poland and the GDR ran the biggest trade deficits; but Romania too ran high trade deficits in the late 1970s, reaching $1.2 billion in 1979.

The Eastern European cumulative trade deficit with the industrialized West during 1961–70 was $6.4 billion (Table 2.2). From

[1] The analysis of debt developments in Eastern Europe in the present study is based on Western estimates. The CMEA countries did not publish data on their hard-currency debt in the 1970s. Most of them (Soviet Union, Bulgaria, Czechoslovakia, GDR) still do not publish such data. The statistics available on the debts of Poland, Romania, and even Hungary are often inadequate, especially for interest payments and the composition of debt. There are some differences in the Western estimates on the CMEA debt (e.g., CIA, OECD Secretariat, Morgan Guaranty Trust, and Wharton Econometric Forecasting Associates). The text does not discuss these differences because they do not affect materially the analysis of the main economic and debt trends in the Eastern European Six and the Soviet Union.
[2] For a discussion of balance-of-payments problems in Eastern Europe until 1970 (the Soviet Union in 1929–32 and 1963, Hungary in 1954–5, and Czechoslovakia in 1962–4), see Oleg Hoeffding, "Recent Structural Changes and Balance of Payments Adjustments in Soviet Foreign Trade," in Brown and Neuberger (1968), pp. 312–37; see also Wiles (1968a).

Table 2.1. *CMEA trade balances (total), 1971-9
(millions of U.S. dollars)*

	1971-3 avg.	1974	1975	1976	1977	1978	1979
Bulgaria	51	−490	−716	−245	−42	−170	351
Czechoslovakia	114	−471	−728	−668	−875	−825	−1,054
GDR	21	−898	−1,202	−1,835	−2,310	−1,305	−1,151
Hungary	47	−446	−889	−607	−700	−1,590	−752
Poland	−659	−2,168	−2,256	−2,853	−2,353	−1,928	−1,333
Romania	70	−269	0	42	3	−830	−1,191
East. Eur. 6	−356	−4,742	−5,791	−6,166	−6,277	−6,648	−5,131
Soviet Union	329	2,511	−3,652	−942	4,293	1,596	6,932
Total	−27	−2,231	−9,443	−7,108	−1,984	−5,052	1,801

Source: The Twentieth Century Fund (1983), p. 66.

the beginning of the 1970s it increased rapidly and reached $12 billion in 1975, twice that of 1974. The trade deficits remained high until the beginning of the 1980s despite some reduction after 1976. The Soviet Union, Poland, GDR, Czechoslovakia, and Romania ran the biggest trade deficits among the Eastern European countries. The deficits of the smaller Eastern European Six increased from $0.63 billion in 1971 to $6.6 billion in 1976, and fell to $5.4 billion by 1979. The Soviet Union reached its highest trade deficit with the industrialized West in 1975 ($6.3 billion).

Current accounts. CMEA hard-currency, current-account balances also had high deficits from 1975 to 1979 (Table 2.3). The smaller CMEA countries increased their deficits from $6.2 billion in 1975 and $5.5 billion in 1977, to $7.4 billion in 1979. Only the Soviet Union was able to reduce its current-account deficit considerably, cutting it from $6.1 billion in 1975 to $1.7 billion in 1978, and achieving a surplus by 1979 ($0.6 billion).

Table 2.2. *CMEA balances of trade with developed market economies, 1961–79* (millions of U.S. dollars)

	1961–70 total	1971	1972	1973	1974	1975	1976	1977	1978	1979
Bulgaria	−563	−20	−5	−21	−409	−700	−470	−386	−415	−43
Czechoslovakia	−450	−14	−9	−221	−349	−396	−740	−707	−804	−803
GDR	−488	−296	−340	−750	−1,028	−1,150	−1,415	−1,326	−1,093	−1,855
Hungary	−499	−257	−102	−89	−741	−550	−674	−817	−1,217	−745
Poland	−303	−53	−313	−1,316	−2,269	−2,746	−3,237	−2,496	−2,052	−1,605
Romania	−1,379	−97	−166	−196	−416	−243	−80	−476	−776	−387
East. Eur. 6	−3,682	−631	−935	−2,593	−5,212	−5,785	−6,616	−6,208	−6,358	−5,438
Soviet Union	−2,704	−303	−1,288	−1,748	−916	−6,300	−3,974	−1,514	−3,345	−1,131
Total	−6,386	−934	−2,223	−4,341	−6,128	−12,085	−10,590	−7,722	−9,703	−6,569

Source: The Twentieth Century Fund (1983), p. 67.

Table 2.3. *CMEA hard-currency current-account*
balances, 1975-9
(billions of U.S. dollars)

	Soviet Union	East. Eur. 6	Total
1975	−6.1	−6.2	−12.3
1976	−3.85	−6.0	−9.85
1977	−1.3	−5.5	− 6.8
1978	−1.7	−5.6	− 7.3
1979	0.6	−7.4	− 6.8

Source: The Twentieth Century Fund (1983), p. 68.

Gross debt. Accompanying the chronic deficit was an increase in hard-currency debt (Tables 2.4–2.6), an increase that was especially rapid in the second half of the 1970s. Total gross debt (at current prices) grew from $8.3 billion in 1970 to $24.0 billion in 1974 and reached $77.1 billion in 1979, more than nine times higher than in 1971.[3] The level of indebtedness by the end of 1970s was roughly half of the indebtedness of the other major debtor group, namely, the Latin American and Caribbean countries (Argentina, Brazil, Chile, Mexico, etc.), and about the same as the debt of the East Asian and Pacific countries (Indonesia, Phillippines, Singapore, etc.).[4]

The gross hard-currency debt of the Eastern European countries increased very rapidly, particularly from 1974 to 1977 (see Figure 2.1). The gross debt of the Soviet Union grew from $5.9 billion in 1974 to $17.7 billion in 1977, and that of the smaller CMEA countries from $16.0 billion to $37.0 billion, respectively. Notably rapid were the tripling of the debt of Poland and the doubling for the

[3] The total debt of the CMEA countries in 1979 excludes the debt of Vietnam and Cuba, which are not considered in the present study. These two non-European CMEA-member countries increased rapidly their convertible currency debt in the second half of the 1970s. The debt of Vietnam grew from $0.5 billion in 1976 to about $3.1 billion in 1979; the debt of Cuba reached an estimated $1.4 billion in 1979 (1976, $0.9 billion). Thus the total CMEA debt may be estimated at $82 billion at the end of 1979. (Estimates are the author's.)
[4] For detailed data, see World Bank, *World Debt Tables* (March 1986), pp. 198, 250.

Table 2.4. *Eastern European gross hard-currency debt, 1970-9*
(billions of U.S. dollars, end-year)

	1970	1971	1974	1975	1977	1978	1979
Bulgaria	n.a.	0.7	1.7	2.4	3.4	4.0	4.5
Czechoslovakia	n.a.	0.5	1.1	1.5	3.0	3.5	4.0
GDR	n.a.	1.4	3.6	4.9	7.5	9.0	10.1
Hungary	n.a.	1.1	2.3	3.2	5.4	7.3	8.0
Poland	n.a.	1.1	4.9	7.8	14.5	17.5	21.1
Romania	n.a.	1.2	2.4	2.8	3.2	4.4	7.0
East. Eur. 6	5.8	6.0	16.0	22.6	37.0	45.7	54.7
Soviet Union	2.5	1.8	5.9	11.4	17.7	17.2	17.2
CMEA banks	n.a.	n.a.	2.1	2.8	5.5	5.8	5.2
Total	8.3	7.8	24.0	36.8	60.0	68.7	77.1

Source: Portes (1977, p. 38; 1980a, p. 38); the data for 1971 and 1979 are
from National Foreign Assessment Center (1980).

GDR and Hungary. In 1977-9, these three countries and Romania
were the most indebted to the West. Romania's debt grew especially
rapidly in the period 1974-9 (it tripled), though in 1977 its gross
debt was the second lowest in the CMEA (after Czechoslovakia).
Poland stood out among CMEA countries in increasing its gross
debt to the West almost 2,000 percent during 1971-9.[5]

Net debt. The general tendencies in the development of Eastern
European gross debt characterize net debt (gross debt minus assets
in Western banks) as well. The total net debt increased from $3.5
billion in 1970 and $5.9 billion in 1971 to $62.8 billion in 1979 (i.e.,
by a factor of more than 10; see Table 2.5). The smaller CMEA
countries' net debt grew from $4.9 billion in 1971 to $48.5 billion in
1979 (i.e., by a factor of almost 10). The Soviet Union's net debt

[5] Note that Poland entered the 1970s with a relatively favorable hard-currency external current account and debt. Its cumulative foreign trade deficit with the Western
countries for the period 1960-70 was $0.28 billion, and its trade balance with OECD
countries showed a surplus of $80 billion in 1970. In the late 1960s Poland tried to
eliminate debt and probably created some convertible currency reserves (Brus 1982,
p. 102).

US$ BILLIONS

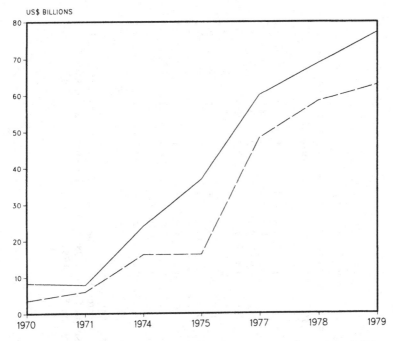

Figure 2.1. Total Eastern European gross (———) and net (- - -) debt, 1970-9. *Sources:* Tables 2.4 and 2.5.

increased from $0.6 billion in 1971 to $9.1 billion in 1979 (more than 15 times greater). Poland, the GDR, and Hungary were the most net-indebted among the Eastern European Six in that period. Their net debt reached $20.2, $8.4, and $7.1 billion, respectively, in 1979. All these countries and Romania increased their net debt particularly in the period 1974-9.

Commercial borrowing. Most of the increase in debt to the West resulted from commercial borrowing, principally from Western banks (Table 2.6). At the end of 1971, commercial bank liabilities totaled $3.1 billion, roughly 40% of gross debt. In the following years, these borrowings grew to $11.5 billion in 1974 and $47.7 billion in 1979, or nearly 48% and 62% of gross debt, respectively. By the end of 1979, commercial bank borrowing by the Eastern European countries was roughly fifteen times above its level in

Table 2.5. *Eastern European net hard-currency debt, 1970–9*
(billions of U.S. dollars, end-year)

	1970	1971	1972	1973	1974	1975	1976	1977	1978	1979
Bulgaria	n.a.	0.7	0.9	1.0	1.4	1.4	2.8	3.2	3.7	3.0
Czechoslovakia	n.a.	0.2	0.2	0.3	0.6	0.6	1.4	2.1	2.5	3.0
GDR	n.a.	1.2	1.2	1.9	2.6	2.6	5.0	6.2	7.6	8.4
Hungary	n.a.	0.8	1.1	1.1	1.5	1.5	2.9	4.5	6.5	7.1
Poland	n.a.	0.8	1.2	2.2	4.1	4.1	10.7	13.5	16.9	20.2
Romania	n.a.	1.2	1.2	1.5	2.5	2.5	2.5	3.4	4.9	6.8
East. Eur. 6	n.a.	4.9	5.7	7.9	12.7	12.7	25.3	32.8	42.2	48.5
Soviet Union	n.a.	0.6	0.6	1.2	1.7	1.6	10.1	11.2	11.2	9.1
CMEA Banks	n.a.	0.5	1.2	1.5	1.8	1.8	3.5	4.2	4.8	5.2
Total	3.5	5.9	7.5	10.6	16.2	16.2	38.9	48.2	58.3	62.8

Note: Totals may not add because of rounding.
Sources: The data for 1970 are from Portes (1977, p. 38); the data for 1971, 1974, 1977, and 1978 are from National Foreign Assessment Center (1980, p. 7); the data for 1972, 1973, 1975, 1976, and 1979 are from Twentieth Century Fund (1983, p. 69).

Table 2.6. *Eastern European gross hard-currency indebtedness to Western commercial banks, 1971–9 (millions of U.S. dollars, end-year)*

	1971	1972	1973	1974	1975	1976	1977	1978	1979
Bulgaria	397	705	748	1,420	2,033	2,433	2,866	3,422	3,640
Czechoslovakia	149	230	278	431	426	1,035	1,532	2,000	2,750
GDR	695	720	1,225	2,130	4,000	4,423	5,227	6,712	7,800
Hungary	943	1,219	1,278	1,938	2,830	3,722	5,135	6,880	7,400
Poland	305	641	1,536	2,895	5,230	7,698	8,894	11,963	15,100
Romania	405	332	357	975	1,189	936	1,379	2,692	3,800
East. Eur. 6	2,894	3,847	5,422	9,789	15,708	20,247	25,033	33,669	40,490
Soviet Union	207	528	1,501	1,752	5,432	7,617	7,618	8,271	7,200
Total	3,101	4,375	6,923	11,541	21,140	27,864	32,651	41,940	47,690

Source: Calculated from National Foreign Assessment Center (1980).

1971. The liabilities of Poland, the GDR, Hungary, and Romania grew particularly fast. At the end of 1979, the commercial bank borrowing of these countries represented 72%, 77%, 92%, and 54% of their gross debt, respectively.

Another feature of the CMEA borrowing during the 1970s was the increased volume raised in the Euromarket. Eastern European Eurocurrency loans grew from $150 million in 1968–72 to $700 million in 1973 and $2.3 billion in 1975. The Euromarket credits to the smaller CMEA countries increased particularly fast in the second half of the 1970s and reached $2.6 billion in 1980. Poland, Hungary, and the GDR have received the greatest part of the Euromarket credits to CMEA (Table 2.7).

Guaranteed debt. A considerable part of the CMEA debt was guaranteed by official agencies in creditor countries at the beginning of the 1970s. The data from Table 2.8 show that the guaranteed debt grew from $3.9 billion in 1971 to $16 billion in 1979, or roughly four times. The share of the guaranteed debt in the gross debt had fallen, however, from 50% in 1971 to 22.3% and 20.6%, respectively, in 1974 and 1979.

Debt-burden indicators. The accumulated debt of the CMEA countries increased their hard-currency debt problem in the late 1970s as shown by two indicators of the debt burden: long-term debt service as a share of hard-currency exports (debt-service ratio), and gross debt as a share of hard-currency exports.[6] The data from Table 2.9 show the particularly rapid growth of the debt service ratio[7] of Poland (from 15% in 1972 to 92% in 1979), GDR (from 18% in 1972 to 54% in 1979), and Hungary (from 14% in 1972 to 37% in 1979). The Bulgarian debt service ratio was also high (1977, 45%; 1979, 38%): In that time Bulgaria faced increased debt-servicing difficulties. Relatively lower debt-service ratios were faced by the Soviet Union, Czechoslovakia, and Romania.

In the late 1970s the debt service ratios of Poland, GDR, Hungary, and Bulgaria were higher than the average debt service ratio for Latin American countries (26%) and East Asian countries (8%). These four CMEA countries had higher ratios than two other major

---

[6] For methodological discussion on debt ratios see Chapter 6.
[7] Most creditworthy countries maintain their debt service ratios below 25%.

Table 2.7. *Medium- and long-term credits raised by Eastern European countries on the international financial markets, 1968–86 (millions of U.S. dollars)*

	1968–72[a]	1973[a]	1975[a]	1980	1981	1982	1983	1984	1985	1986 (Jan–June)
Bulgaria	—	115	125	—	—	—	—	—	475	n.a.
Czechoslovakia	—	—	60	475	30	—	50	—	121	n.a.
GDR	10	15	280	397	516	69	386	903	1,173	n.a.
Hungary	140	90	250	550	591	483	567	1,146	1,578	821
Poland	—	430	475	736	—	—	—	235	—	n.a.
Romania	—	—	6	458	337	—	—	—	150	n.a.
East. Eur. 6	150	650	1,196	2,616	1,464	552	1,003	2,284	3,497	n.a.
Soviet Union	—	—	650	50	25	153	68	867	1,489	1248
CMEA banks	—	50	480	—	100	—	—	140	250	n.a.
Total	150	700	2,326	2,666	1,600	704	1,071	3,291	5,236	2,219

[a]The data for 1968–72, 1973, and 1975 are only for Eurocurrency loans.
Source: Portes (1977, p. 42); United Nations, *Economic Bulletin for Europe* 36:82 (1984); OECD (1985b, p. 2; 1986, p. 39); *World Financial Markets* (Sept. 1986, p. 14); Dillon et al. (1985, p. 62).

Table 2.8. *Officially guaranteed debt of Eastern Europe, 1971–9: Western external bank claims plus nonbank trade-related credits (millions of U.S. dollars, end-period)*

	1971	1972	1973	1974	1975	1976	1977	1978	1979
Bulgaria	301	244	202	183	187	320	313	328	320
Czechoslovakia	201	195	199	227	206	287	326	408	470
GDR	553	609	626	641	703	813	1,005	1,165	1,340
Hungary[a]	103	98	89	76	54	51	59	93	120
Poland	718	708	845	1,057	1,467	2,324	3,574	4,414	5,100
Romania	642	652	814	797	706	659	715	800	905
East. Eur. 6	2,518	2,506	2,775	2,981	3,323	4,454	5,992	7,208	8,255
Soviet Union[a]	1,400	1,551	1,708	2,389	3,631	5,185	5,870	6,911	7,700
Total	3,918	4,057	4,483	5,370	6,954	9,639	11,862	14,119	15,955

[a]Officially guaranteed export credits.
Source: Calculated from National Foreign Assessment Center (1980).

Table 2.9. *Debt service and gross debt as ratios to hard-currency exports, 1972–9*
(in percentages)

	Debt service ratio					Gross debt/exports ratio				
	1972	1974	1975	1977	1979	1972	1974	1975	1977	1979
Bulgaria	36	33	33	45	38	198	185	282	292	195
Czechoslovakia	10	13	14	17	22	46	46	48	95	112
GDR	18	21	25	38	54	95	104	169	210	223
Hungary	14	19	19	25	37	140	126	185	259	239
Poland	15	23	30	59	92	87	120	194	286	333
Romania	27	22	23	19	22	99	98	101	99	130
Soviet Union	17	15	23	27	24	68[a]	55[a]	104[a]	94[a]	64[a]

[a]Gross debt as a share of total revenues.
Source: National Foreign Assessment Center (1980).

debtor countries in Latin America – Brazil (31%) and Argentina (27%). The debt service ratio of Poland was considerably higher than the ratio of Mexico (55%).[8]

The gross debt/exports ratios show similar rising trends. The gross debt/export ratio for Poland grew from 87% in 1972 to 333% in 1979. The data for the GDR and Hungary were, respectively, 95% and 140% in 1972, and 223% and 239% in 1979. Bulgaria's ratio was also high, particularly in 1977: 292%. The gross debt/total foreign exchange revenues ratio of the Soviet Union was relatively lower: 1972, 68%; 1979, 64%. (Note that the gross debt/export ratios of most of the Eastern European countries at the end of the 1970s were higher than the averages for the Latin American and East Asian countries: 137% and 76%, respectively. The debt ratios of Poland and Hungary were higher than those of the most indebted Latin American countries: Brazil, Mexico, and Argentina.)[9]

East European debt in the early 1980s

Trade balances. In 1980 and 1981 the total trade balance of the Eastern European Six and the Soviet Union with market economies remained negative (Table 2.10). Trade performance since 1982 improved considerably leading to positive balances in 1982, 1983, and 1984 of $9.5, $11.8, and $10.9 billion, respectively; the trade surplus was reduced to $5.1 billion in 1985 due mainly to the fall in trade surplus with developed market economies.

The six Eastern European countries ran a negative trade balance of $4.2 billion in 1980, which improved to a surplus of $400 million in 1981. A further improvement occurred during 1982–5: The positive trade balance increased from $5.2 billion in 1982 to $6.8 billion in 1984, but then fell to $4.4 billion in 1985. Czechoslovakia was the only CMEA country to have positive trade balances in the whole period 1980–5. Bulgaria ran trade balance surpluses until 1984, but registered an $0.3 billion negative trade balance in 1985, due to increased imports of food, raw materials, and crude oil from the Middle East. The GDR, Poland, and Romania had negative trade balances in 1980 and positive ones during 1981–5. Hungary was the

---

[8] World Bank, *World Debt Tables* (March 1986), pp. 199, 201, 251, 253, 255, 257, 275, 277, 327, 329.
[9] *Ibid.,* pp. 198, 201, 274, 277, 326, 329.

Table 2.10 *CMEA current-account balances with market economies, 1980–5 (billions of U.S. dollars)*

	Trade balance with market economies		Net services plus transfers		Current account
	Total	Of this, DMEs	Total	Invest. income	
Bulgaria					
1980	1.0	0.1	-0.1	-0.4	1.0
1981	0.7	-0.6	—	-0.3	0.7
1982	0.7	-0.5	-0.1	-0.2	0.6
1983	0.4	-0.3	—	-0.2	0.4
1984	0.6	-0.6	—	-0.1	0.5
1985	-0.3	-0.6	0.2	-0.1	-0.3
Czechoslovakia					
1980	0.1	-0.4	-0.4	-0.3	-0.4
1981	0.3	-0.3	-0.5	-0.5	-0.2
1982	0.4	—	-0.4	-0.4	—
1983	0.8	0.1	-0.3	-0.3	0.5
1984	0.8	0.9	-0.2	-0.2	0.6
1985	0.6	-0.04	-0.06	0.1	0.5
GDR					
1980	-1.7	-1.7	-0.1	-1.2	-1.8
1981	—	-0.5	-0.4	-1.6	-0.4
1982	1.5	0.7	—	-1.3	1.5
1983	1.4	1.0	0.3	-1.0	1.7
1984	1.1	0.7	0.3	-0.8	1.1
1985	0.9	0.7	0.1	-0.6	1.0

Table 2.10 (*cont.*)

	Trade balance with market economies		Net services plus transfers		Current account
	Total	Of this, DMEs	Total	Invest. income	
Hungary					
1980	-0.7	-0.6	-0.6	-0.4	-1.3
1981	-0.8	-1.0	-1.2	-1.1	-1.9
1982	-0.3	-0.6	-0.8	-1.0	-1.2
1983	-0.1	—	-0.6	-0.7	-0.6
1984	0.6	0.2	0.2	-0.8	0.3
1985	0.2	-0.14	-0.49	-0.56	0.03
Poland					
1980	-1.0	-0.7	-1.8	-2.3	-2.8
1981	—	-0.5	-2.1	-2.9	-2.1
1982	1.5	0.6	-2.7	-3.0	-1.2
1983	1.4	0.9	-2.3	-2.7	-0.9
1984	1.5	0.7	0.1	-2.7	-0.8
1985	1.0	0.6	-1.8	-2.5	-0.7
Romania					
1980	-1.9	—	-0.9	-0.8	-2.8
1981	0.2	0.5	-1.0	-1.0	-0.8
1982	1.4	1.4	-0.9	-1.0	0.5
1983	1.6	2.3	-0.8	-0.7	0.8
1984	2.2	3.6	-0.7	-0.6	1.5
1985	2.0	2.55	-0.54	-0.54	1.5

East. Eur. 6					
1980	-4.2	-3.2	-3.9	-5.4	-8.1
1981	0.4	-2.4	-5.3	-7.4	-4.8
1982	5.2	1.7	-4.9	-6.8	0.3
1983	5.5	3.9	-3.6	-5.5	1.9
1984	6.8	5.5	1.1	-5.1	3.2
1985	4.4	3.0	-2.6	-4.2	2.0
Soviet Union					
1980	3.4	2.4	0.2	-1.2	3.6
1981	-0.7	-0.7	-0.1	-1.4	-0.8
1982	4.3	0.6	-0.2	-1.5	4.1
1983	6.2	2.5	-0.1	-1.4	6.1
1984	4.1	7.5	0.3	0.03	4.3
1985	0.7	-0.6	-0.1	0.2	0.6
Total					
1980	-0.8	-0.8	-4.3	-7.1	-5.0
1981	-0.3	-3.1	-5.9	-9.4	-6.2
1982	9.5	2.3	-5.5	-8.8	4.0
1983	11.8	6.5	-4.0	-7.2	7.7
1984	10.9	13.0	1.4	-5.1	7.5
1985	5.1	2.4	-2.7	-4.0	2.6

Note: Trade balance FOB–FOB, except for Hungarian imports, which are shown CIF in the national returns. The group of market economies includes the Western industrialized countries, the developed countries of the Southern Hemisphere, and the developing countries, most of which conduct trade on a convertible-currency basis.

Source: United Nations, *Economic Bulletin for Europe* 36:77–7 (1984); the data for 1984 are from Vanous and Movit (1985); the data for 1985 (except for Hungary and Romania) are from WEFA, *CPE Current Analysis*, April 1986.

only Eastern European country that ran a negative trade balance in the period 1980-3; its improvement in 1984-5 was marginal.

The Soviet Union also considerably improved its balance of trade, which was positive with market economies in the period 1980-5 with the exception of 1981, from $3.4 billion in 1980 to $6.2 billion in 1983 and $4.1 billion in 1984; the trade surplus was reduced to only $0.7 billion in 1985 due mainly to a decline in oil and gold revenues.

The total Eastern European balances of trade with the Western industrial economies (also in Table 2.10) had a development similar to that of the trade balances with the market economies overall. It was negative in 1980 and 1981 and positive during 1982-5. The surplus quintupled from $2.3 billion in 1982 to $13.0 billion in 1984, but was reduced to $2.4 billion in 1985, due to the fall in exports (primarily machinery, equipment, and fuels) and to increased imports. In 1983 and 1984, the greater part of the CMEA surplus with the market economies stemmed from trade with the developed West and not from the trade with LDCs as in previous years and in 1985. The Eastern European Six ran a balance-of-trade deficit in 1980 and 1981 and a surplus in 1982-5. They increased their positive balance of trade from $1.7 billion in 1982 to $5.5 billion in 1984 and $3.0 billion in 1985. The Soviet Union ran a positive balance of trade throughout 1980-4 (with the exception of 1981, when it had a deficit of $0.7 billion); this grew from $2.4 billion in 1980 to $7.5 billion in 1984 (but became a $0.6 billion deficit in 1985). Czechoslovakia, GDR, and Poland had trade balances that were negative in 1980 and 1981 and positive in 1982-5 (except Czechoslovakia, with a 1985 deficit of $40 million). Hungary ran a negative trade balance in 1980-3 and 1985. Bulgaria was the only CMEA country with a steadily negative trade balance during 1981-5. Romania ran a positive trade balance throughout 1980-5, which increased fivefold from $0.5 billion in 1981 to $2.5 billion in 1985.

Current accounts. The data from Table 2.10 and Figure 2.2 show the development of the CMEA current accounts since the beginning of the 1980s. The current-account surplus, which the Eastern European countries and the Soviet Union first ran with the market economies in 1982, widened in 1983 to $7.7 billion and fell to $7.5 and $2.6 billion in 1984 and 1985, respectively. The six CMEA

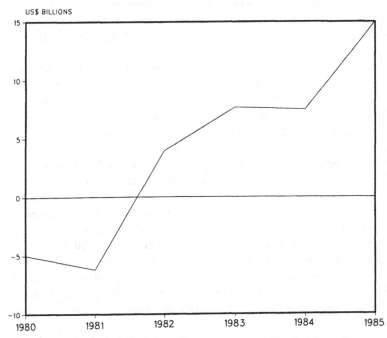

Figure 2.2. Eastern European hard-currency current account, 1980–5.
Source: Table 2.10.

countries ran a current-account surplus in 1982, which in 1983 reached almost $2 billion. The Soviet Union increased its current-account surplus from $3.6 billion in 1980 to $6.1 billion in 1983; this was reduced, however, to $4.3 billion and $0.6 billion in 1984 and 1985, respectively. Czechoslovakia, GDR, and Romania had positive current accounts after 1982. Hungary and Poland were the only Eastern European countries to run current-account deficits for the whole of 1980–3; Poland's current account remained negative in 1984–5.

The change in the development of the current account of the Eastern European Six and the Soviet Union since 1982 was due mostly to the increase in the trade surplus with developed and developing market economies. However, fall in the deficit on invisibles (the deficit on investment income fell from $9.4 billion in 1981 to $4.0 billion in 1985) played an important role as well.

Gross debt. The above tendencies in the development of the balances of trade and the current-account balances of the CMEA countries have influenced the development of their hard-currency debt from the beginning of the 1980s. Gross debt grew from $88.7 billion in 1980 to $92.9 billion in the "crisis" year 1981, declining to $88.0 billion in 1982, $86.6 billion in 1983, and $87.1 billion in 1984 (Table 2.11, Figure 2.3). However, the debt of the Soviet Union and the six Eastern European countries considerably increased in U.S. dollar terms in 1985, to $25 and $66 billion, respectively. The total gross debt amounted to $93.7 billion (including CMEA banks), thus reaching its highest level in the first half of the 1980s.[10] The rapid rise in debt was mainly a result of the depreciation of the U.S. dollar at end-1985, which considerably increased the dollar value of nondollar liabilities and of the increased borrowing of Hungary, GDR, and the Soviet Union. Compared with the debt of the Latin American and East Asian countries (increase in gross debt respectively 54% and 63% in 1980–4), the Eastern European debt position was relatively less constrained by debt problems in the first half of the 1980s: It decreased by 2% during 1980–4, and debt in 1985 was "only" 6% higher (in nominal terms) than in 1980.[11]

The six Eastern European countries reduced their gross debt from $66.2 billion in 1980 to $61.9 billion in 1984. It is important, however, to stress that only a part of the reduction of their gross debt was achieved by actual repayment through the generation of current-account surpluses. Another important factor in the fall of the dollar value through 1984 was the strength of the U.S. dollar, which considerably reduced the value of nondollar liabilities.[12] A

[10] In the period 1982–5 the annual gross debt level of the CMEA group (including non-European member countries) could be approximately $10 billion higher, allowing for the debt developments of Cuba and Vietnam (author's estimates):

	1980	1981	1982	1983	1984	1985
Cuba	1.4	2.2	5.3	5.2	5.3	4.8
Vietnam	3.9	4.6	5.3	5.9	6.4	5.8

[11] See Table 2.11 and World Bank, *World Debt Tables* (April 1986), pp. 198, 250.
[12] Between the end of 1980 and the end of 1983, the value of the dollar increased 39% against the DM, 64% against the British pound, and 85% against the French franc (WEFA, *CPE Current Analysis* No. 24–25, 1984, p. 10).

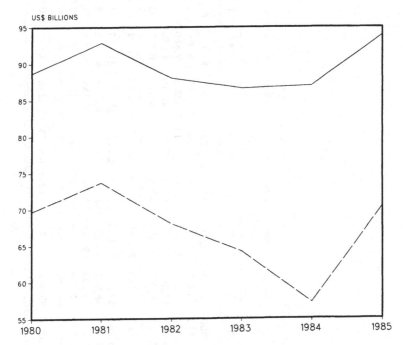

Figure 2.3. Total Eastern European gross (———) and net (---) debt, 1980–5. *Source:* Table 2.11.

further factor was the writing down of Eastern European liabilities by Western banks (particularly for Poland and Romania). The rise in debt in 1985 resulted from borrowing to cover hard-currency current-account deficits (Bulgaria and Hungary) and to build up reserves (GDR, Hungary, Bulgaria). The borrowed funds were used also in the case of Hungary to provide export credits to developing countries (often at negligible interest rates).

The Soviet Union's gross debt grew at relatively lower rates than in the seventies, increasing from $17.8 billion in 1980 to $20.0 billion in 1982 and $21.6 billion in 1984; the sharp increase in debt in 1985 was due mainly to borrowing to build up external reserves and to finance exports of arms and machinery to the developing countries.

Poland, the most indebted CMEA country, increased its gross debt from $25.0 billion in 1980 to an estimated $27 billion in 1984

Table 2.11. *Eastern European hard-currency debt, 1980–5 (millions of U.S. dollars, end-period)*

	Gross debt						Net debt					
	1980	1981	1982	1983	1984	1985	1980	1981	1982	1983	1984	1985
Bulgaria	3,560	3,060	2,760	2,610	2,300	2,409	2,771	2,220	1,736	1,501	850	635
Czechoslovakia	4,930	4,500	4,050	3,700	3,350	3,013	3,674	3,403	3,308	2,769	2,000	1,943
GDR	14,100	14,900	13,000	12,650	12,880	13,108	11,604	12,320	10,714	9,000	7,880	7,415
Hungary	9,090	8,699	7,715	8,250	8,900	11,260	5,856	5,856	5,089	4,940	4,550	9,358
Romania	9,557	10,160	9,766	8,880	7,480	6,000	8,305	8,793	8,055	8,648	6,551	5,500
CMEA 5	41,227	41,309	37,281	36,090	34,910	35,790	32,210	32,592	28,902	24,858	21,831	24,851
Poland	25,000	26,411	26,975	26,396	26,980	30,204	23,646	24,663	25,725	25,253	24,115	28,606
East. Eur. 6	66,227	67,720	64,256	64,486	61,890	65,994	55,856	57,255	54,627	50,111	45,946	53,457
Soviet Union	17,800	20,900	20,000	20,500	21,600	25,193	9,628	12,520	9,896	10,783	10,493	14,545
CMEA banks	4,650	4,250	3,800	3,600	3,600	2,500[a]	4,250	3,950	3,550	3,350	3,300	2,500[a]
Total	88,677	92,870	88,056	86,586	87,090	93,687	69,734	73,725	68,073	64,244	59,739	70,502

Note: Net debt is gross debt minus foreign assets of CMEA countries. In the case of Bulgaria, Czechoslovakia, and the Soviet Union, only BIS-area bank deposits are taken into account. For the GDR, only deposits in BIS-area banks and estimated deposits in West German banks are taken into account. For Hungary, Poland, and Romania, all foreign hard-currency assets are substracted from gross debt for the period 1980–4; for 1985 only BIS-area deposits are taken into account. (These three countries adopted the definition of gross debt in convertible currencies, which determines the gross debt, as a sum of liabilities vis-à-vis BIS/OECD-reporting countries and the following types of debt: all convertible currency credits extended by the financial institutions of Eastern and other countries that do not report to BIS/OECD; nonguaranteed nonbank credits, i.e., supplier credits not held by banks; and convertible-currency credits from international institutions.)

[a]Author's estimates.

Sources: WEFA, *CPE Current Analysis*, No. 25–6:23 (1985); id., CPE Service, April 1986; the data for 1984 are from Vanous and Movit (1985).

and $30 billion in 1985; the rise in debt in 1985 entirely reflects the effect of the U.S. dollar depreciation on the nondollar liabilities.

Net debt. The Eastern European net debt (Table 2.11, Figure 2.3) peaked at $73.7 billion in 1981, declining to $68.0 billion in 1982 and to $59.7 billion in 1984. It sharply increased in 1985, once more approaching the level of 1980 – around $70 billion. The net debt for 1985 is estimated as the difference between gross debt and the assets held only in BIS-area banks; hence, the net debt level, particularly for Hungary, GDR, and the Soviet Union, might be considerably lower.

The Soviet Union decreased its net debt from $12.5 billion in 1981 to roughly $10.5 billion in 1984; the increase of debt in 1985 was in excess of $4.0 billion (without CMEA banks), which represents the largest increase since 1970. The six Eastern European countries reduced their net debt from $57.2 billion in 1981 to $45.9 billion in 1984. This was mostly due to the fall in the net debt of Bulgaria, Czechoslovakia, GDR, Hungary, and Romania. Poland's net debt continued to increase in 1981 and 1982, and fell only slightly in 1983 and 1984.

However, in real terms, the CMEA countries' net debt decreased in 1980–4 by more than the level represented in Table 2.11. Besides assets held in BIS-reporting banks these countries have other reserves, including deposits in banks outside the BIS-reporting area, short-, medium-, and long-term claims on sovereign borrowers, gold, and so on. Unfortunately, data on these holdings are available only for Hungary, Romania, and Poland among the CMEA countries; but these data are often inadequate (even for Hungary).

Commercial borrowing. Most Eastern European debt to the West since 1980 resulted from commercial borrowing. Appendix Table A.1 shows the development of the CMEA debt to Western commercial banks since 1980. The six Eastern European countries reduced their total gross liabilities from $46.4 billion at end-1980 to $31.6 billion at end-1984 (i.e., by more than 31%). In the first three months of 1985, their liabilities declined further to $31.4 billion. However, in the second half of 1985 the liabilities sharply increased (due to developments described earlier) and reached $37.6 billion at end-December 1985, representing a rise of 20%. The GDR's borrowing increased by $2 billion at end-December 1985, and that of Hungary by more than $1.5 billion as compared with the first quarter of 1985.

All of the smaller CMEA countries considerably lowered their liabilities during 1980–4. Poland and Romania decreased them respectively from $15.1 billion and $5.3 billion at end-1980 to $8.8 billion and $3.1 billion at end-March 1985, representing for both countries a decline of 42%. That was primarily the result of restricted Western bank lending to the CMEA countries after Poland's and Romania's debt-servicing difficulties surfaced in 1981 and 1982. In addition, the reduction of debt in U.S. dollar terms reflects the strength of the U.S. dollar until mid-1985, the writing off of credits to these countries in the West (particularly in the United States and West German banks), and the transfer to Western export credit agencies of debt previously owed to commercial banks but guaranteed by the agencies (which was especially relevant to Poland).[13] The Soviet Union was the only CMEA country to increase its liabilities in 1982–4. They rose from $13.4 billion at end-1980 to about $17 billion in end-1984 and $16 billion in the first quarter of 1985. The Soviet Union's borrowing continued to increase and its liabilities reached $22.6 billion at end-December 1985.

Asset positions in commercial banks. A feature of the financial position of the CMEA countries during 1982–5 was the substantial rise in their deposit (asset) positions in BIS-reporting banks. Soviet deposits in Western commercial banks more than trebled from $3.6 billion in mid-1981 to a record level $13.0 billion at end-December 1985. The six Eastern European countries' assets rose from $5.0 billion in mid-1982 to $10.8 billion at end-December 1984, and $13.9 billion in December 1985 (i.e., more than 216% and 278%, respectively). Poland's deposits (although still at a very low level) roughly doubled, and those of the GDR and Bulgaria quadrupled reaching $6.5 billion and $2.1 billion, respectively, by the end of 1985. Romania's reserves remained very low (at end-1985, $0.4 billion), making this country particularly vulnerable to external shocks (e.g., falling oil prices, reduced access to Western commodity and capital markets).

---

[13] Note that because writing off does not extinguish the commercial banks' claims on Poland, that country's debt to commercial banks has not acutally declined to $8.8 billion.

This development of the Eastern European countries' asset position at the BIS-reporting banks determined the decline of the net debt (net liabilities), in the period 1983–4. The Soviet Union's net liabilities decreased from $10.5 billion in mid-1981 to $4.7 billion in mid-1984, and $5.3 billion at end-1984. However, the liabilities sharply rose in U.S. dollar terms in 1985 due to the depreciation of the dollar and increased borrowing.

The six smaller Eastern European countries reduced their net debt to BIS-reporting banks from $37.4 billion in mid-1981 to $20.3 billion in mid-1985 and $23.7 billion at end-1985. Poland decreased its net liabilities from end-1980 to end-1985 by more than $6 billion, Romania by almost $2.4 billion, the GDR by about $3.7 billion, Bulgaria by $1.1 billion, and Czechoslovakia by roughly $0.5 billion. Hungary's net liabilities remained high: $6.4 billion at end-1985 as compared to $6.1 billion at end-1980.

The buildup in Eastern European assets in 1983–5 was mostly the result of the combination of hard-currency trade surpluses, which the six Eastern European countries and the Soviet Union have run since 1982, and borrowing on the Western financial markets which started to pick up in 1983. The inflow of funds appears to have been added to the deposit positions. The rapid rise in assets reflected the desire of the CMEA countries to rebuild reserves and their intention to effect changes in banks' perceptions of CMEA creditworthiness. The costs of holding assets is not that high; with the falling interest rates and spreads in 1985 and 1986, interest earned offsets in large part the interest paid on borrowed funds. However, the building up of assets and paying off of liabilities has the same effect on the level of net debt of the CMEA countries.

The strong asset positions of the Soviet Union, GDR, Hungary, Bulgaria, and Czechoslovakia reflect also the policy of these countries to reduce their vulnerability to swings in Western bank lending. The debt difficulties of Eastern Europe during 1981–2 showed that large financial needs could not be handled with the low level of assets held in BIS-area and other banks. Hungary and the GDR are particularly favored by Western banks at present; however, the heavy borrowing by Hungary in order to increase its reserves may prove costly to it in the next few years because of its large financial needs (including the provision of export credits to developing countries at very low – in some cases, even zero – interest rates).

Maturity structures. The maturity structure of liabilities also shows relative improvement since 1981 (Table A.2). In the case of the six Eastern European countries, the proportion of liabilities due in up to one year decreased by mid-1985 as compared to end-1981. Liabilities due after two years or more increased from 34% to 40%. This debt management policy reduced pressure on their balances of payments. The share of the Soviet Union's liabilities due in over two years slightly declined in mid-1983, but afterwards increased to 34% at end-1984 and 32% mid-1985. Poland's maturity structure changed considerably between mid-1981 and mid-1985: Liabilities due within a year decreased from 32% to 20%; those due in one to two years dropped from 15% to 10%; and liabilities due in over two years rose from 36% to 56%. Romania's maturity structure changed as well: Liabilities due in up to one year declined from 43% in mid-1981 to 22% at end-1984, but rose again to 25% in mid-1985; at the same time, liabilities due in over two years increased from 25% to 40%. These changes in the maturity structures of the debt of Poland and Romania were due mainly to rescheduling, as discussed in Chapter 3. Hungary, GDR, and Bulgaria were the only Eastern European countries that increased considerably their short-term liabilities (used in 1981–3 not only for financing trade flows but also for meeting payments on medium-term credits due) while decreasing those due in over two years (except GDR) in the period mid-1981–mid-1985.

New credits. During 1983–6 there was a recovery in new credits to Eastern Europe in the form of Western medium- and long-term bank loans, after the crisis years 1981 and 1982. Table 2.7 shows the medium- and long-term funds raised by the six Eastern European countries and the Soviet Union on the international financial markets since the beginning of 1980. Poland's and Romania's debt difficulties in 1981 led to increased caution by the Western banks in their lending to Eastern Europe in 1981 and 1982. Banks sharply reduced their exposure and canceled short-term lines to the CMEA countries during the first quarter of 1982. As a result, the new funds raised by these countries on the international financial market fell to $704 million in 1982, from a level of $2.7 billion in 1980 and $1.6 billion in 1981. The lending to Eastern Europe was restricted to credits with maturities of only two to three years and interest rates approximately 3% above LIBOR. The CMEA countries had limited access to the syndicated Euromarkets, the only exception being Hungary, which was able to remain in the market by paying higher spreads and having the "seal of approval" of the IMF and the World Bank.

The high-cost borrowing, the precluded access to routine refinancing, and the withdrawal of short-term Western deposits from Hungary, GDR, Poland, and Romania in early 1982 (see section "Historical origins of the debt problem") led to serious liquidity difficulties in those countries. The loss of confidence in CMEA creditworthiness also hit Hungary and GDR, countries with reputations as reliable borrowers. By contrast with Poland and Romania, which had to reschedule their debt (see Chapter 3), Hungary and GDR avoided rescheduling with the help of the international financial community. Hungary entered the IMF and the World Bank, received "bridging" credits from BIS and also credits from commercial banks. The special relationship between GDR and West Germany (the so-called West German umbrella for the GDR), was an important factor in avoiding rescheduling, as the GDR was able to service its debt. However, GDR did not receive credits from West Germany in the crisis year 1982; it received two credits guaranteed by the West German government in 1983 and 1984 in the amounts of 1 million DM and 950 million DM, respectively (OECD 1985b, p. 25).

Table A.3 provides data on the Eastern European borrowing sources in 1982 and 1983, when the level of supplier credits was particularly high. A lower level of funds was borrowed in the Euromarket. At a lower level still was the flow of funds from Arab banks and factoring, forfeiting, and switch activities.

The credits recovered in 1983 to $1.0 billion with syndicated or club funds raised by Czechoslovakia, GDR, Hungary, and the Soviet Union. In 1984 the new credits to Eastern Europe increased to $3.3 billion, with funds raised by the GDR (which reentered the market successfully in late 1984 after the loans received from West Germany), Hungary, the Soviet Union, the international CMEA banks, and Poland (after the rescheduling agreement with the Western commercial banks from April 1984). Lending conditions improved with loan maturities of not less than three years. Japanese banks were particularly involved in lending to Eastern Europe.

The Western lending activity rose in 1984 and 1985 to the highest level since 1980.[14] The credits reached $5.2 billion in 1985, and in the first three months of 1986 the raised funds equaled the amount provided for the whole of 1983. The syndicated loans were often oversubscribed, indicating that Western lenders were again confident of the creditworthiness of Eastern Europe (except for Poland), compared to their still negative assessments of the creditworthiness of the Latin American debtor countries.

Although Bulgaria and Czechoslovakia did not raise funds in 1984, preferring to rely upon intrabank credits, which are relatively cheaper and on which no separate statistics are available, in 1985 and in early 1986 they were active in the market and received credits of seven-to-eight-year maturity (OECD 1986, p. 38). Romania also relied upon intrabank loans and did not have access to the Euromarket in 1982–3. However, in 1984 Romania failed to borrow not only because Western lenders were reluctant to provide credits but because of its politically motivated decision to reduce debt and to avoid Western loans. In 1985, Romania reentered the market with a $150 million loan. In early 1986, it once more experienced difficulties in servicing debt to commercial banks and the World Bank, but it again avoided the market. Romania has built up arrears, which would have been avoidable had it borrowed in order to ease short-term payments problems and to avoid rescheduling of its commercial bank debt in July 1986.

Poland's debt crisis largely precludes its access to Western syndicated loans and government credits. In August 1985, Poland received for the first time since 1980 an officially guaranteed credit from a Western country: The Austrian government guaranteed a credit line in the amount of $40 million to finance imports from Austria. In mid-1986 France, West Germany, and Great Britain decided to reopen official credit lines to Poland. The British government, for example, agreed to provide a $30 million revolving line for short-term business (*Financial Times,* June 10, 1986, p. 3). However the improvement of the credit relations between Poland and the Western banks and government agencies will be a slow process in the second half of the 1980s and will depend on the ability of

---

[14] Not all syndicated lending to the Eastern European countries is reflected in the BIS and OECD data, as the part held as assets outside the banking system or by banks outside the BIS-area is not known. Consequently, syndicated and club lending to the Eastern European Six and the Soviet Union could be higher than the figures shown in Table 2.7.

this country to limit its debt increase and meet principal and interest payments as contractually due.

Credit terms. The terms on Western bank syndicated credits, measured in terms of margins over LIBOR, were more favorable for the Eastern European countries during 1984–5 and in 1986 in comparison to their levels in 1982 and 1983. Annual average spreads (hundredths of a percentage point over LIBOR) on international bank loans (Table 2.12) decreased from 103 basis points in 1982 and 112 in 1983 to 88 in 1984 and 55 in 1985. Their level in 1985 was far below the level in late 1970s and early 1980s. Although the terms were better than the average to all borrowers (62 basis points) they remained not as favorable as those obtained by Western borrowers from the OECD area (43).

The conditions offered by Western banks were judged to be too expensive by the CMEA borrowers during 1982–4, and in some cases borrowings were postponed because no agreement was reached. Czechoslovakia was unwilling to pay one percentage point over LIBOR (including fees) for a five-year loan in 1984 (*International Herald Tribune,* September 17, 1984, p. 21). The Soviet Union also considered as too expensive the credit conditions on a loan and preferred to pay cash for imported French equipment destined for the Astrakhan gas-condensing plant (Schmeljov 1984, p. 91).

In general, however, compared with the debtor countries in Latin America, borrowing conditions during 1984–5 and in 1986 have improved in both relative and absolute terms for the CMEA countries, and particularly for the Soviet Union. The Soviet Union raised funds with eight-year maturity and a highly favorable interest rate of one-quarter percentage point above LIBOR in 1985–6. Czechoslovakia, GDR, and Bulgaria borrowed with spreads of three-eighths to one-half percent above LIBOR (OECD 1986, p. 38), and Hungary raised considerable funds in 1985–6 at three-quarter percent above LIBOR. After signing a new credit in the amount of $300 million in June 1986, the Hungarian banker Janos Fekete said his country was able to borrow at very good terms, and optimistically stated that Hungary was a "star of the credit market" (*Financial Times,* June 11, 1986, p. 2).

The relatively low borrowing by some of the Eastern European countries in 1984 and early 1985 was a result of not only the high credit costs at that time but also a weak demand for new funds. They

Table 2.12. *Average annual spread on international bank loans
(basis points*[a]*)*

	1979	1980	1981	1982	1983	1984	1985
OECD area	62	59	58	56	64	62	43
Eastern Europe	70	88	62	103	112	88	55
OPEC	105	77	79	94	85	69	58
Other developing countries	85	91	104	114	170	158	91
General average	79	74	80	77	114	117	62

[a]Hundredths of a percentage point over LIBOR.
Sources: United Nations, *Economic Bulletin for Europe* 36:82 (1984); OECD (1985, p. 21; 1986, p. 39); World Bank, *World Debt Tables* (April 1986), pp. XV-XVI.

were hesitant in accumulating additional debt, given the financial difficulties of earlier years; such was the policy particularly of Bulgaria and Czechoslovakia. The accelerated borrowing in 1985 and early 1986 of the Eastern European countries (except Poland and Romania) indicates that they have reestablished their credibility in the Western financial markets.

The six Eastern European countries and the Soviet Union benefited from the rise of interest rates on commercial credits in 1984, which contributed to higher earnings on their growing deposits in Western banks. At the same time this put upward pressure on their debt-servicing capacity, since inflation rates in the Western countries continued to ease and the real interest rates increased as well. The average interest rates on a basket of Eurocurrencies rose from 8.6% in 1983 to 9.2% in 1984 (9.8% in the last quarter of 1984); however, this is significantly below the average interest rates in 1981 (14.3%) and 1982 (11.6%). The average interest rates on new credits fell to 8% in 1985, which decreased considerably the pressure on servicing debt (Table 2.13).

Another feature of the borrowing activity of the six Eastern European countries and the Soviet Union since the 1981 crisis has been the diversification of financial instruments employed. These include club and syndicated loans, IMF credits, cofinancing with the World Bank (for Hungary), various guaranteed credits and credit

Table 2.13. *Average interest rate on a basket of*
Eurocurrencies, 1978–85 (percentage)

Year	Rate	Year	Rate	Year	Rate
1978	6.8	1981	14.3	1984	9.2
1979	9.3	1982	11.6	1985	8.0
1980	11.6	1983	8.6		

Sources: United Nations, *Economic Bulletin for Europe* 36:84
(1984); World Bank, *World Debt Tables* (April 1986), p. XII.

lines, bankers' acceptances, floating rate notes, note issuance facilities, Eurobonds, BIS bridge lines (for Hungary), and others. Hungary is the only Eastern European country particularly active in the
securities market at present.[15] It appears that, in the future, commercial banks will play a less direct role in international lending
whereas the provision of credit through the international securities
markets will increase. Because of a lack of market experience, the
Eastern European countries (except for Hungary and the Soviet
Union) probably will enter the market cautiously in the next
years.

Guaranteed debt. The share of the guaranteed debt[16] in the gross debt
of the Eastern European countries and the Soviet Union (Table
2.14) increased from 21% in 1979 to 48% in 1982 and 44% in 1985.
The Soviet guaranteed debt (including the CMEA banks) had the
highest level among the Eastern European countries (1982, 74%;
1983, 69%; 1985, 47%) followed by Bulgaria (1982, 32%; 1983, 34%;
1985, 33%) and Poland (1982, 41%; 1983, 45%; 1985, 62%).[17] The
share of the guaranteed debt in the gross debt was relatively lower
for Czechoslovakia, GDR (except for 1985), Romania (particularly
the share of nonbank credits), and Hungary (see Tables 2.11 and

[15] During 1984–5, access to the securities market was precluded for many LDCs. Of
the NICs only Korea, Malaysia, and Thailand were successful issuers in the capital
market (World Bank, *World Debt Tables,* April 1986, p. XIX).
[16] This covers guaranteed bank credits plus guaranteed nonbank credits, the latter
including export credits extended by governments or government agencies and
officially guaranteed or insured buyers and suppliers' credits.
[17] Calculated on the basis of data from Tables 2.4, 2.8, 2.11, and 2.14.

Table 2.14. *Guaranteed debt of Eastern Europe: Western commercial bank claims plus nonbank trade-related credits, 1980–5 (millions of U.S. dollars)*

	1980	1981	1982	1983	1984	1985
Bulgaria	1,000	890	883	808	708	795
Czechoslovakia	740	790	846	838	736	1,356
GDR	2,100	2,300	2,503	2,930	2,866	6,030
Hungary	220	320	464	536	390	1,362
Poland[a]	10,500	12,336	11,200	11,900	16,818	18,726
Romania[b]	1,750	1,845	1,428	1,226	1,083	960
Soviet Union	7,800	7,900	17,644	16,584	8,417	11,937
Total	24,110	26,381	42,252[c]	40,976[c]	31,018	41,166

[a]Guaranteed convertible-currency debt to all Western countries, including interest arrears.
[b]All export credits under governmental guarantee.
[c]Including CMEA banks.
Sources: United Nations, *Economic Bulletin for Europe* 26:88 (1984); Vanous and Movit (1985); WEFA, CPE Service (April 1986).

2.14). These tendencies are typical of the shares of guaranteed credits in total CMEA bank liabilities vis-à-vis BIS/OECD-reporting countries as well (see Tables A.1, A.2, and 2.14).

The increase of guaranteed credits in the total gross debt of Eastern Europe since 1982 has been due to the willingness of the Western official credit and guarantee agencies to provide or insure credits to most of the Eastern European countries in order to maintain export shares in their markets during a period of slowdown of economic activity in the West. In most cases these credits were tied to the purchase of machinery, equipment, and so on. The CMEA countries preferred to use guaranteed credits to finance their imports because of the difficulties in raising funds on the Western market. Since 1984, however, the guaranteed credits have been provided by the Western agencies on relatively more expensive terms. In accordance with the new pricing formula adopted in October 1983 (and effective as of July 15, 1984) by the OECD countries, the officially supported export credit interest rates were raised by 120 basis (1.2 percentage) points. Three of the CMEA countries – Czechoslovakia, GDR, and the Soviet Union – are classified in the

Table 2.15. *Currency composition of Eastern European debt, 1981–5*
(weighted average in percentage)

	1981	1982	1983	1984	1985
U.S. dollar	53	53	53	55	55
Deutsche mark	16	16	16	16	16
Swiss franc	15	15	14	14	14
French franc	5	5	5	4	4
British pound	5	4	5	4	4
Other currencies[a]	6	7	6	7	6

[a]Japenese yen, Austrian schillings, etc.
Source: Calculated from WEFA, CPE Service, April 1986.

group of relatively rich countries, and their interest rates are 13.35% (for 2–5-yr maturity) and 13.60% (for 5–8.5-yr maturity). Poland, Hungary, Romania, and Bulgaria belong to the intermediate countries, and their interest rates are 11.55% and 11.90%, respectively (United Nations, *Economic Bulletin for Europe,* 1984, p. 89).

Currency composition. The currency composition of debt as shown in Table 2.15 has not changed much since the beginning of the 1980s. More than 50% of the borrowed funds are denominated in U.S. dollars, followed by Deutsche marks (16%), Swiss francs (14%–15%), French francs (4%–5%), and British pounds (4%–5%). More than 6% of the credits are denominated in Japanese yen, Austrian schillings, and other convertible currencies. This composition of debt indicates the extent of the effects of appreciation/depreciation of the major Western currencies, and particularly of the U.S. dollar, on the level of debt and debt servicing.

Indicators of debt burden and creditworthiness. Indicators of the burden of external debt and of creditworthiness have improved for Eastern European countries (except Poland and Hungary) since 1982, mainly as a result of the reduction of the CMEA gross and net debt and increased exports to the Western industrialized economies in 1983–4 (Table A.4). In particular, the debt service ratios, the liquidity ratios, and the ratios of gross debt to exports and net debt to exports improved in 1982–5 (Tables 2.16 and 2.17). Developments varied widely among countries. For example, the debt ratios of Poland and Hungary were very high: The debt service ratios of these countries were 109% and 70%, respectively, in 1985; the debt service ratios of GDR and Romania (both 26%) were very close to the "critical" 25% level.

The Eastern European liquidity ratios improved considerably during 1983–5 (Table 2.16). The Soviet Union's liquidity ratio increased from 21% in 1981 to 28% in 1983 and reached 36% and 35%, respectively, in 1984 and 1985. The GDR (70%), Bulgaria (51%), and Hungary (44%) had the highest liquidity ratios among the six Eastern European countries in 1985. These improvements were due to the substantial buildup in the CMEA asset positions with BIS-reporting banks (Tables A.1 and A.2) and to the cut in CMEA imports from the developed market economies in 1982 and 1983 (Table A.4). The liquidity ratios deteriorated in 1984 (except for the Soviet Union and Hungary) mainly as a result of increased hard-currency imports. Although the Eastern European Six increased their imports in 1985, their liquidity ratios improved because of the substantial buildup of assets in BIS-area banks.

Compared to developments in the debt service ratios of the most heavily indebted countries (World Bank, *World Debt Tables,* April 1986, p. XXV), the ratios of the Eastern European Six show similar trends in 1980–5. However, the debt service ratios of Poland and Hungary were much higher in 1985 than those of Brazil (40%), Mexico (44%), Argentina (20%), and Yugoslavia (14%). The ratios of all of the Eastern European countries were considerably higher than those of the debtor countries in East Asia (Korea, Singapore, and others) and reflect the weakness of debt management and export strategy in Eastern European countries compared to those of East Asia. The gross debt/exports and net debt/exports ratios show similar development. A peculiarity of the indicators of the credit-worthiness of Eastern European countries was the higher level of liquidity ratios in 1983–5 compared to Latin American countries, East Asian countries, and Yugoslavia. The most indebted CMEA country, Poland, had a liquidity ratio of 30% in 1983; Brazil's was 24%, Mexico's 28%, Yugoslavia's 28%, and Korea's 14%.[18]

---

[18] Calculated from World Bank, *World Debt Tables* (April 1986) for the individual countries.

Table 2.16. *CMEA debt service and liquidity ratios, 1980–5*

	Debt service ratios[a]						Liquidity ratios[b]					
	1980	1981	1982	1983	1984	1985	1980	1981	1982	1983	1984	1985
Bulgaria	35	33	34	29	16	14	36	29	35	44	23	51
Czechoslovakia	24	19	18	22	25	31	25	23	17	23	17	32
GDR	58	60	50	40	36	26	28	30	28	44	43	70
Hungary	25	40	36	34	50	70	29	19	16	30	35	44
Poland	99	87	80	68	70	109	8	13	24	30	17	32
Romania	27	38	41	42	15	26	3	4	6	12	8	10
Soviet Union	8	9	8	8	1	14	25	21	26	28	36	35

[a]All interest and amortization of medium- and long-term debt as a percentage of exports to market economies.
[b]Ratio of liquid assets to imports from market economies.
Sources: United Nations, *Economic Bulletin for Europe* 36:106–8 (1984); OECD (1985b, p. 32); author's estimates.

Table 2.17. *Gross debt/exports and net debt/exports ratios of the CMEA countries, 1980–5*

	Gross debt/exports ratios						Net debt/exports ratios					
	1980	1981	1982	1983	1984	1985	1980	1981	1982	1983	1984	1985
Bulgaria	117	92	84	91	73	76	91	88	80	52	27	20
Czechoslovakia	109	105	99	88	81	74	81	84	79	66	49	48
GDR	267	222	165	148	148	144	219	183	136	105	90	81
Hungary	184	178	155	165	182	253	118	120	102	99	93	210
Poland	314	458	470	448	431	500	299	427	489	428	385	474
Romania	145	140	157	142	108	88	126	121	129	106	58	80
Soviet Union	57	65	56	57	61	81	31	31	39	30	30	47

Sources: OECD (1985b, p. 30); author's estimates.

Insolvency or illiquidity

Was the debt crisis in Eastern Europe at the beginning of the 1980s one of insolvency or illiquidity? The anlaysis of the debt situation of the six Eastern European countries and the Soviet Union, given the discussion of sovereign illiquidity and insolvency in the "Note on state creditworthiness," admits the following conclusions:

The debt difficulties of Poland and Romania at the beginning of the 1980s were *insolvency* problems, leading to a failure of these countries to fulfill obligations to the Western governments and commercial banks lenders (suspending payments) and to reschedulings of their debt. The Polish official debt was not serviced during 1982–6. The debt problem of Poland generally is still one of insolvency, because it is not able to restore creditworthiness in the short-term, and new reschedulings of commercial and official debt will be necessary in the next several years.[19] The debt crisis is so severe that it will not be possible for Poland to restore the full servicing of the debt before the 1990s.

Hungary and the GDR also faced debt problems in the beginning of the 1980s, but these were (and remain) manageable in the short-term through temporary financing combined with policy adjustment. Hence the situation is best described as temporary *illiquidity*, not insolvency.

The Soviet Union, Bulgaria, and Czechoslovakia do not belong to either of the above-discussed groups of "debt crisis" countries in Eastern Europe. However, the debt-servicing difficulties of Bulgaria in the late 1970s stemmed from the lack of liquidity.

---

[19] According to the vice-president of the Polish Planning Commission, a sufficiently large positive balance of trade can appear no earlier than in 1987–8 (Fallenbuchl 1984, p. 16). In a speech at the Polish Parliament in November 1985, former Finance Minister S. Nieckarz noted that the payment situation regarding the Western countries was tense, and predicted that the expected surplus in hard-currency trade balance in 1986 would be insufficient to arrest the debt increase (*Wall Street Journal,* November 29, 1985, p. 16). According to the director of the Research Institute of Foreign Trade in Warsaw, J. Soldaczuk, Poland will be able to balance its hard-currency current account no earlier than 1990 (Soldaczuk 1985, p. 9). Taking into account the steadily negative Polish current account since the beginning of the 1980s, the pessimistic prospects for improvement of the balance of trade, and the restricted borrowing on the Western financial markets, it must be concluded that continued rescheduling of the debt is unavoidable. (See the discussion of Poland's reschedulings in Chapter 3).

Historical origins of the debt problem

I have analyzed how the debt of Eastern Europe evolved during the 1970s and how foreign borrowing led to more or less severe debt-servicing problems. The origins of those problems are found in two groups of factors: (1) the internal economic (growth) performance of CMEA countries; (2) the external disturbances of the early and late 1970s.

Internal factors

High growth targets were characteristic of the plans for the Eastern European Six and Soviet Union economies at the beginning of the 1970s. Increased growth required rapid enlargement of the share of investment in the national economies. As described in Chapter 1 this was accompanied by the typical centrally planned economies' expansion drive and investment "hunger." The investment "hunger" led to increased demand for machinery, equipment, and so on, and enforced the import "hunger" that is the driving force behind the foreign trade of the CMEA countries.

The demand for imported Western investment goods and modern technologies grew rapidly with the liberalization of imports during the 1970s – the period of détente in East–West relations, when the CMEA countries changed attitudes toward East–West trade and financial relations. As discussed in Chapter 1, in the 1950s and 1960s these countries relied on domestic savings and intrabloc bilateral credits to finance investment. Strong preference was given toward import substitution. The trade flows were oriented primarily to the intra-CMEA market, which limited trade and credit relations with the West. Political considerations restricted external borrowing in hard currency, which was regarded as counter to the national independence of the Eastern European countries. As a result of the policy to balance trade with the West, the CMEA external borrowing was restricted primarily to short-term trade-related credits.

At the beginning of the 1970s the East European Six and the Soviet Union attempted to introduce productivity and aggregate output gains through accelerated imports of Western technology, which were expected to help modernize CMEA industries, introduce sophisticated products (electronics, electrical industry,

Table 2.18. *National income (net material product) in Eastern Europe,*

	1966-70	1971-5	1974	1975	1976	1977
Bulgaria						
Produced	8.7	7.9	7.6	8.8	6.5	6.3
Used domest.	n.a.	8.6	9.0	11.1	0.7	2.2
Czechoslovakia						
Produced	6.9	5.7	5.9	6.2	4.2	4.2
Used domest.	n.a.	6.1	8.0	4.5	3.1	1.4
GDR						
Produced	5.1	5.4	6.4	4.9	3.7	5.2
Used domest.	n.a.	4.7	6.0	2.7	5.7	4.8
Hungary						
Produced	6.8	6.3	6.9	5.4	3.0	7.8
Used domest.	n.a.	5.6	12.6	5.8	1.2	6.0
Poland						
Produced	5.7	9.8	10.4	9.0	6.8	5.0
Used domest.	n.a.	11.6	12.0	10.9	7.0	2.7
Romania						
Produced	7.7	11.3	12.3	10.3	10.5	9.0
Used domest.	n.a.	n.a.	n.a.	n.a.	n.a.	n.a.
Soviet Union						
Produced	7.8	5.7	5.4	4.5	5.9	4.5
Used domest.	n.a.	5.1	4.8	4.1	5.0	3.5

Note: National income used domestically = Absorption = $C + I + G$. Net
Sources: Portes (1980a, p. 33); WEFA, *CPE Current Analysis,* No. 26-7:5
the Soviet Union and Eastern Europe, No. 7-11:15-16 (1986); Plan Econ, *Review*

etc.), enhance the competitiveness of CMEA exports in Western
markets, boost labor productivity, and thereby lead to faster
economic growth. The Eastern European Six (particularly Poland,
Romania, Hungary, and Czechoslovakia) undertook many energy-
intensive investment projects in steel and in modern petrochemicals production. Some of them (Hungary, Bulgaria) were almost
completely dependent on imported energy sources. Although
imports of machinery and equipment clearly had to be financed by
raising funds on the Western capital markets, it was expected that
the resultant debt would be repaid in the 1970s and 1980s through
accelerated exports to the West. The differences in the implementation of this development strategy among the Eastern European
countries were attributable mainly to differences in their internal
policy choices.

1966–85 (Average annual growth rates, in percentages)

1978	1979	1976–80	1981	1982	1983	1984	1985
5.6	6.5	6.1	5.0	4.2	2.9	4.6	0.7
5.5	3.2	2.8	7.7	1.9	1.5	2.8	1.9
4.0	n.a.	3.7	−0.1	−0.3	2.2	2.8	3.1
2.7	2.7	2.2	−3.4	−1.5	0.9	1.5	1.3
4.0	4.0	4.1	4.8	2.5	4.4	5.5	4.8
1.4	n.a.	3.6	1.3	−3.4	2.8	3.3	2.3
4.0	1.2	3.2	2.5	2.3	0.2	2.9	−0.7
10.0	6.0	1.9	0.7	−1.4	−2.5	−0.4	0.2
2.8	−2.0	1.2	−12.0	−5.5	4.5	5.1	3.0
0.7	n.a.	−0.2	−10.5	−10.5	3.5	5.0	3.5
7.6	6.2	7.3	2.2	2.6	3.4	7.7	5.9
n.a.	n.a.	6.9	−5.7	−2.6	−0.3	3.4	1.6
n.a.	n.a.	4.2	3.3	4.2	3.6	3.1	3.1
4.0	2.0	3.8	3.2	3.6	3.1	2.6	3.1

material product is net of intermediate inputs.
(1984), No 25–6:2 (1985); PlanEcon Report, *Developments in the Economies of and Outlook,* December 1985.

The direct impact of the net inflow of foreign resources on the overall position of disposable resources can be seen from the difference of the rates of growth of national income produced and national income used domestically. The latter includes the balance of foreign trade as the main additional item. The data from Table 2.18 show that in the first half of the 1970s the growth rates of the CMEA national income (produced and used domestically) were high.[20] Poland (9.8% and 11.6%), Romania (11.3% produced),

---

[20] The data on economic growth, consumption, and investment are based on the official statistics of the Eastern European countries. Note that there are varying degrees of distortions among these countries in publishing such data (see Marer 1985a).

Table 2.19. *Gross investment in fixed capital in Eastern Europe,*
1971–84 (average annual growth in real terms, percentage)

	1971–5	1976–80	1981	1982	1983	1984
Bulgaria	8.6	4.0	10.5	3.6	3.4	1.0
Czechoslovakia	8.2	3.5	−4.6	−2.3	2.2	4.4
GDR	4.8	3.4	2.8	−3.0	4.0	−0.2
Hungary	7.0	2.4	−5.2	−2.2	−5.0	−1.0
Poland	17.5	−3.0	−22.3	−12.2	4.8	8.0
Romania	11.5	8.5	−7.1	−3.1	2.9	6.1
Soviet Union	7.0	3.4	3.8	3.5	5.0	2.0

Sources: WEFA, *CPE Current Analysis,* No. 26–7:11 (1984), No. 25–6:6 (1985).

Table 2.20. *National income used for net investment*
(accumulation fund) in Eastern Europe, 1971–84,
(average annual growth in real terms, percentage)

	1971–5	1976–80	1981	1982	1983	1984
Bulgaria	12.9	0.1	14.8	−3.3	−5.2	1.4
Czechoslovakia	8.4	1.4	−21.7	−3.4	−5.1	−3.3
GDR	2.9	3.0	−3.4	−19.9	11.9	−0.6
Hungary	8.1	−2.0	−8.6	−13.2	−11.6	−6.2
Poland	18.1	−11.8	−27.6	−6.6	8.5	6.3
Romania	n.a.	6.6	−22.1	−5.4	−2.1	2.4
Soviet Union	3.3	3.2	0.9	11.0	4.3	1.4

Sources: WEFA *CPE Current Analysis,* No. 26–7:5 (1984), No. 25–5:2 (1985).

Hungary (6.3% and 5.6%), and Bulgaria (7.9% and 8.6%) had particularly high annual growth rates. The average growth rates of gross investment in fixed capital (Table 2.19) peaked at 17.5% in Poland and at 11.5% in Romania during 1971–5. The average annual rates of growth of national income used for net investment (Table 2.20) during 1971–5 were 18.1% in Poland, 12.9% in Bulgaria, 8.4% in Czechoslovakia, and 8.1% in Hungary. The growth rates in the Soviet Union (3.3%) and the GDR (2.9%) were relatively lower. At

Table 2.21. *National income used for consumption (consumption fund) in Eastern Europe, 1971-84 (average annual in real terms, percentage)*

	1971-5	1976-80	1981	1982	1983	1984
Bulgaria	7.0	4.0	5.3	3.7	3.8	3.2
Czechoslovakia	5.3	2.5	2.6	−1.1	2.4	2.6
GDR	5.3	3.8	2.7	1.2	0.8	4.2
Hungary	4.7	3.1	3.0	1.2	−0.2	0.5
Poland	8.7	4.5	−4.6	−11.5	2.1	4.6
Romania	n.a.	7.1	3.1	−1.5	0.4	3.8
Soviet Union	5.8	4.7	4.0	1.2	2.7	3.0

Sources: WEFA, *CPE Current Analysis,* No. 26-7:5 (1984), No. 25-6:2 (1985).

the same time the growth rates of national income used for consumption were lower (Table 2.21): Poland (8.7%), Hungary (4.7%), Bulgaria (7.0%), and so on.

The Eastern European imports of machinery and equipment from OECD countries increased by a factor of almost four in 1970-5 (in current prices). The increases in the Soviet Union, Poland, and Hungary were by factors of 4.5, 8.6, and 3.4, respectively.[21]

As discussed earlier, the consequences of CMEA imports of Western machinery and equipment and external debt that grew more rapidly than hard-currency exports during the 1970s were negative current-account balances with the industrialized West (Tables 2.2 and 2.3) and a deterioration in indicators of credit-worthiness.[22] One reason for this was that Western credits were not used to implement an outward-oriented development strategy and to raise exportables production, as was the case for the NICs in East Asia.

The average growth rates of national income, along with the gross and net investment in CMEA countries declined in the second half of the 1970s (Tables 2.18, 2.19, and 2.22). Some of the countries (Bulgaria, Hungary, and Romania), however, sustained their 1976-7 growth at rates close to those of 1971-5. Industrial production

---

[21] Author's estimates from the national foreign trade statistics.

[22] J. Fekete, the deputy chairman of the National Bank of Hungary, writes that Hungary does not strive for an equilibrium in the balance of trade. Furthermore, he stresses that a trade deficit is considered by the policymakers to be acceptable in the years of structural transformation of the economy (Fekete 1982, p. 198).

Table 2.22. *Net investment in fixed capital[a] in Eastern Europe,*
1971-84 (average annual growth in real terms, percentage)

	1971-5	1976-80	1981	1982	1983	1984
Bulgaria	n.a.	n.a.	12.3	0.4	−0.2	n.a.
Czechoslovakia	9.5	0.3	−11.1	−11.4	−1.5	n.a.
GDR	3.4	2.2	0.6	−9.0	1.9	n.a.
Hungary	n.a.	n.a.	−16.4	−14.6	−22.7	n.a.
Poland	19.6	−9.2	−24.2	−19.9	4.0	6.0
Romania	n.a.	8.4	−13.8	−9.6	−0.7	n.a.
Soviet Union	n.a.	n.a.	2.5	2.2	5.3	−1.1

[a]Including investment in unfinished construction.
Sources: WEFA, *CPE Current Analysis,* No. 26-7:11 (1984), No. 63-4:12
(1985), No. 61-2:3 (1985).

steadily increased (Table A.5). The imports of machinery and
equipment from OECD countries almost doubled during 1975-9
(in current prices). These imports and intermediate products imports were financed, as in the first half of the 1970s, by heavy
borrowing abroad. The increased imports of machinery and equipment forced significant acceleration also of Western imports of raw
materials and intermediate products in order to utilize imported
technology. After 1975, borrowed funds in Eastern Europe, as in
many Latin American countries (e.g., Costa Rica, Mexico), were
used not only to pay for imported machinery, equipment, and
intermediates but also for consumption goods. The Soviet Union,
for example, considerably increased its grain imports. However, the
use of Western credits to finance consumption was not offset by
increasing the domestic funds used for investment in import
replacement or efficient development of more exportables. This
was characteristic of the borrowing of all CMEA countries, particularly Poland.[23] The consequences of that policy were borrowing
for general balance-of-payments purposes (particularly for the East-

[23] In the second half of the 1970s, a big part of the Polish debt to the U.S. government was borrowings from the Commodity Credit Corporation to finance imports of
agricultural products (Crane 1985, p. 12).

ern Europe Six) and a rapid increase of hard-currency debts in the late 1970s. Czechoslovakia was the only Eastern European country to restrict borrowing in that period, but Bulgaria did so a few years later, after experiencing a liquidity crisis in 1978-9.

What, then, were the main characteristics of the economic and borrowing policies of Poland, Hungary, GDR, and Romania, countries that faced severe debt-serving difficulties at the beginning of the 1980s?

Poland. In the late sixties Poland had the same economic difficulties as other Eastern European countries: poor export performance of industry, lagging growth rates, and low labor productivity. In 1968 the Gomulka leadership discussed a strategy for the reconstruction of Polish industry, primarily oriented toward maximizing the growth of the more profitable exports (machine building and manufactured consumer goods). This strategy was expected to generate growth and to contribute to an increase in the "social productivity" (Brada and Montias 1985, p. 204) of the economy. After the serious political crisis in December 1970, which brought down the Gomulka leadership, the new secretary of the party, E. Gierek, announced a "new development strategy" for the reconstruction and modernization of the economy. Its main goals, which determined Polish economic and borrowing policy during the seventies were as follows:

rapid increase in living standards;
accelerated economic growth, generated by imported Western
     technology;
improved incentives for agriculture; and
economic reform.

The "new development strategy" aimed to raise per-capita consumption and living standards through increased labor productivity. In order to raise labor productivity, the Gierek leadership boosted real wages in the early 1970s (annual growth rates around 7% in 1971-5) and made more consumption goods available to households. It was expected that rapid growth in productivity would be generated in the long run both by a high rate of investment and sizable increases in real wages. Policymakers anticipated that a dynamic foreign trade policy would help to achieve a high rate of investment. They recognized that faster economic development would require importing capital from OECD countries. Borrowing on the Western financial markets was expected to fill the savings and trade resource gaps and to provide opportunities to buy high-technology licenses, machinery, and equipment from the OECD countries, which would help to modernize the industries and enhance the competitiveness of Polish exports in the West. Poland made large energy-intensive investments in steel production and petrochemicals (as did Hungary, Romania, Bulgaria, and Czechoslovakia), which required increased fuel imports, especially in the second half of the 1970s.

During the 1970s, Poland obtained Western credits estimated at $58 billion: $27 billion in 1971–6 and $31 billion in 1977–80.[24] Many agreements on industrial cooperation with Western firms were signed in the expectation that they would stimulate both imports and exports. Imports from nonsocialist countries rose 97% in 1972, 67% in 1973, 50% in 1974, and 23% in 1975. In the second half of the 1970s, import growth considerably decelerated. Balance-of-payments difficulties required a revision of the economic program and forced a halt to imports of Western machinery, which fell 25% in 1979 compared to their value in 1975 (in current prices). The share of imported Western machinery in total domestic machinery investment fell from 20% in 1976 to 12% in 1979 (1972, 7%; see Table 2.23).

Furthermore, Poland could not develop a successful export strategy. The drive for imports was not compensated by a simultaneous drive for exports, although Poland did diversify its exports to the West, which included consumer electronics, construction machinery, and cars and trucks (Poznanski 1986, p. 470). Exports grew by 5%–14% in nominal terms from 1973 to 1979.[25] A large number of the acquired foreign licenses were of little or no use. Of the licenses in heavy industry, 20% were never used, only 55% were

---

[24] The Western credits were used as follows (Kaminski 1985, pp. 10–11):

	1971–6	1977–80	% change in share
Fuels and energy (%)	4	8	+100
Intermediate products (%)	35	33	−6
Capital goods (%)	35	25	−29
Agricultural goods (%)	18	25	+39
Other consumption products (%)	8	9	+12

[25] Estimated from *Rocznik statystyczny* (Statistical Yearbook), various years.

Table 2.23. *Percentage shares of imported Western machinery
in total domestic machinery investment in the Soviet Union,
Poland, and Hungary, 1971–9*

	Soviet Union	Poland	Hungary
1971	3.9	n.a.	23.4
1972	3.0	7.4	27.4
1973	3.3	12.3	23.1
1974	3.7	16.2	23.7
1975	4.0	18.5	21.8
1976	6.7	20.2	22.9
1977	6.6	15.3	26.6
1978	6.0	13.5	28.6
1979	5.4	11.5	25.4

Source: Hanson (1982, p. 136).

realized in the planned period, and another 10% were subsequently
deemed to have been unnecessary because of the existence of
domestic alternatives; about 50% of the utilized licenses were highly
import-intensive.

However, poor export performance was partly due to factors
beyond the control of the Polish authorities. Some export items,
such as foodstuffs and manufactures, suffered from trade barriers in
the European community during the 1970s. Higher prices for coal
boosted exports from this sector, but coal exports stagnated after
the recession in 1974. Because of the rise in oil prices, the increased
cost of oil imports could not be compensated by the coal exports;
by the end of the decade, Poland became a net importer of fuels.
Agricultural production declined in 1975 due to poor weather.
Because the planning authorities devoted insufficient investment to
agriculture in the period 1970–2, and because of excessive emphasis of the state agricultural sector to the detriment of the dominant and more efficient private sector, Poland became a net
importer of foodstuffs in 1973, increasing considerably its imports
of grain and meat bought with hard currency. As a result of these
policies, debt to Western commercial banks and government agencies grew rapidly in the late 1970s (see Tables 2.4–2.6). Even so,
Poland avoided serious debt-servicing difficulties until the beginning of the 1980s.

The "new development strategy" failed because of the systemic inability of the Polish planning authorities to implement it properly. Instead of increasing productivity, the production of high-technology goods, and exports to Western countries, the "development strategy" resulted in the following: a large number of unfinished investment projects; inefficient use of the borrowed resources;[26] expanded productive capacities in industries producing investment goods and shortages of capacity in industries producing consumption goods (food, light industry, etc.); increased dependence on Western imports; serious agricultural crises (accompanied by several bad harvests); strong inflationary pressures; shortages of consumption goods and services; and, as a result, rapidly growing trade and balance-of-payments deficits. Corrupt practices were stimulated (Davies 1985, p. 2), and the economic reform ("experiment" would be a better term) failed.[27]

Hungary. Economic policy mistakes and shortcomings of the economic system were also responsible for the debt problems of Hungary. They were connected primarily with the import-led economic growth strategy and the failure to implement fully the economic reform (the so-called New Economic Mechanism) of 1968, which pursued decentralization and an increase in the efficiency of the domestic economy. The external shocks in the 1970s (see section "External factors") exacerbated the deterioration of the country's external balance. An import-led economic growth strategy was pursued by the Hungarian policymakers with little consideration for external disturbances, which were thought to be only temporary. The policymakers, believing that their economy was insulated from the effects of external shocks, accelerated the growth of investments and associated convertible currency imports of energy, raw materials, and intermediates. Many industrial projects

---

[26] I will mention here two of the many examples of inefficient use of Western credits in Poland. A consortium of West German banks lent DM 850 million to finance exploration for vanadium in Poland in 1979. Vanadium was not found, but these funds were all spent (Delamaide 1984, p. 75). The industrial Komplex Huta Katowice was of doubtful value: Using inflated wages, it drew thousands of new workers, many of them from agricultural employment.

[27] Brus argues that any effort to introduce economic reform in Poland acquires its own peculiar logic that leads nowhere. The vicious circle is particularly visible in the persistent attempt to eliminate any political connotations of the reform process, thus depriving it of very important social support, necessary for its successful implementation (Brus, cited in Davies 1985, pp. 9–10).

with long gestation periods were undertaken. The export performance to the Western countries was poor. Meaningful adjustment to the external imbalance was postponed until 1979.

In the sphere of industrial policy, the Hungarian economic reform of 1968 was generally oriented to decentralization of the allocation of investments. It allowed enterprises to control half of the investment resources, with the other half remaining under the control of the planning authorities. Enterprises had greater decision-making power over production, and profits and market prices were supposed to govern their production decisions. The stimulus to export-oriented production and the competition for imports was expected to be provided by a functioning exchange rate.

There is little evidence that the economic reform led to a rise in the productivity of domestic production. In practice, the main goals of the reform failed to be fully implemented. Especially in the seventies, the enterprises strove to increase output, rather than profits and quality, and they were aided by often receiving investment resources in the form of grants rather than loans (Crane 1985, p. 63). Concentration in industry reduced the intended decentralization of the economic reform. The elimination of the central allocation of inputs has been replaced by micro-level bargaining over prices and tax rates, not by market determination (Bauer 1983, p. 304). In fact, many industrial projects were undertaken in the second half of the 1970s at pre-1973-4 prices, without considering the adverse effects of the increases in the world market prices for oil and raw materials. The reform did not bring full autonomy to enterprises. The managers' decision making was limited; even worse, the autonomy granted was not fully respected. The exchange rate system did (and does) not provide sufficient incentives for the efficient allocation of resources and for expanding exports. In general, the sellers' market still characterizes economic activity in Hungary; that was true particularly in 1973-8, when the government began to retreat from the initial reforms introduced in 1968. Even at the present stage of the implementation of the economic reform, most economic regulators – prices, exchange rates, interest rates, and taxes – are established not by the market but by the central authorities, who try to manipulate them and to simulate what a market would do (Marer 1985d, p. 1).

During the seventies, the so-called Central Development Programs (CDPs) were introduced. They were approved during 1968–73 and implemented during 1968-78.[28] These programs were designed to promote key sectors of the economy (natural gas utilization, petrochemicals, aluminum and motor vehicle industries, computer production and utilization, and the use of light-weight structures in construction) and relied on Western technology and equipment to develop large-scale production. The share of Western machinery in total domestic machinery investment reached 27% in 1972 and remained above 21% during 1971-9 (see Table 2.23). Financing was borrowed primarily from Western commercial banks (mainly Euromarket syndicated credits at floating interest rates and, in the second half of the 1970s, short-term credits frequently refinanced), which drove the rapid increase in Hungarian hard-currency debt (see Tables 2.4-2.6). Net resource inflows enabled the national income used domestically to rise faster than the national income produced in the period 1971-79.

The products of the industries covered by the Central Development Programs, however, were mainly oriented toward import substitution (from the West and other Eastern European countries) and the needs of Comecon, not toward exports to the Western market. Many of the inputs into exports to the CMEA countries were available only on Western markets in return for convertible currency; but exports to the CMEA countries earned only inconvertible transferable rubles, which could not be used to finance Western imports. The goods produced under the CDP were of insufficient quality to attract much interest from the West. The result of all this was increased deficits in the Hungarian hard-currency balance of trade and balance of payments in the second half of the seventies.

GDR. The GDR, the most developed CMEA country, shared common features of development strategy with Poland and Hungary during the 1970s. Its policy was characterized by the following three tendencies:

1. rapid modernization of its industries (machine building, electronics, electrical machinery) through increased access to Western high technology;
2. modernization of agriculture and further improvement of

---

[28] See the discussion of Hungarian Central Development Programs in Balassa (1975).

agricultural goods supply on domestic market through imports of grain and other products; and

3. increased imports of manufactured goods, energy, and raw materials from Western and developing countries in order to compensate for the stagnating deliveries from CMEA countries.

The détente in East-West relations generally, and especially the "Ostpolitik" of Willy Brandt and his Social Democratic Party Liberal coalition, created a favorable climate for the relations of the GDR with the OECD countries, West Germany in particular. As in the other Eastern European countries, it was expected that the increased convertible-currency imports would be financed by borrowing and that the accumulated debt would be repaid through exports in the West.

The GDR expanded its foreign trade with West Germany, Austria, Sweden, France, Japan, and other Western industrialized countries. The trade with West Germany, the so-called inner-German trade, has special advantages for the GDR: Financial transactions are conducted on a clearing basis and both sides have granted each other a revolving, interest-free overdraft credit line (called the "swing"), which, in practice, is utilized only by the GDR. European Community tariff restrictions do not apply to the GDR's exports to West Germany, and trade flows from or to the GDR are subject to considerably reduced West German value-added tax. The GDR also enjoys the option for *Drehgeschaefte* – purchase of West German goods on credit for immediate export in return for convertible currency: West Germany is the GDR's major supplier of high-quality technology goods. The GDR benefits from its "special relationship" with West Germany also in the field of nonfactor convertible-currency trade (transport, tourism, etc.).

The convertible-currency debt of GDR rose rapidly in the second half of the 1970s, mainly because of increased imports of intermediate products and capital goods, particularly from West Germany. A small proportion of the borrowed funds was used also for consumption, but this borrowing did not add considerably to foreign debt, as it did in Poland and the Soviet Union. However, like its CMEA partners, the GDR was neither able to develop a successful export strategy nor to improve its competitiveness on Western markets. Its trade deficits were financed by easy available Western credits. External disturbances late in the 1970s (oil-price shocks, deterioration of terms of trade both with the Western countries and the Soviet Union) exacerbated its external balance difficulties, and the GDR's convertible-currency debt and debt ratios reached alarming levels in the early 1980s, when it became the second largest debtor country in the CMEA Six after Poland.

Romania. The debt problems of Romania have a specific political background. Efforts at rapid industrialization were characteristic of its economic policy in the 1960s and the 1970s. At the time of communist consolidation of power in 1944, Romania was one of the least developed countries in Europe (as it still is). The overwhelming majority of the population lived in rural areas; only 8% was engaged in industry. In the 1960s, the Romanian leadership actively opposed the policy of the Soviet Union and the other CMEA countries, which sought to impose specialization in raw materials and agriculture within the Eastern European economic community on Romania, because it saw industrialization as the key tool to economic growth. Under Ceausescu's leadership the drive toward industrialization and modernization of the society has been expanded.

The policy goal of a "multilaterally developed society" drove Romanian development after 1965. Sustained industrialization was its main feature. All branches of industry were supposed to be developed, but preference was given to heavy industry (steel, chemicals, refining) and the electronics industry. In primary production, the Romanian leadership intended to make the country self-sufficient in the production of all major raw materials[29] and to establish it as a supplier to the rest of the world in such fields as petroleum, oil, petrochemicals, and coal (Gilberg 1975, p. 18). In contrast to Poland, no substantial increase in domestic consumption was planned. Industrialization and modernization were based on rigid centralized planning and supervision and, as in the other CMEA countries, on "artificial" full employment and a lack of incentives to firms and individuals to raise efficiency.

Romania's gross rates of investment in fixed capital were the highest among the CMEA countries in the 1970s (see Table 2.19).

---

[29] Romania is the second richest country within the Comecon (after the Soviet Union) in raw materials and fuels.

The national income also showed the most rapid growth rates in Eastern Europe (see Table 2.18). Continued expansion of Romanian trade with the Western countries, and particularly imports of advanced technology and equipment, were financed by borrowing on Western financial markets, leading to a rapid rise in hard-currency debt. However, until the mid-1970s the debt level remained relatively low compared to that of Poland, Hungary, and GDR.

Romania pursued an active policy of import substitution. By 1980, it produced its own passenger aircraft, automobiles, and some types of machine tools (Crane 1985, p. 108). Romania reduced the share of imported Western capital goods in total domestic investments in the 1970s, but the investment drive that accompanied the import substitution policy created the shortages typical of such a highly centrally planned economy. Demand for domestically produced raw materials increased, as did demand for imported investment goods and intermediates. Many of the domestically produced raw materials (oil, gas, coal) are important exports to the Western markets. Shortages in inputs bred shortages in exports, leading to a deterioration in the balance of trade.

In the second half of the 1970s Romania began importing oil in large quantities from the Arab countries because of declines in domestic production and unused capacities of refining and petrochemical plants.[30] Refined products are important exports to the Western markets and a source of hard-currency earnings; but the earnings from refined oil, coal, and traditional agricultural exports were insufficient to compensate for the chronic excess demand and convertible-currency deficits in machinery, equipment, intermediates, and raw materials after the oil price shock of 1973-4. A World Bank analysis shows, however, that Romania has exported refined products for as much as $25 per ton less than the price of the imported crude oil for their production (M. Jackson, cited in Crane 1985, p. 109).

More than 50% of Romania's deficits in its balance of payments

---

[30] Romania enlarged its refinery capacity from 16 million metric tons a year in 1970 to more than 30 million metric tons in the early 1980s; but Romania's surplus in its oil trade turned into a deficit in the second half of the 1970s. Most of the oil it imported came from OPEC countries (*Economist,* October 26, 1985, p. 54). These imports increased from 8 million metric tons in 1976 to over 15 million metric tons, valued at $3.8 billion, in 1980 (Crane 1985, p. 109).

were financed by short-term Euromarket credits in 1978–80. At the same time, the reserves were kept at very low levels, which made the country particularly vulnerable to changes in the Western financial markets' perception of its creditworthiness. The consequence of Romanian production, trade, and credit policies was a deterioration of the trade and payments balance, which exacerbated the difficulties in servicing debt at the beginning of the 1980s.

Romanian economic problems were also worsened by losses from a 1977 earthquake and the poor harvests in 1980 and 1981 due to bad weather. Romania's unsophisticated approach to debt management must also be considered a factor. For example, after the introduction of a new law in 1981 stipulating that the foreign trade enterprises had to balance imports from the West with exports earnings, many of these enterprises did not pay their import bills as they fell due, but instead waited to receive payment for Romanian exports. The Romanian government's refusal to alleviate the concerns of Western commercial banks over this problem led to loss of confidence in the country's creditworthiness. As a result, Western commercial and supplier credits were withdrawn and normal refinancing was impeded.

External factors

Eastern Europe shared with many developing countries (e.g., the NCIs in Latin America and East Asia) the detrimental effects of external disturbances that increased its difficulties in servicing hard-currency debt. The main external origins of the Eastern European debt problems in the seventies and the beginning of the eighties were the oil-price shocks of 1973–4 and 1979–80, the deterioration of the Eastern European countries' terms of trade (both with the Western countries and the Soviet Union), the global recession in the West and the resulting rise in real interest rates, and the Western credit squeeze after the Polish hard-currency payments crisis in 1981.

Oil-price shocks. The two oil-price shocks led to a rapid increase in international payment imbalances. The increased prices of oil and oil products generated great demand for balance-of-payments financing by the oil-importing countries. At the same time, Western commercial banks found themselves with huge deposits from the oil-exporting countries, which the banks desired to use as loanable funds. These events in the international commodity and financial markets had two main impacts on the CMEA members.

First, these countries faced large and wide-ranging changes in foreign relative prices within quite disaggregated commodity groups. The relative prices of raw materials increased faster than those of manufactures – which, for the Soviet Union, as a major world supplier of energy resources, as well as for Bulgaria, Poland, and Romania, as countries exporting predominantly primary products to the West, was a windfall to their external position. However, the slowdown of investment activity in Western countries after 1975 and again at the beginning of the 1980s created difficulties for CMEA exports generally,[31] and especially for their exports of manufactures, which were (particularly for the CMEA Six) supposed to be the main source of hard-currency export earnings. At the same time, the Eastern European Six and to lesser degree the Soviet Union were forced (especially in the late seventies) to increase imports of raw materials at relatively higher prices. Western technology could not operate with domestic raw materials either of lower grade or in insufficient quantities to utilize productive capacities fully. The result was that Eastern European convertible-currency export earnings were not balanced with the growth of import outlays. The gap was financed by borrowing on the Western financial markets.

Second, competition among the Western commercial banks to recycle the oil-exporting countries' deposits after 1974 made available "cheap" credits to Eastern Europe to finance their payments deficits. The six Eastern European countries and the Soviet Union had new opportunities to borrow from private sources, particularly in the Eurocurrency market. The Western (mostly European) commercial banks increased the growth in their exposure to CMEA. It has to be noted, however, that the banks (as was the case for many developing country borrowers, particularly in Latin America) did not have precise information on the level, maturity, and interest rate structures of the Eastern European debt (commercial or government guaranteed). The Berne Union (International Union of

---

[31] The volume of OECD imports from the Eastern European countries and the Soviet Union fell 10% below trend in 1974 and 15% below trend in 1975 (Portes 1980a, p. 26).

Export Credit Insurance Agencies) began to seek such information from its members in the second half of the 1970s. The BIS also began to require information (through its central bank members) on the commercial banks' positions with the CMEA at that time.

The supply of medium-term credits to Eastern Europe after 1974 was effectively unconstrained for these countries. Some of the Eastern European countries (Poland, GDR, and Hungary) became major borrowers in the Euromarket. The levels of real interest rates in the international financial markets during 1973-4 and 1977-80 were negative, which made borrowing economically justified. The spreads above LIBOR applied to credits to CMEA were better than those available for the OPEC members and substantially lower than for developing country borrowers (Portes 1980a, p. 31). Dornberg writes:

Western bankers . . . in some cases seem to be tripping over each other in the rush to provide [money] at rates and conditions highly favorable to the borrowers . . . one keeps hearing that these borrowers must fall into line and provide potential lenders much more information. Yet for all the caveats . . . there remains a distinct atmosphere of euphoria surrounding the business of lending to the Communists. (cited in Portes 1977, p. 25)

According to R. Davies, U.S. ambassador to Poland in the period 1975-80, bankers and businessmen from the West "were thrusting financial and technological resources at [Polish] officials who all too often have a strong self-interest in taking them, regardless of the possibility that they might be used in unproductive fashion" (Davies 1985, p. 5).

The Eastern European countries were regarded by the Western commercial banks as responsible borrowers, which anyway would have the support of the Soviet Union to pay back their financial obligations (the so-called Soviet umbrella). In the case of the GDR it was further expected that its "special relationship" with West Germany guaranteed normal debt servicing. The West assumed that the Soviet Union would not, for economic, political, strategic, and prestige reasons, allow any CMEA member to default or even reschedule. In Western financial circles, the Eastern European countries were regarded as borrowers for which "repayment is the No. 1 priority" (Janssen 1977, p. 12). This view certainly contributed to the overlending by Western commercial banks to the CMEA in the 1970s; but during that period and in the early 1980s the Soviet Union allowed its allies only to run high trade deficits. When Poland experienced serious debt-servicing difficulties in 1981, it did *not* receive Soviet oil to substitute for deliveries in return for convertible currencies that were reduced from 500 million metric tons in 1980 to 3.5 million in 1981. The Soviet Union did *not* provide direct financial assistance, with the exception of a $500 million grant to Poland in 1981 (Poznanski 1986, pp. 476, 483); thus, the "Soviet umbrella" did not work as expected.[32]

One can only speculate on whether the Soviet Union consciously pursued such a policy in the early 1980s. The accumulated debt of the Eastern European countries created problems not only for them but also for the Western commercial banks and governments. Poland, Hungary, and Romania became increasingly dependent on Western capital imports; this, for economic, political, and strategic reasons, was not favored by the Soviet Union. Poland's intensive relations with the West were of particular concern. Portes argued in 1977 that "one way to make sure that the Poles don't go too far is to let them get into trouble. Then Russia won't have to impose any constraints on Poland's relations with the West, the Western bankers will do that for them" (Portes, cited in U.S. Senate 1977, p. 4). The events in the early 1980s confirmed that, not only for Poland but also for Romania and to some extent for the other Eastern European countries.

Deteriorating terms of trade. The two oil-price "shocks" caused deterioration in the terms of trade of the Eastern European Six both with the world in general (Tables A.6–A.8) and the Soviet Union. However, as noted earlier, after the first oil-price increase in 1973–4 some of the Eastern European Six (Bulgaria, Poland, Romania) and particularly the Soviet Union registered improvements in their terms of trade with developed market economies because of the predominantly raw-material nature of their exports to the West. At the same time, Czechoslovakia, the GDR, and Hungary suffered losses. After the second oil-price increase in 1979–80 the terms of trade for the Eastern European Six further deteriorated (Table A.6); in particular, their terms of trade with the Soviet Union deteriorated considerably. Both shocks increased the external imbalances of the Eastern European Six and "the tax on their GNP" to be paid

---

[32] According to CIA estimates, the Soviet Union did in fact provide direct convertible-currency assistance to Eastern Europe and other communist countries in 1981: $2 billion for Poland, $1.3 billion for the other five Eastern European countries, $1.9 billion for Cuba, and $1 billion for Vietnam (Portes 1983, p. 39).

abroad. After 1975 the price of Soviet energy exports to Eastern Europe doubled.[33] The formula applied for intra-CMEA trade prices based on a moving average of world market dollar prices[34] covering the five preceding years led to a significant increase of the Soviet energy export prices vis-à-vis Eastern European machinery and industrial consumer goods prices. Compared to 1970 (= 100), Soviet terms of trade with the Eastern European Six after the first oil shock improved in 1975 and 1976 to 115 and 114, respectively. In particular, Hungary, Bulgaria, Czechoslovakia, and Poland have had a significant deterioration in their terms of trade with the Soviet Union (Portes 1980a, p. 29). After the second oil shock, the deterioration in Eastern European terms of trade with the Soviet Union compared to 1980 was 6% annually during 1981-2 and 4% in 1983. The cumulative deterioration was nearly 15% during 1980–3.[35] Romania, because of its lower share of imported Soviet energy, was the only Eastern European country that was not seriously affected.

This development in the Soviet Union's terms of trade with most of its CMEA partners proved that, after 1974, intra-CMEA trade became sensitive to changes in the world markets and was not protected from external shocks by the intrabloc system of planning and mutual exchange. The changes in terms of trade with the Soviet Union created additional tension in the balance of trade and payments of the Eastern European Six (particularly for Hungary, the GDR, and Czechoslovakia). If the growth in trade deficits in nominal prices with the Soviet Union was to be avoided, the same quantity of Soviet imports (primarily raw materials) had to be offset by larger quantities of Eastern European exports (primarily manufactures) to compensate for higher-priced imports.[36] The increased exports to the Soviet Union required additional resources that could be mobilized for convertible-currency exports.

[33] WEFA *CPE Current Analysis*, No. 24-5:1-2 (1984).
[34] World market dollar prices are converted into transferable rubles at the official Soviet ruble–dollar exchange rate for each year.
[35] WEFA, *CPE Current Analysis*, No. 24-5:4 (1984).
[36] In 1982-3, the Soviet Union increased the pressure on the Eastern European Six to boost the physical quantity of export deliveries in order to reduce the large nominal surpluses in its trade and payments balance with these countries. Because the Six have been unable to expand their exports to the Soviet Union in proportion to the increases in prices, the Soviet Union opened credit lines for trade with Eastern Europe in the amount of more than 11 billion transferable rubles ($15 billion), which it was unable to put to use in the period 1974-2 (Tiraspolsky 1984, p. 33).

Global recession. Just as for Latin American countries, but in contrast to East Asia, the global recession in 1974–5 and 1979–80 led to increased difficulties for CMEA exports to Western markets, and consequently for the servicing of CMEA hard-currency debt. The OECD countries introduced protectionist measures against imports of textiles, clothing, footwear, steel, electric motors, basic chemicals, meat products, and agricultural items, which were (and are) important commodities in CMEA exports. In addition to that the Eastern European Six and the Soviet Union have lost and are losing market shares because of the increased exports from newly industrialized countries such as South Korea and Taiwan, which, although poor in raw materials and energy resources, have an industrial sector capable of generating products competitive in the world market.

The excess supply of investment goods in the Western countries from 1973 led to strong and highly competitive efforts to find Eastern European markets for these goods. That led to an increase of officially supported long-term export credit lines with CMEA. This policy of the Western countries was welcomed by the Soviet Union and the Eastern European Six because of their investment booms in the seventies. The consequence was overlending to CMEA.

Rising interest rates. Most of the OECD countries responded to the global recession in the late 1970s and the beginning of the 1980s with tight monetary policy designed to keep inflation under control. That resulted in a surge of nominal and real interest rates. Short-term dollar interest rates peaked at 18% in 1981. Real interest rates reached very high levels in 1981 and 1982: 9.4% and 6.0%, respectively (Heller 1984, p. 9). Government deficits put pressure on capital markets in the Western countries, thus preventing real interest rates from falling.

The nominal average interest rate on a basket of Eurocurrencies increased from 6.8% in 1978 to 11.6% in 1980 and 14.3% in 1981 (see Table 2.13). The surge of interest rates put great pressure on the debt-servicing ability of the CMEA countries, which had accumulated large hard-currency debt by that time (especially Poland, the GDR, Hungary, and Romania).

The effects of external disturbances on the economies of Eastern Europe increased the tension in trade and payments balance. The planners had to acknowledge their illusion concerning the impact of external shocks on centrally planned economies. The Hungarian banker J. Fekete writes:

After the oil and raw material price explosion the situation changed very swiftly. A 20 percent loss in the terms of trade, a deterioration in foreign markets because of the recession in the Western world and the structural weakness of our industry came to the fore ... We had to recognize very quickly that we have some illusions:

We believed that there were two world markets and negative events on the capitalist market did not affect our economic relations with our socialist partners.

We thought that the unrealistic oil prices, not based on any economic calculations whatsoever, would not last long.

We hoped that the oil consuming countries, both industrially advanced and developing, would form some common front against the excessive price increases of the OPEC and other oil producing countries ... (1982, p. 332)

Hungary and other Eastern European countries (without the Soviet Union) had to pay a high price for their illusions. Balassa and Tyson (1985, pp. 66-8) have estimated that Hungarian losses due to external disturbances on the balance of payments equaled 6% of GNP in trade with market economies and 2% of GNP in trade with the other socialist countries during 1974–6; values were 2% and 7%, respectively, during 1979–81. The losses due to increased interest rates equaled 2% of GNP in 1979–81. The terms of trade losses were 6% of GNP in 1974–6 and 4% of GNP in 1979–81. Furthermore, Hungary's losses due to declines in the demand for its exports were estimated to be 2% of GNP in 1974–6 and 8% of GNP in 1979–81. Losses averaged 10% of the volume of overall exports between 1974 and 1978. It seems reasonable to assume that the experience of the other members of the Eastern European Six was similar to that of Hungary because of their common size, openness, and sensitivity to external disturbances.

Credit squeeze and capital withdrawal. One of the reasons for the debt-servicing problems of many Latin American countries (Argentina, Brazil, Mexico, and others) in the early 1980s was the global credit squeeze, accompanied by the flight of capital from their economies. In the case of Eastern Europe, the Western credit squeeze in 1981–3, after the Polish hard-currency payments crisis and similar Romanian difficulties, also increased the strain on this region. Short-term credits to CMEA countries were sharply curtailed, and, as described earlier, access to medium- and long-term credits on the Western financial markets also became difficult for them. A significant decline in loan rollovers occurred. The one remaining source of finance for CMEA purchases in the West was supplier credits; but, given the depressed demand for CMEA exports, this caused further tension in the Eastern European trade and payments balance.

In addition to the credit squeeze, Western deposits in hard-currency in Romania, Hungary, Poland, and the GDR were withdrawn. In 1981 Poland lost short-term credit lines and deposits in the amount of $2 billion. In the first quarter of 1982, Hungary lost approximately $1.1 billion in deposits, mainly because of withdrawals by the Soviet Union (Moscow Narodny Bank and other Soviet banks), and some Arab countries (Lybia, Iraq). The withdrawal of Western short-term deposits from the GDR was relatively small and totaled only $0.2 billion; but Romania lost credit lines by Western banks in the amount of $1.5 billion, which was one of the reasons for the suspension of debt servicing in 1981 and 1982.

The withdrawal of capital and the loss of confidence in CMEA creditworthiness caused serious liquidity difficulties in Hungary and the GDR in 1982, which like Poland and Romania were considered to be very close to rescheduling their debt. Hungary's reserves in the West dropped to less than $500 million in the first quarter of 1982. At the same time, its financing requirements totaled approximately 50% of gross debt ($7.7 billion). The growth-cum-debt response of Hungary to the external shocks and the increased short-term borrowing in the late 1970s and in 1980–1 led to rapid accumulation of debt with maturities due in the early 1980s. The low level of reserves, the Western credit squeeze, and the inability to push the trade surplus beyond $1 billion exacerbated the concern of Western banks and government agencies. Rescheduling of the Hungarian debt seemed to be on the agenda, but the Hungarian government pursued policies designed to avoid rescheduling at any cost. Rescheduling was considered as an action that would weaken political support, both in the East and West, for the Hungarian economic reform; it also would impose an additional financial burden. Hungary found the goodwill needed to overcome the liquidity crisis and to avoid rescheduling in the West. It joined the IMF and the World Bank and received new credits from these institutions and from commercial banks and the BIS (with strong support particularly from the Bank of England and the Deutsche Bundesbank) in 1982 as well (see Chapter 4).

In 1982, roughly 40% of the GDR credits to Western commercial banks fell due. The debt-servicing pressures in 1982–3 were exacerbated by the Western credit squeeze, which precluded the GDR's access to new or revolving Euromarket loans and funds from government agencies. In addition, the "swing" credit line for intra-German trade was reduced in 1983, from DM 850 million to DM 770 million,[37] as a political riposte of the West German government to GDR increases in the compulsory travelers' exchange with West Germany. All that further contributed to loss of confidence in the GDR's creditworthiness, but the GDR was able to avoid rescheduling at that time, partly because of the provision of two West German government-backed credits in the amount of roughly DM 2 billion. There is no doubt that the good standing of the GDR on the Western financial markets depended heavily on the liquidity and financial security provided by West Germany.

Macroeconomic adjustment

As discussed in Chapter 1, demand-mix management measures cannot be applied easily in the CMEA countries in the event of external disturbances, because of the different roles that the traditional market economy instruments of fiscal, monetary, income, and exchange-rate policy play in the centrally planned economies. Macroeconomic adjustment in the latter relies on only two possible responses to external shocks: borrowing abroad and deflationary economic policy conducted through direct control.

What have been the main features of the policy responses to the external disturbances in the Eastern European countries since the beginning of the seventies? Those responses are best considered over two subperiods: up to the end of the 1970s and from the beginning of the 1980s.

Characteristically, the Eastern European countries did not take strong external adjustment measures after the oil price shock in 1973–4. For the Soviet Union and Romania, the oil-price shock was a windfall for their external balance. The rest of Eastern Europe pursued a growth-cum-debt policy relying on foreign borrowing.

[37] Deutsches Institut für Wirtschaftsforschung, *Wochenbericht*, No. 10:121 (1986).

Thus, during the 1970s, the external shocks fundamentally affected the trade balances and the borrowing policies of the CMEA countries, but not their domestic economic policies. This strategy was considered favorably by borrowers at that time because real interest rates were negligible or even negative. The CMEA countries increased their industrial and agricultural production (Tables A.5 and A.9) and absorption grew further (see Table 2.18). In the period 1976–80 the absorption showed relatively lower growth rates than in 1971–5. The investment booms continued, however, in most of the CMEA countries until 1978, although the national income used for net investment decreased in the second half of the 1970s (see Table 2.20). The countries did not respond to external disturbances by reducing domestic demand mainly for three reasons: (1) the centrally planned authorities were wrong in their forecasts that the external shocks would be transitory and future output would cover the cost of borrowing; (2) they were unable to ensure efficient investment; and (3) they were unwilling (unable) to cut consumption. (The data from Tables 2.20 and 2.21 show that, although the planned growth rates of national income used for consumption were lower in 1976–80 than in 1971–5, they were higher than the growth rates of national income used for net investment.)

The ability to finance the deficits in the balance of payments by borrowing abroad,[38] however, made adjustment unnecessary. The problem in the 1970s was (as the previous analysis showed) that heavy borrowing in the Western capital markets allowed the continuation of economic growth and investment policies, which gave little promise of helping to modernize the CMEA industries, improve weak competitiveness of their exports, boost labor productivity, and, consequently, to improve the external trade and payments balance in the long run.

Ultimately, however, the policy response of the six Eastern European countries and the Soviet Union to the external disturbances in the late 1970s and the beginning of the 1980s had to be deflation. It resulted in a substantial reduction in domestic absorption, which enabled the countries to restrict hard-currency imports and to free additional goods for export. Bulgaria and Hungary were the first

---

[38] In some of the Comecon countries (Hungary, Poland) additional net external financing nearly equaled the balance-of-payments deficits that resulted from the external disturbances in the seventies.

among the Eastern European countries to introduce a deflationary economic program in the late 1970s. Ferenc Havasi, one of the secretaries of the Hungarian Party Central Committee, stated the main goal of the Hungarian program of 1979: " . . . economic growth, production and development, as well as living standard improvements, must be subordinated in the interest of improving our international financial balance" (Hewett 1983c, p. 12). Such a policy has been characteristic of the other CMEA countries during the 1980s, particularly in 1981 and 1982 when the need for austerity was recognized and deflationary measures were applied. The forced austerity in Eastern Europe actually preceded the forced austerity policies in Latin America (Brazil, Mexico, etc.)

The data from Table 2.18 show that the national income used domestically decreased considerably in 1981 and 1982; only two of the CMEA countries raised domestic absorption (Bulgaria in 1981 and the Soviet Union). Bulgaria's improved external position was mainly a result not of cuts in imports, but of the increased revenues from reexport of Soviet oil, purchased in transferable rubles and sold in return for convertible currency in the West. The decrease of national income used domestically was particularly high in the case of Poland (1981–2, −10.5%) and Romania (1981, −5.7%; 1982, −2.6%). Czechoslovakia, GDR, and Hungary also cut domestic absorption substantially.

The decrease in domestic absorption mainly reduced investment activity. As discussed in Chapter 1, the first reaction of the policy-makers in the CMEA countries in case of external imbalances is to cut investment, because to place the burden of adjustment on the other two components of domestic absorption – aggregate consumption and government expenditures – is politically difficult. The data from Tables 2.24 and 2.25 show that, although in 1981 and 1982 the share of net investment was reduced significantly (the exceptions were Bulgaria in 1981 and the Soviet Union in 1982), the share of consumption rose. Only in three of the CMEA countries – Poland (1981 and 1982), Romania (1982), and Czechoslovakia (1982) – were the growth rates of consumption negative in that period[39] (see Table 2.21).

Gross investment in fixed capital and net investment in fixed

---

[39] In Romania and Poland the shortages for food and consumer goods were severe in 1981 and 1982, and the decline in living standards was substantial.

Table 2.24. *Share of consumption in national income used in the CMEA countries, 1980–4*

	Constant prices of year	In constant prices					In current prices		
		1980	1981	1982	1983	1984	1980	1981	1982
Bulgaria	1981	0.748	0.731	0.745	0.761	0.762[a]	n.a.	n.a.	n.a.
Czechoslovakia	1977	0.751	0.798	0.802	0.814	0.827	0.740	0.799	0.794
GDR	1980	0.773	0.783	0.820	0.804	0.831[a]	n.a.	n.a.	n.a.
Hungary	1982	0.752	0.773	0.799	0.818	0.878	0.785	0.790	0.799
Poland	1982	0.744	0.793	0.784	0.774	0.783	0.811	0.901	0.737
Romania	1977	0.653	0.714	0.722	0.727	0.719	0.672	0.717	0.734
Soviet Union	1982	0.750	0.756	0.738	0.736	0.735[a]	0.761	0.766	0.738

[a]These data are based on constant prices of the following years: Bulgaria, 1982; Hungary, 1981; Soviet Union, 1983.

Sources: WEFA, *CPE Current Analysis*, No. 26–7:10 (1984), 25–6:15 (1985).

Table 2.25. *Share of net investment (accumulation) in national income used in the CMEA countries, 1980–4*

	Constant prices of year	In constant prices					In current prices		
		1980	1981	1982	1983	1984	1980	1981	1982
Bulgaria	1981	0.252	0.269	0.255	0.239	0.238[a]	n.a.	n.a.	n.a.
Czechoslovakia	1977	0.249	0.202	0.198	0.186	0.173	0.260	0.201	0.206
GDR	1980	0.227	0.217	0.180	0.196	0.169[a]	n.a.	n.a.	n.a.
Hungary	1982	0.248	0.227	0.201	0.182	0.122	0.215	0.210	0.201
Poland	1982	0.256	0.207	0.216	0.226	0.217	0.189	0.099	0.263
Romania	1977	0.347	0.286	0.28	0.273	0.281	0.328	0.283	0.266
Soviet Union	1982	0.250	0.244	0.262	0.264	0.265[a]	0.239	0.234	0.262

[a]These data are based on constant prices the following years: Bulgaria, 1982; Hungary, 1981; Soviet Union, 1983.

Sources: WEFA, *CPE Current Analysis*, No. 26–7:10 (1984), No. 25–6:15 (1985).

capital fell substantially in most of the CMEA countries (the exceptions were Bulgaria and the Soviet Union) during 1981-2 (see Tables 2.19 and 2.22). Industrial production in the Eastern European countries fell in 1981 and increased only slightly in 1982. The Soviet Union also showed lower rates of growth of industrial production during 1980-2, in comparison to the average growth rates in the period 1971-9 (Table A.10).

Most of the decline in gross investment resulted from cutbacks in inventories. These are a typical response of the CMEA policymakers when domestic absorption has to be reduced and short-term adjustment has to be achieved.[40] The cutback of inventory investment (Table A.11) was particularly high in Romania, Poland, and Czechoslovakia in 1981 and in the GDR in 1982. Another method to cut gross investment is to reduce the funds devoted to unfinished construction. This strategy was pursued especially in Czechoslovakia, Poland, and Romania.

Although deflationary economic policy was the principal response to external shocks at the beginning of the 1980s, some CMEA countries (Hungary, Romania) also adjusted through an increase of their exports in convertible currencies in the intrabloc trade. The limited available data show that the Hungarian positive balance of trade in convertible currencies with the Soviet Union reached $646 million in 1982 (from $14 million in 1979 and $372 million in 1980). Romania increased its positive trade balance in hard currencies with the Soviet Union from $80 million in 1979 to $210 million in 1982. These earnings were used primarily to finance the balance-of-payments deficits with the market economies. However, the Soviet Union reduced significantly its deficit trade balance in convertible currencies with Hungary and Romania in 1983 and 1984 (Vanous and Marrese 1984, pp. 188, 194). Hungary's positive trade balance was reduced in 1984. Romania ran a trade deficit with the Soviet Union of $11 million in 1983, but trade was balanced in 1984. The Soviet Union showed unwillingness to trade with Hungary on a hard-currency basis in 1985.

The deflationary economic policy in Eastern Europe required that the share of national income devoted to reduction of convertible currency grow substantially in 1981 and 1982. Eastern Euro-

[40] The centrally planned economies in the Comecon countries operate with much higher inventory levels than market economies at comparable development levels.

pean exports increased particularly in 1982 and 1983. At the same time import (and demand) restrictions led to a reduction of import volume (with the exception of the Soviet Union in 1982), as shown in the data from Tables A.4 and A.12. The Eastern European Six countries reduced their imports from the developed market economies by 19% in 1982 and 3.3% in 1983, while their exports fell by 1.1% in 1982 and grew by 7.1% in 1983. In the case of the GDR the orientation of convertible-currency trade to the "inner-German" trade (on a clearing basis) in 1982 reduced the pressure on its external balance. It imported steel, oil, and grain from West Germany instead of from France, Great Britain, and the United States as in previous years. Some of these imports purchased on credit were reexported for convertible currency (*Drehgeschaefte*). Soviet exports to Western countries grew relatively faster than imports from these countries during 1982–3 (Table A.4). The domestic and foreign trade policies of the CMEA countries allowed significant reduction of their gross and net hard-currency debt in 1982–4.

The Eastern European economies in general recovered in 1983 and particularly in 1984–5. The most important contributing factors were good performance by agriculture in 1984, the continued improvements in energy efficiency,[41] and the ensuing reduction of convertible-currency debt (except for Poland). During 1983–4 most of the Eastern European countries increased their national income growth rates. Hungary and Romania (1983) were the only countries that reduced domestic absorption. The Soviet Union showed stagnant national income growth rates (see Table 2.18).

An important question arises: What impact will the adjustment policies of 1981–2 have on the economic development of Eastern Europe in future years? The decision to place the burden of adjustment on investment reduced the long-term potential for expansion and modernization of the industrial base, thereby threatening the competitiveness of CMEA exports. The cut in investment was general and not selective. One may argue that if the "sacrificed" investment was inefficient, growth prospects have been greatly improved; but it is difficult to give a clear-cut answer to such a question. The reduced investment in sophisticated areas – for example,

---

[41] Poland, Romania, Czechoslovakia, and the GDR increased their reliance on domestic energy sources: lignite, hard coal, nuclear power, and so on. This enabled them to operate with less oil imported from either the Soviet Union or the Arab countries (WEFA, CPE *Current Analysis*, No. 25–6:7, 1985).

in electronics and computers – would have an adverse impact on the competitiveness of CMEA goods in the international markets. This lack of competitiveness will be one of the main problems in raising exports to the West. Many developing and newly industrializing countries have also expanded their exports to developed market economies and are serious competitors to the Eastern Europe Six and the Soviet Union in manufactured products.[42] In addition to that, the widening technological gap between East and West (even in the case of GDR, which, through its "special" relationship with West Germany, has easier access to high-technology products) will make CMEA exports more difficult to market.

The depressed level of investments makes it very difficult to effect the structural adjustment[43] in CMEA necessary to expand production of exportables. Without changes in economic structure the prospects for economic growth are not bright. In some of the Eastern European countries (Poland, Romania, Czechoslovakia) the nonreplacement of obsolete or worn-out machines and equipment has reached high levels in various industries. Thus, the deflationary adjustment to the debt crisis in the beginning of the 1980s has sown the seeds of serious structural problems in the CMEA countries in the late 1980s.

There is little prospect that the necessary structural changes in Eastern Europe will be financed by borrowing on the Western market or, in the case of the Eastern European Six, through assistance from the Soviet Union. (The Soviet Union itself has serious structural problems and is currently facing a sharp deterioration in its terms of trade with the market economies as a result of the decline in prices for exported raw materials, particularly oil and gas, vis-à-vis imported manufactured goods.) The alternative of considerably improving the efficiency of resource utilization through economic reforms is also generally unlikely in Eastern Europe

---

[42] For example: electromechanical machinery – Argentina, Brazil; iron and steel – Brazil, Mexico, India; shipbuilding – Taiwan, South Korea; petrochemicals – Iran, Saudi Arabia, Mexico, Singapore; light-industry products – Hong Kong, South Korea, Taiwan.

[43] The structural disequilibrium in Eastern Europe results from the excessive domination of heavy industry, which requires major investments of capital, energy resources, and raw materials. A disproportionate share of the Comecon products have become obsolete and thus cannot be sold readily on the world markets. Domestic production is excessively wasteful of inputs. Changes in the composition of expenditures and the production structure are necessary in order to stimulate the production of exportables and to correct the external imbalance.

because of the many problems that the reforms cannot solve in the fields of monetary, fiscal, exchange rate, and pricing policy. Economic experiments will, however, continue in the Eastern European Six and the Soviet Union. It is expected that the Soviet Union will widen the scope of the ongoing economic experiments in the next few years.[44] The new party leader Gorbachev made a statement at the Polish Communist Party congress in 1986 that a failure to modify economic and political methods in time could lead to crises such as in Poland in 1981 (*Financial Times,* July 7, 1986, p. 12). However, radical Soviet "modification" of economic and political methods of management is an unlikely scenario for the rest of this decade and probably even for this century. More likely are partial reforms aimed at increasing discipline, dismissing inefficient workers, and increasing financial incentives to meet the targets imposed by the central authorities – all of which would have negative political and economic impacts on the economic reforms and growth in the Eastern European Six (particularly in Hungary, GDR, and Bulgaria). It would be too optimistic to expect that Eastern Europe will pursue a new outward-oriented development strategy in the years to come; and yet the successful implementation of such an economic strategy seems to be the only way to improve permanently the CMEA convertible-currency external balance.

[44] *Ekonomiceskaja gazeta,* Moscow, No. 11:24, March 1986.

3

Rescheduling Eastern European debt

The Eastern European gross convertible-currency debt peaked at $93 billion in 1981. The rapid rise in foreign borrowing resulted in increased debt-servicing difficulties for most of the CMEA countries and particularly for Poland, Romania, GDR, and Hungary.[1] As discussed in Chapter 2 the liquidity crisis in GDR and Hungary did not result in restructuring of their debt obligations. Poland and Romania (and their Western lenders), on the other hand, faced the dilemma either of repudiating the debt, with all the resulting political and economic consequences of isolation from the international community, or of pursuing a cooperative strategy and restructuring debt owed to Western governments and banks. Poland and Romania chose the second alternative. The nature of debt consolidation and the main characteristics of this phenomenon in the Eastern European debt crisis are the subjects of this chapter.

---

[1] Debt-servicing difficulties in the early 1980s were faced by the non-European CMEA countries Vietnam and Cuba as well. Vietnam has rescheduled its debt with Libya, Iran, West Germany, Japan, and other countries. It has arrears on an IMF standby credit (SDR 28 million) from 1981. Cuba rescheduled its debt both with the Soviet Union and Western lenders (commercial banks and government agencies). The rescheduled debt with the Soviet Union is estimated at 7.5 billion rubles (roughly $7.5 billion) (*Latin America Weekly Report*, London, January 4, 1985, WR-85-01). Cuba made the following rescheduling agreements with Western commercial banks: $125 million falling due in 1983 (rescheduled on the terms 7 yr, 2 yr grace, interest 2.25% above LIBOR); $100 million due in 1984 (9 yr, 5 yr grace, 1.875%); $82 million (out of $94 million) due in 1985 (10 yr, 6 yr grace, 1.5%) (*Latin America Weekly Report*, January 24, 1986, WR-86-04). Cuba reached an agreement to reschedule $140 million in debt to the Paris Club (see note 2) member countries in 1984. New debt-servicing difficulties forced Cuba to request rescheduling of commercial and government credits in 1986 (*Wall Street Journal*, May 13, 1986, p. 35; *Financial Times*, April 25, 1986, p. 1).

Nature of debt consolidation (rescheduling)

A debt consolidation is a rearrangement of a sovereign country's external debt by agreement with its creditors, either on a bilateral, country-to-country basis, or multilaterally with a group of creditor countries or banks. The majority of the postwar international debt rearrangements (Argentina – 1956, 1962, 1965, 1983; Turkey – 1959, 1965, 1979, 1982; Brazil – 1961, 1983, etc.) have been conducted on the basis of multilateral negotiations involving the debtor country on the one hand and its principal creditors on the other (Brau, Williams, et al. 1983, pp. 30–32; Hardy 1982, p. 2). Multilateral negotiations enable the debtor to deal with all of its creditors at the same time and to avoid uncertainty and delay.

Debt consolidation usually takes one of two main forms: rescheduling or refinancing. These do not solve the debt problem; they simply buy time. In the case of *rescheduling* the repayment schedule of the existing debt is either amended or replaced by a new schedule extending the date of repayment, altering the rate of interest, and (possibly) granting a grace period. Basically, the main goal of this operation is to provide temporary relief by reducing the debtor country's debt profile in order to make the debt service more manageable. Reducing the total outstanding debt is not an objective. In the case of *refinancing* the debtor is given a new loan or credit line in order to continue to meet existing service payments or to resume repayments if these have been temporarily suspended.

Debt refinancing was the form of debt consolidation in the case of Hungary in 1982; for the GDR it is less clear. Debt rescheduling was the consolidation form applied to both Poland and Romania in 1982, 1983, and 1986 and to Poland during 1984–6. Poland and Romania expected in the late 1970s and in the 1980 that their Western creditors as a group would refinance on a large scale, but these overly optimistic expectations were not fulfilled. After encountering severe debt-servicing problems, Poland and Romania turned to their creditors and requested rescheduling. They waited too long, however. Early advice by some of their Western creditors was ignored (Eichler 1986, p. 200). In the case of Romania, which is a member of the IMF and the World Bank, intensive efforts by the IMF were required to reach an agreement on its debt rescheduling.

In Eastern European reschedulings four main groups of creditors were involved: commercial banks, commercial suppliers, the Paris

Club,[2] and governments and central banks of some oil-exporting countries. In some of the negotiations, CMEA banks also participated.

The main stages of the process of rescheduling the Eastern European commercial debt during 1982–6 were as follows:[3]

formulation of terms of rescheduling, including: categories of debt to be rescheduled; maturities of such debts to be rescheduled; whether to provide new credits and in what form; conditions of rescheduling and of provision of new credits; maturity, grace period, and interest rate (LIBOR) to be applied to the rescheduled debt and new credits; permitted currencies of rescheduled debt and new credits; provision of economic data and required information for the IMF (in the case of Romania); payment of fees and expenses of the rescheduling process;

determination of the structure of the rescheduling;

negotiation on the terms of rescheduling by the Western creditors (represented by a working group) with the Central Bank and the Ministry of Finance of the debtor country;

preparation of the legal documents by the working group to the coordinating (steering) committee[4] to implement the terms of rescheduling;

---

[2] The Paris Club is neither a legal entity nor an organization. It is the name given to an ad hoc group of fifteen creditor governments that assembles in Paris at meetings organized and chaired by the French Treasury. The Club is the forum in which intragovernment debt is renegotiated. It originated in 1956 when Argentina requested that bilateral negotiations be replaced with a multilateral meeting of her creditors. There is no handbook describing the functioning of the Paris Club, but over the past 30 years a number of procedures and practices have evolved. The most important ones: Creditors agree to a meeting only when default is imminent; the type of debt eligible for debt relief is limited to officially insured suppliers' credits and governments loans; the amount of debt to be rescheduled is determined by consolidating the repayments of principal (and part or all of the interest) due on the eligible debt over a 2–3 year period and rearranging the terms of the consolidated amount; the consolidated debts are rescheduled usually for 2½–10 yr at market rates of interest.

[3] This section is based on information provided to the author in interviews with the IMF, the World Bank, and commercial banks.

[4] Coordinating or steering committees of bankers were established to act as advisory and liaison groups for all bank creditors. In the case of Poland's rescheduling it was called a "multinational task force," in which twenty banks participated from twelve countries. A working group of seven banks from six countries was also established to work out key issues in detail and to prepare the legal documentation. Further, an international economic committee was formed to deal with economic and conditionality issues. In the Romanian reschedulings an advisory committee of nine banks was established.

negotiation of the legal documents by the working group, the Cen-
    tral Bank, and the Ministry of Finance;
presentation of the resulting legal documents to all bank creditors
    and signing of these documents by all parties.

The reschedulings agreed for bank and official credits owed by
the developing countries were made conditional on the agreement
of a program with the IMF. Mostly, the rescheduling discussions
with the commercial banks have not been concluded before an
agreement with the official creditors (Paris Club) was achieved.
However, some countries restructured debt to banks without having approached the Paris Club. Poland led the way followed by
Mexico, Brazil, Argentina, and others. The commercial banks were
willing to negotiate and act before the official creditors and the
international financial institutions in the reschedulings of Poland
and Romania in 1982, 1983, and 1984. After the imposition of martial law in Poland, rescheduling discussions with the Western
governments were suspended in January 1982. A decision on
Poland's application of November 1981 to join the IMF was
postponed; for that reason, the IMF played no role in Poland's
rescheduling before 1986. In the Romanian reschedulings the
agreement of the Paris Club simply copied the terms of the commercial banks' agreement (Eichler 1986, p. 201).

The commercial debt reschedulings of both Eastern European
countries were extremely laborious, slow, and more complicated
than the reschedulings of their official debt, mainly for two reasons:
First, many banks were involved (more than 300 banks from over
twenty countries), which made the organization of reschedulings a
long and difficult process. For example, negotiations among the
Western banks themselves on different economic and financial
issues concerning both the creditor and the borrowing countries
had to take place more often than those between the banks and the
CMEA countries. Second, Poland and Romania did not provide
required information in time, or, in some cases, refused to provide
data on their credit and economic relations with creditors not
involved in the rescheduling (Eastern European or Arab countries, et.).

There were other problems as well. One was the restructuring
of the debt to nonbank private creditors, primarily unguaranteed
suppliers' credits (Brau, Williams et al. 1983, p. 13). A signifi-

cant portion of these credits was transferred to the debt that Poland and Romania owed to official (Paris Club) creditors.[5] Unfortunately, there is little available information on the terms involved.

Another obstacle to rapid renegotiation of the Eastern European debt concerned also the short-term lines of credit. Many of the creditor institutions felt that the easiest and most rapid way to reduce their commitments in Poland and Romania lay in not renewing short-term loans. As a result, it was difficult to maintain lines of credit, which are vital for the proper functioning of trade at the projected levels.

Another problem, which is partly related to the foregoing, involved interest payments. Traditionally, reschedulings do not include interest payments; if they did, the banks would run the risk of having their loans classified as unprofitable assets by the national regulatory authorities. As a result, banks have sought other ways to reduce the burden of interest payments, particularly for Poland.[6] The main form was the granting of new credits (revolving short-term trade) to refinance a portion of the outstanding interest commitments. Thus the banks have introduced, in the Polish case, a de facto rescheduling of interest payments, since they have capitalized a portion of their income under this heading. Capitalization of interest payments, however, was and remains a very delicate point in negotiations with some banks.

Two questions arise: Did rescheduling solve Poland's and Romania's debt problems? What are the dangers involved for both Western creditors and Eastern European debtors?

Rescheduling medium-term commercial debts into medium-and long-term obligations (6½–10 yr; see Table 3.1) merely postponed the problem. The two Eastern European debtor countries seem to have identified their problem as one of illiquidity, assuming that, given a relatively brief respite, the problem would correct itself. However, time alone was (and is) not the solution, at least not in the

---

[5] Nonbank supplier credits are sometimes excluded from the debts to be rescheduled, thereby facilitating the repayment of existing, and the extension of future, supplier credits and other trade financing.
[6] In mid-1983, Poland suggested as an initial negotiating position the rescheduling of its entire debt to the West over twenty years with an eight-year grace period during which no interst would be paid (Cline 1984, p. 92).

sense that the Western creditors and the Eastern European debtors considered it to be. What Poland and Romania needed (and need) is not more time to service their external debt, so much as time to restructure their economies and achieve a rate of growth that would enable them to meet debt obligations without jeopardizing their future economic performance.

The deflationary economic policy applied in these two Eastern European countries (as was discussed in Chapter 2) does not raise hopes that this will be achieved. The measures that Poland and Romania took to improve their trade and current-account balances were too austere (especially in Romania) for the countries to adhere to over the time required for those measures to be successful. That is one of the reasons that both Eastern European countries have ransomed their future economic performance to their debts. They have reduced imports, cut domestic absorption, and compromised on the level and efficiency of investment projects. However, the roots of the pessimistic prospects for the economies of these countries lie in their inefficient use of borrowed funds during the 1970s.

In the case of Romania, the austerity policy applied after 1981 allowed the external hard-currency debt to be significantly reduced over 1982–5 and further reschedulings of its debt were not necessary during 1984–5. However, debt-servicing difficulties were again experienced in 1986, and repayments both to the World Bank and the commercial banks had to be deferred. The gross and net debt level is still higher than in the mid-1970s and could easily rise further if Romania tries to restructure (which would require imports of Western technology, equipment, etc.) in the next few years.

Poland's capacity to service external debt remains marginal, and the rescheduling process will have to be repeated over and over again. That may mean increased exposure for the commercial banks and increased official credits. Ultimately creditors could face the imminent Polish default they are trying to avoid and with larger amounts of debt involved. Especially for Poland's creditors rescheduling may have put off "the evil day." One risk is that rescheduling has enabled both Western creditors and Eastern debtor countries to avoid taking more decisive action. For example, the Western debtors were able to provide the minimum possible level of relief. This relief allowed the Eastern debtor countries to postpone the introduction of domestic structural adjustment programs.

The mistakes in debt management that led to reschedulings of Poland's and Romania's debt made it harder for these countries to service debt as well as to borrow. The access of Poland to international capital markets is still limited, and Romania resumed borrowing only in 1985. The low levels of reserves and uncertain economic prospects of both countries only exacerbate their situations. Poland and Romania have become high-cost borrowers of capital as compared to other CMEA countries. This further increases the costs, through interest and fees, of their external obligations and, particularly in the case of Poland, intensifies the pressure to start the process all over again.

Poland's rescheduling

The debt-servicing difficulties of Poland in the late 1970s led Western commercial banks to be cautious about lending to this country. The banks wanted more information about the Polish economic situation before providing new credits. In early 1979, a discussion in Warsaw on the Polish austerity economic program had preceded the lending of a new $550 million syndicated credit (in which participated representatives of major commercial banks from the United States, Canada, Great Britain, and Japan). In 1980, when Poland requested a new syndicated credit for $550 million, many banks were reluctant to provide fresh funds. Several banks suggested a rescheduling of the Polish debt. Most of the Western European and American banks continued, however, to maintain their level of loan exposure by refinancing maturing credits on an ad hoc basis. These rollovers were mainly for export financing but could not provide debt relief for Poland. The accumulated debt required a comprehensive debt consolidation.

Poland requested a rescheduling of its debt in 1981. Shortly after this announcement several hundred million U.S. dollars in short-term deposits in Poland were withdrawn by Western banks, one of the reasons for Poland's severe debt-servicing difficulties in 1981. The ensuing reschedulings decreased, at least temporarily, the tension in the credit relations with the Western creditors. From 1981 to 1986, eight reschedulings were arranged, three with official and five with commercial bank creditors.

Agreements with official creditors

The first rescheduling agreement covered medium- and long-term government guaranteed debt due in 1981 (Tables 3.1 and 3.2). Short-term obligations were excluded. The terms and conditions of the agreement (Table 3.1) included rescheduling of 90% of the principal and interest (which provided estimated debt relief of $2.5 billion), to be repaid, after a four-year grace period, between January 1986 and July 1989; interest on the rescheduled interest was to be charged during the grace period. The greatest part of the rescheduled credits was due to the United States ($0.54 billion) and West Germany ($0.36 billion).

The agreement of April 1981 was followed by bilateral agreements with the participating governments before year end. The agreement with the United States was signed in August 1981 and that with West Germany in October 1981. However, Poland had to make debt payments in the amount of $1 billion during 1981. These payments were strictly met (Schroeder 1983b, p. 18).

After the imposition of martial law in Poland in December 1981, the ministers of foreign affairs of the NATO countries proposed a cessation of rescheduling discussions with Poland in January 1982. As a result, the discussion on the debt payments due in 1982 did not take place. However, the agreement of April 1981 was not suspended. Several meetings of Western government agencies took place in Paris during 1983–4 without a Polish representative; only technical issues on the Polish debt were discussed. The Polish official debt has not been serviced since 1981, but the Western governments have in the meantime paid their exporters the government-insured amount of the credits due from Poland.

The negotiations between Poland and its official creditors were resumed at the end of 1983, and the second agreement was signed in July 1985. The main terms and conditions of this rescheduling agreement are debt relief in the amount of $11.3 billion, five years grace, and eleven years maturity.

The third rescheduling agreement with the Paris Club was signed in March 1986. Its main terms are debt relief of $1.6 billion due in 1986, five years grace period, and ten years maturity. Poland will not receive new financing, but funds will effectively be provided to pay interest. The conditions for the deal are that Poland will adhere strictly to agreed payments and that commercial banks will not

Table 3.1. *Terms and conditions of debt reschedulings of Poland and Romania*

	Basis	Amount provided ($U.S. billions)	Grace period (yr)	Maturity (yr)	Spread over LIBOR (%)	Resched. fee (%)
Poland						
Agreement of April 1981; government-guaranteed medium- and long-term debt due in 1981	90% of principal and interest	2.5	4	7.5	n.a.	n.a.
Agreement of April 1982;[a] medium-term debt due March 26–December 31, 1981	95% of principal	2.3	4	7	1.75	1
Agreement of November 1982; medium-term debt due in 1982, including arrears on nonrescheduled maturities due in 1981	95% of principal	2.3	4	7.5	1.75	1
Agreement of November 1983; medium-term debt due during 1983	95% of principal	1.4	5	10	1.875	1
Agreement of April 1984; medium- and long-term debt due during 1984–7	95% of principal	1.615	5	10	1.75	1

Table 3.1. (cont.)

	Basis	Amount provided ($U.S. billions)	Grace period (yr)	Maturity (yr)	Spread over LIBOR (%)	Resched. fee (%)
Agreement of July 1985; government-guaranteed debt due in 1981–5	n.a.	11.3	5	11	n.a.	n.a.
Agreement of March 1986; government-guaranteed debt due in 1986	n.a.	1.6	5	10	n.a.	n.a.
Agreement of June 1986; medium-term debt due in 1986–7	95% of principal	2.06	—	4^b	1.125	n.a.
Romania						
Agreement of July 1982; government-guaranteed medium- and long-term debt due in 1981 and 1982	80% of principal and interest	0.486	3	6.5	1.75	n.a.
Agreement of December 1982; arrears on the 1981 debt obligations	80% of such debt obligations	1.598	3	6.5	1.75	1
Obligations due in 1982 on all debts (including short-term)	80% of principal		3	6.5	1.75	1

Agreement of May 1983; government-guaranteed medium- and long-term debt due in 1983	10% of principal	0.022	1.5	1.5	1.75	1
	60% of principal	0.134	3.5	6.5	1.75	1
Agreement of June 1983; medium- and long-term due in 1983	10% of principal	0.081	1.5	1.5	1.75	1
	60% of principal	0.486	3.5	6.5	1.75	1
Agreement of July 1986; medium- and long-term debt upon rescheduling agreements of 1982 and 1983	see above	see above	3		1.375	0.25

1982

May 1986	May & Nov. 1989
November 1986	May & Nov. 1990
May 1987	May & Nov. 1991
November 1987	May & Nov. 1992

1983

March 1987	May & Nov. 1991
September 1987	May & Nov. 1992

[a] The agreement, which covers maturities due from March 26 to December 31, 1981, was effective May 10, 1982. Short-term facilities and interbank deposits were specifically excluded.

[b] The credits will be rolled over for four years.

Sources: Brau, Williams, et al. (1983, pp. 31–2); Eichler (1986, p. 209); BIS (1984, p. 112); Schroeder (1983b); *Wall Street Journal*, November 29, 1985, p. 16, June 13, 1986, p. 27; OECD (1985b); Dillon et al. (1985, pp. 58, 62).

Table 3.2. *Poland's and Romania's debt reschedulings, 1982–6*

	Med.- & long-term public sector debt	Short-term debt	Arrears		Future debt service	New med.-term loan	Bridge loan	Other new financ.	Official debt resched.	IMF arrangement	
			Princ.	Int.						In place	Condit'l. upon
Poland											
April 1981	Yes	No	No	No	Yes	No	No	No	Yes	No	
April 1982	Yes	No	No	No	Yes	No	No	No	No	No	
November 1982	Yes	No	Yes	No[a]	Yes	No	No	No	No	No	
November 1983	Yes	No	No	No[b]	Yes	No	No	No	No	No	
April 1984	Yes	No	No	No[c]	Yes	No	No	Yes[d]	Yes	No	
July 1985	Yes	No	Yes	Yes	Yes	n.a.	n.a.	n.a.	Yes	No	
March 1986	Yes	No	Yes	Yes	Yes	n.a.	n.a.	n.a.	Yes	No	
June 1986	Yes	No	Yes	No[e]	Yes	n.a.	n.a.	n.a.	No	No	
Romania											
July 1982	Yes	No	Yes	Yes	Yes	No	No	No	Yes	Yes	Yes
December 1982	Yes	Yes	Yes	No	Yes	No	No	No	No	Yes	Yes
May 1983	Yes	No	No	No	Yes	No	No	No	Yes	Yes	Yes
June 1983	Yes	No	No	No	Yes	No	No	No	No	Yes	Yes
July 1986	Yes	No	Yes	Yes	Yes	No	No	No	No	Yes	No

[a] A six-month, $375 million trade credit, revolving for up to three years, was extended under separate agreement.
[b] A six-month, $175 million trade credit, revolving for up to five years, was extended under separate agreement.
[c] A six-month trade credit, revolving for up to five years, was extended under separate agreement. The credit totaled $U.S. 465 million. The short-term credit facility was rolled over in 1985.
[d] New trade financing amounting to $U.S. 235 million (5-yr maturity).
[e] A six-month, $180 million trade, revolving facility was extended under separate agreement.

Sources: See sources for Table 3.1.

receive preferential treatment with regard to repayment of principal.

Agreements with commercial banks

The first Polish rescheduling agreement with commercial banks was signed in April 1982 in Frankfurt, West Germany, after long negotiations. The Western banks agreed on the main terms and conditions of the rescheduling in July 1981. Poland announced that it accepted them in August 1981, but delayed signing for tactical reasons, trying to take advantage of differences about the rescheduling terms among the Western banks. It further insisted on 100% rescheduling of principal payments and, after the imposition of martial law, on a new credit of $350 million. At the end of 1981, Poland had fallen $500 million into arrears on interest payments, which also contributed to the delay in negotiations.

The main terms of the rescheduling agreement of April 1982 were as follows: exclusion of short-term obligations; rescheduling of 95% of principal; repayment of the rescheduled debt of $2.3 billion, after a grace period of four years, between 1986 and 1989; three-quarters[7] of a percentage point spread above LIBOR; and a rescheduling fee of 1%.

The second rescheduling agreement with Western commercial banks was signed in November 1982. It rescheduled 95% of principal payments on medium-term debt, with the debt relief covering $2.3 billion due in 1982, including arrears on nonrescheduled maturities due in 1981. The grace and the maturity periods were 4 and $7\frac{1}{2}$ years, respectively, the spread above LIBOR was $1\frac{3}{4}$%. Interest payments were excluded. A short-term trade credit ($375 million, or about 50% of the interest payments due on non-rescheduled debt), revolving for up to three years, was extended under a separate agreement; the rescheduling fee was 1%.

The third rescheduling agreement with commercial banks was signed after long discussion one year later in November 1983. It

---

[7] The spreads of LIBOR in Poland's reschedulings are relatively low in comparison to the spreads applied in some of the most indebted developing countries' (Brazil, Mexico) reschedulings (see Brau, Williams et al. 1983, pp. 35–40; Cline 1984, pp. 80–2).

covered medium-term commercial debt due during 1983, with its main terms as follows: rescheduling of 95% of principal payments; debt relief in the amount of $1.4 billion due after five years grace between 1989 and 1993; a spread above LIBOR of 1⅞%; and a re-scheduling fee of 1%. Under a separate agreement a short-term trade credit (equivalent to approximately 60% of the $300 million in interest due on outstanding obligations other than those arising from the rescheduling in 1981 and 1982) was also extended, in order to facilitate Polish imports from the West.

The fourth rescheduling agreement with commercial banks, in April 1984, was on medium- and long-term debt due in 1984–7. The basic terms included rescheduling of 95% of principal; debt relief covering just over $1.6 billion due, after a grace period of five years, between 1990 and 1994; a spread of 1¾% above LIBOR. A revolving trade credit in the amount of $465 million was extended under separate agreement (Dillon et al. 1985, p. 62). (The short-term credit facility was rolled over in 1985. Further trade credits revolving every six months for up to 4–5 yr are to be extended.) Poland received for the first time since 1981 a new $235 million trade credit (maturity 5 yr, interest rate spread of 1¾% above LIBOR).

The fifth rescheduling agreement with commercial banks was negotiated in June 1986 in Vienna. The debt relief covered $2.06 billion of medium-term debt due in 1986–7; $0.86 billion were due in 1986 and $1.2 billion in 1987. During this period, the commercial banks will receive only the interest payments due; the principal repayments will be rolled over for four years and then paid. Interest on the rescheduled credits was reduced from a 1¾% to a 1⅛% spread above LIBOR.

This fifth agreement completed the process of reschedulings with commercial banks in the first half of the 1980s. The total debt rescheduled amounts of $9.7 billion (excluding the revolving trade credits and the new financing) or roughly 83% of the commercial debt. The accumulated commercial and official debt and the minimal increases in the capacity to service it certainly require a new rescheduling "wave" in the coming years.[8]

---

[8] The restructured debt repayment schedule (Table 3.1) indicates that the debt negotiated in 1981, 1982, and 1983 will fall due largely over 1986–9.

Romania's rescheduling

Even before the debt problems of the 1980s, Romania was known to the Western financial community as a country that might not always fully meet its external financial obligations. Romania rescheduled a small amount of debt in hard currencies to the West in 1970 (Schroeder 1983b, p. 25). Its increased debt during the seventies resulted in new debt-servicing difficulties at the end of that decade. During 1978–80 Romania received short-term credits of approximately $2 billion, when more than half of its deficits of the balance of payments were financed by short-term funds raised on the Euromarket. However, the Polish debt crisis led in 1981 to increasing caution by bankers in providing new short-term loans to Romania. At that time, $1.5 billion in Western deposits were withdrawn, creating serious liquidity problems. The amount roughly corresponded, however, to Romanian hard-currency obligations in 1981. Romania received a confirmation of a new credit (about $1.5 billion spread over 3 yr) from the IMF. The first tranche of the IMF credit line of $0.4 billion was not enough to cover hard-currency payments falling due without raising other medium-term credits on the Euromarket. This proved impossible. In addition, the failure to fulfill debt obligations (in an estimated gross amount of $600 million) to Western commercial banks in mid-1981 led to a freeze in their credit relations with Romania. The second IMF disbursement was suspended at the end of 1981 because of Romania's failure again to fulfill economic targets agreed with the IMF. The comprehensive rescheduling of official and commercial hard-currency debt became unavoidable in this situation.

Negotiations with the Paris Club were concluded in the summer of 1982 (after reaching accord on a new stabilization program with the IMF) and the rescheduling agreement was signed in July 1982. The latter was followed by the specific bilateral agreements with Western governments – many of which were signed only after considerable delays because Romania failed to meet fully its rescheduling obligations. This was particularly evident for the agreement with West Germany.

The main terms and conditions of the first Paris Club agreement included rescheduling of 80% of principal and interest due in 1981 and 1982 (ca. $0.6 billion) and grace and maturity periods of 3 and $6\frac{1}{2}$ yr, respectively. The interest rate was not determined multilaterally, but agreed in bilateral negotiations with different Western governments at a spread of $1\frac{3}{4}\%$ above LIBOR. The remaining 20% of (nonrescheduled) debt was due after signing the agreements with the Western governments.

Romanian commercial debt was rescheduled in 1982, 1983, and 1986. The reschedulings of 1982 and 1983 covered roughly 60% of the commercial debt outstanding at end-1983. The first agreement was signed, after almost a year of negotiations, in December 1982 in London. It covered commercial debt due to more than 300 Western banks. It rescheduled 80% of the arrears of principal on the 1981 debt obligations plus the maturities (including short-term) due in 1982. Debt relief amounted to about $1.6 billion to be paid, after three years grace, over 1986–9; the nonrescheduled 20% remainder of the debt had to be paid by March 1983; the interest rate spread was $1\frac{3}{4}\%$ above LIBOR, and the fee was 1%.

A few weeks after signing the 1982 agreement Romania requested a new rescheduling of its commercial and official debt due in 1983. A basic agreement on the commercial debt was achieved in February 1983 and the final rescheduling document was signed after the Paris Club agreement in June 1983. The debt relief provided covered 10% of the principal and 60% of the principal, respectively, and totaled $567 million; the grace periods were $1\frac{1}{2}$ and $3\frac{1}{2}$ yrs, respectively; the maturities were $1\frac{1}{2}$ and $6\frac{1}{2}$ yr; the interest rate spreads were $1\frac{3}{4}\%$ above LIBOR, and the rescheduling fees (as in the previous agreements) were 1%. The main conditions of the Paris Club agreement of May 1983 were the same as those of the agreement with the commercial banks (Table 3.1). The debt relief provided totaled $156 million. Until 1986 Romania met its financial obligations under the rescheduling agreements of 1982 and 1983, but in early 1986 it experienced new debt-servicing difficulties and required some $800 million in debt falling due in 1986–7 to be deferred (*Financial Times*, July 15, 1986, p. 3). These payments included part of the principal rescheduled by the commercial banks in 1982 and 1983. Romania reduced its reserves to only $200 million in the first half of 1986, and consequently was exposed to liquidity difficulties. In July 1986 Romania requested new rescheduling of its com-

mercial bank debt rescheduled in 1982 and 1983 (see Table 3.1).
The prospect remains that the need for new reschedulings may
reappear.

4

The role of international financial institutions in resolving the Eastern European debt problems

Although the Soviet Union took part in the Bretton Woods conference in 1944, which led to the establishment of the International Monetary Fund (IMF) and the World Bank, it did not ratify the treaty and thus did not become a member of these international financial institutions. Poland and Czechoslovakia participated in both organizations until the early 1950s. Throughout the 1950s and 1960s no Eastern European country belonged to either the IMF or the World Bank. Romania joined both international financial institutions in 1972, the first CMEA country to do so, followed by the non-European CMEA member Vietnam in 1975. Beside having economic motives Romania wanted to demonstrate its foreign policy independence from the Soviet Union.

In the early 1980s, some other Eastern European countries changed their policies toward the IMF and the World Bank. Poland and Hungary applied to enter these financial institutions in 1981. Hungary became an IMF member in May 1982 and a World Bank member two months later. After the imposition of martial law in Poland in December 1981, the decision on its application was postponed. Poland joined both institutions five years later in June 1986.

Romania, Hungary, Poland, Bulgaria, and Czechoslovakia are members of the Bank for International Settlements (BIS) and are represented through their central banks. The BIS has been an active participant in financial rescue packages. The membership of the five aforementioned Eastern European countries in the BIS and that

of Romania, Hungary, and Poland in the IMF and the World Bank
prove that these countries value the assistance of the international
financial institutions in dealing with economic problems, especially
those concerned with external payments.

This chapter discusses the role of the IMF, the BIS, and the World
Bank in resolving the CMEA debt crisis in the beginning of the
1980s.

International Monetary Fund

The International Monetary Fund and its sibling organization the
World Bank were established to promote economic and financial
cooperation among their member countries and to play a central
role in the international monetary sphere. An essential aspect of this
role is the provision of financial assistance by the IMF to members
facing potential or actual balance-of-payments difficulties. International debt problems, which reached the point of crisis in 1982,
have thrown into unusual prominence the activities of the Fund. Its
name has been frequently in the headlines as Mexico, Brazil,
Argentina, Yugoslavia, Hungary, Romania, and other debtor countries have turned to it for critical assistance in managing their external finances.

Why did two of the Eastern European countries turn to the IMF
for assistance in the early 1980s? What was the influence of the
Fund's policy on Hungarian and Romanian adjustments to their
debt problems?

The Eastern European countries' main reasons for *not* joining the
Fund in the early postwar period were political. The Soviet Union's
(and the other CMEA countries') arguments against membership in
the IMF and the World Bank were as follows (Fomin, cited in Zloch
1984, p. 193);

the requirement to provide sensitive economic information (such as
    the national gold and foreign exchange reserves) and even to
    transfer a portion of gold and foreign exchange reserves to the
    United States, where the Fund and the World Bank are
    headquartered;
the procedure adopted for allocating votes to the Fund and World
    Bank members, which were felt to play down the position of

the Eastern European countries in the world economy and politics;[1]
the policy conditionality required for access to IMF credits; and
the requirement of free convertibility of foreign exchange payments and transfers.[2]

The Mason and Asher study describes the motives of the Soviet Union in not ratifying the Bretton Woods Articles of Agreement as follows:

No veto power was given to any member, and the Fund quota relegated the Soviet Union to third place in number of votes in both the Fund and the [World] Bank, after the United States and the United Kingdom. Fund membership required making available a substantial amount of information hitherto nondivulged, and borrowing from the Bank involved exacting investigations. Furthermore, a general purpose of the Bank and Fund to promote private trade within freer markets was of little interest to the Soviet Union . . . [3]

The requirements for membership in the IMF and the World Bank are still in force.[4] Obviously, in the early 1980s Hungary and particularly Poland turned for assistance to the IMF because their economic difficulties were so serious that political considerations paled beside them. However, Poland and Hungary were interested in rejoining the Fund and initiated preliminary consultations as long ago as the late 1950s and late 1960s, respectively.[5]

One can only speculate on whether both countries, as members of the Eastern European political, military, and economic community, obtained the Soviet Union's tacit agreement before joining

[1] The United States initially held 31% of the total IMF quota. If the Soviet Union had ratified the treaty, it and the other communist countries (Poland, Czechoslovakia, and Yugoslavia) combined would have had only 17% of the vote; 20% of the vote was required to exercise a veto (Marer 1984, pp. 2–3). At present, the United States has a 20% share in the total quota, and 15% of the vote is now required to exercise a veto.

[2] This requirement was considered to be unacceptable to the Eastern European countries because of their state monopoly on foreign exchange payments and foreign trade.

[3] Edward S. Mason and Robert E. Asher, *The World Bank since Bretton Woods,* cited in *Bank's World* 5(6):6, June 1986, Washington, D.C.

[4] Since 1971, gold contributions to the IMF are not required.

[5] There is evidence that the Soviet Union is interested in joining the IMF and World Bank at present (see, e.g., *PlanEcon Report,* July 31, 1986; *Washington Post,* Oct. 17, 1986, pp. F1, F10). It might be expected that other Eastern European countries (e.g., Bulgaria) might also try to apply to join both international financial institutions in the future.

the Fund (and the World Bank) in the early 1980s. As the liquidity problems of Poland and Hungary mounted to the point of crisis in 1981, and the Soviet "umbrella" failed to work as anticipated by the Western countries and the Eastern European debtors, the Soviet Union may have given its (implicit) "permission" for Hungary and Poland to apply for IMF membership. Both countries wanted access to additional and favorably priced IMF credits to overcome their serious balance-of-payments problems. They could borrow new loans from Western government and commercial bank sources only at high cost in 1981. The Hungarian economist L. Scaba writes that the Eastern European countries in the early 1980s increasingly recognized that "being at the private banks' mercy is not better than being dependent on the IMF, because credit conditions and re-scheduling arrangements are much tougher with the former than with the latter" (1984, p. 17).

Thus, the main motives of Hungary and Poland[6] in joining the IMF were economic. This is also true of Romania, but, as mentioned earlier, political considerations prevailed when this country applied to join the Fund (and the World Bank) in the early 1970s.

There are two main economic benefits for the three Eastern European countries from IMF membership: first, access to significant standby credits and funds from the Fund's special compensatory facilities; second, the Fund's "seal of approval" improves their creditworthiness with the international financial community and strengthens their position in negotiations with commercial bank lenders.

The Fund developed standby credits (arrangements) as the main instrument through which it could make financial resources available on a conditional basis. These arrangements can be described as a line of credit, contingent on prescribed circumstances, under which a member can draw on the Fund.[7] An important prerequisite

---

[6] Marer argues that a secondary reason for Poland's interest in membership may well be a desire by the authorities for support in pursuing unpopular policies, such as reducing the large gap between the purchasing power of the population (owing to large wage increases during the 1970s) and the availability of goods and services at prevailing prices (Marer 1985b, pp. 60–1).

[7] The Fund holds a substantial pool of liquid resources, which it can use to provide foreign exchange to members in need of balance-of-payments assistance. It does this by making available SDRs, or currencies of members that are currently in a relatively strong balance-of-payments and reserve position. The Fund does not

for a member's access to the Fund's standby credits is that it should have a balance-of-payments need. In accordance with recent IMF policy to make resources available in substantially larger amounts and for longer periods, a member can receive a standby credit of 115% of quota a year within a maximum of 345% of quota over a three-year period.[8] This enlargement of the credit possibilities from the Fund appears to be favorable for the Eastern European members.

In the case of Poland, its subscription to the Fund's capital is a quota[9] of SDR 680 million (about $796 million) of which 75% is subscribed in Polish zloty and the rest in convertible currencies.[10] Consequently, under a three-year program, Poland would have potential access to a total of approximately $2.5 billion in standby credits from the Fund. The interest rates on these credits are in the range 4.5%–7%, and the maturity period is 3–7 yr. These credit conditions are quite favorable for Poland, if one takes into account the high cost of rescheduling Polish debt from 1981 to 1986; for example, these were approximately 16%–17% in 1982–3, that is, more than twice as high as the rates on the IMF's standby credits. The maximum standby credits amount to about 8% of the country's gross debt in 1985 and could provide considerable financial assistance. However, Poland was not able to secure an IMF standby loan and to draw on it soon after it joined the organization.[11]

"lend" the foreign exchange, using instead the technique of a currency swap. The member receiving assistance purchases foreign exchange from the Fund in exchange for an equivalent amount of its own currency, and is obliged to reverse the transaction by installments over a period of several years.

[8] In the early 1980s access limits were 150% of quota within a three-year maximum of 450% of quota (*IMF Survey,* October 7, 1985, pp. 293–4). These earlier, more favorable limits were reduced after an approved quota increase.

[9] Upon joining the IMF, each member is allocated a quota whose relative size broadly reflects the size of the member's economy and its importance in world trade. The member's quota determines the amount it must subscribe to the capital of the institution, its voting rights, and the amount of the assistance it can receive from the Fund.

[10] IMF Press Release No. 86/17, June 12, 1986.

[11] The United States did not support Polish membership in the Fund and the Bank in 1986 (*Wall Street Journal,* May 23, 1986, p. 22). However, after the lifting of U.S. sanctions against Polish imports and the improvement of the conditions for providing new credits from Export-Import Bank and the Commodity Credit Corporation to Poland in early 1987, one might expect that the United States would change its policy regarding Polish membership in the international financial institutions (*New York Times,* Feb. 19, 1987, p. A8).

To receive a standby credit from the Fund a member must not only have a balance-of-payments need, but must also meet certain policy conditions, which increase in severity as the total amount of credit extended to it increases. In the Fund's special language, this is known as "conditionality." The key element of the Fund's conditionality is that the member is required to adopt a comprehensive adjustment (stabilization) program designed to correct its economic difficulties and bring it into a sustainable payments position over a reasonable period.

The Fund programs are complex packages of policy measures geared to the particular circumstances of the country, and the choice and nature of the policy mix result from negotiations between the country and the Fund.[12] The starting point in the adjustment program is the estimation of how large an improvement in a country's current-account deficit has to be achieved, taking into consideration the availability of foreign capital inflow and its sustainability. The next stage deals with the level of domestic demand that can be sustained consistent with stabilizing the external sector. The Fund adjustment programs are aimed primarily at noninflationary growth and dampening demand by controlling income flows to households, enterprises, government, and the banking system. The main monetary, fiscal, and income policy instruments applied to dampen the demand are controls on wages to lower real household income and consumption; controls on aggregate credit (by high interest rates) in order to lower investment expenditures; reductions in government expenditure; increases in taxes; and decreases in the rate of growth of the money supply designed to control inflation. An important part of many adjustment programs is a substantial devaluation of the national currency – an expenditure-switching policy to encourage exports and discourage imports. Special attention has been focused also on measures to improve resource allocation primarily by increased reliance on price mechanisms.

The institutional structure and incentive systems of the Eastern European centrally planned economies differ from those of the market economies. The role of the above-mentioned policy instruments in Fund adjustment programs are designed principally for market economies. This indicates that CMEA members Hun-

[12] See for more details de Larosiere (1984b) and Khan and Knight (1985).

gary, Poland, and Romania may differ significantly from other developing countries in their ability to apply standard Fund stabilization measures fully, as well as in their responses to these measures. For example, Hungary and (particularly) Romania resisted substantial cuts in price subsidies, real wages, and income, because associated with these measures are wage differentials and income inequality, which contradict the ideological and political legitimacy of their communist regimes. They resisted price desubsidization also because of concern for inflationary increases in prices. Hungary and Romania were reluctant for the same reasons to cut government expenditures, which will have as a consequence a reduction in social services (health, education, etc.). The burden of adjustment fell on a cut in investments. It has to be noted, however, that Hungary cooperated quite well with the Fund in negotiating the standby policy measures, whereas Romania did not pursue such a policy.

The cut in absorption in Hungary and particularly in Romania in the early 1980s was achieved through well-known centrally planned administrative measures and not by the application of a standard IMF package for reducing aggregate investment by limiting the availability of credit, raising interest rates, and so on. In the condition of persistent excess demand for investment in the Eastern European countries, the use of these incentive policy instruments would do little to reduce the investment demand. In Hungary, however, the administrative measures were accompanied by a 2% increase in interest rates and the imposition of additional taxes on new investments except those intended to increase hard-currency exports or to diminish the use of energy and raw material inputs. In Romania, interest rates were increased to 5%–8% (against 2%–5% previously) by January 1983 and to 7%–10% in January 1984. A tax on investment funds granted to the enterprises from the state budget also has been introduced since the beginning of 1984 (Romania, *Economic Memorandum,* 1983, p. 4).

The reduction of investment in both Eastern European countries was general and not selective. Furthermore, investments important for structural adjustment have been constrained. The effort to improve resource allocation by increased reliance on the price mechanism has also been limited because most prices are administratively controlled (even in Hungary) and are not determined primarily by market conditions. For the same reason, both CMEA countries are unable to pursue an effective expenditure-switching policy through devaluation. It appears that devaluation of the leu and also of the forint[13] cannot help considerably to promote exports and increased import substitution because the trade deficit with the Western countries is a structural problem. The Western demand for Eastern European goods is fairly price-inelastic. The influence of the devaluation on imports is also limited because the hard-currency imports are mostly capital goods and intermediate items for which there are no acceptable domestic substitutes. It appears, therefore, that the Eastern European demand for Western imports is also fairly price-inelastic. Even more important is the fact, especially for Romania, that the exchange rate is not a real price: World prices and domestic prices are not related and cannot be varied relative to each other by changing the exchange rate. Thus, the effectiveness of devaluation as a policy for adjustment in the centrally planned economies is limited. However, a forint devaluation would certainly have some impact on the balance of payments in Hungary, in contrast to a leu devaluation under Romania's rigid centrally planned economic system.

The adjustment process in both Eastern European countries has been quite similar to the response of other CMEA countries to external disturbances since the beginning of the 1980s. The IMF's (and the World Bank's) policy recommendations have not inspired a radical change in the adjustment efforts of either Hungary or Romania. The Fund and the Bank helped the policymakers in these countries to implement economic measures that they were either ready or inclined to introduce independently.[14] The Fund and Bank did play an important role in the adjustment process in Romania and particularly in Hungary, but mainly through their assistance in establishing an access to foreign credits. It should be noted,

---

[13] The forint was devalued by 22$ and 40%, respectively, against the U.S. dollar in the periods 1976-80 and 1980-3. In June 1984, the forint was further devalued by 12% against the U.S. dollar and 5% against the DM. The forint was devaluated also in 1985 and 1986. The leu commercial rate was devalued by 43.7% between January 1, 1983 and January 1, 1984. From July 1, 1983, a six-currency basket weighted according to the hard-currency structure of the Romanian foreign trade was adopted to determine the exchange rate of the leu (Romania, *Economic Memorandum,* 1983, p. 3).

[14] Marer argues that only when the authorities in the Eastern European countries are themselves convinced of the advantages of cooperation with the Fund and the World Bank, and have a firm commitment to such a course, are the prospects of meaningful external influence assured (Marer 1985c, p. 32).

Table 4.1. *Selected IMF quotas (in millions of SDR and percentages)*

	Quotas in millions of SDR	Quotas in percentages
United States	17,918.3	19.9
United Kingdom	6,194.0	6.9
Germany	5,403.7	6.0
France	4,482.8	5.0
Japan	4,223.3	4.7
Canada	2,941.0	3.2
Yugoslavia	613.0	0.68
Romania	523.4	0.58
Hungary	530.7	0.59
Poland	680.0	0.76
Other countries	46,406.1	52.0
Total	89,987.6	100.0

Sources: IMF, *Annual Report,* 1985, pp. 157–9; Press Release No. 86/17, June 12, 1986.

however, that the Fund and the Bank strengthened the position of the Hungarian policymakers advocating market-oriented economic reform, enabling them to introduce more rapidly price, exchange rate, subsidy, and other reforms because the top leadership pursued a policy to avoid rescheduling of debt at any cost.

Hungary was allocated a quota of 375 million SDR upon joining the Fund. In 1983 it was raised to 530.7 million SDR (Table 4.1). Eighty percent of quota is subscribed in forint, and 20% in convertible currencies or SDR. Shortly after joining the Fund in November 1982, Hungary received 72 million SDR (about $78.5 million) from the compensatory financing facility to offset declines in certain Hungarian exports. It was part of a 547-million-SDR (about $600 million) credit line approved by the Fund in November 1982, 475 million SDR of which were provided under a standard standby arrangement.[15] Hungary received 142 million SDR in December 1982; the remaining 333 million SDR were disbursed in four

[15] It has to be noted, however, that the Hungarian authorities informally asked the IMF what kind of program the Fund might recommend if a standby agreement were negotiated. They then adopted on their own an economic program along the lines informally suggested to them (Mendelson 1983, pp. 7–8).

installments during 1983, which showed that the Fund regarded the economic program as satisfactory, even though Hungary failed to fulfill some of the performance criteria. The IMF credit helped directly as well as indirectly, through the "seal of approval" effect on Hungarian creditworthiness in 1982-3, so that a rescheduling of debt was avoided. The second standby agreement was approved in January 1984, providing for a credit line of 425 million SDR. The "conditionality" required a further application of demand management and structural reform policies in Hungary. This standby credit line was disbursed during 1984. By the end of that year, Hungary initiated preliminary consultations with the Fund on a new standby agreement; this new agreement, however, was not achieved during 1985-6, although Hungary is moving ahead with market-oriented reform, which is broadly in accord with the Fund's (and the World Bank's) views.

Romania was allocated a quota of 367.5 million SDR when it joined the IMF in 1972. Upon the last general review of quotas from December 1983, the subscription to Fund capital was raised to 523.4 million SDR (Table 4.1). Romania made relatively little use of IMF credits during the seventies. In 1981, the Fund approved a credit line in the amount of $1.48 billion, which was approximately three times more than the total drawings by this country since 1972. Part of this credit line was provided under a standby agreement. The standby credit was not tied to special "conditionality" but had to be disbursed fully in three years (Schroeder 1983b, p. 33). This relatively long disbursement period (compared to that for Hungary) reflects the Fund's judgment that Romania's problems were too severe to be resolved rapidly. The main purpose of the 1981 credit line was to assist Romania in adjusting to the deterioration in its current account. This large drawing was provided at the relatively favorable interest rates of 6.25%-13.5%. The first installment in the amount of $400 million was disbursed in 1981. The second disbursement was scheduled for the end of 1981. Financial observers expected that, with this assistance from the IMF, Romania would be able to meet its debt obligations in 1981 and the beginning of 1982. However, because of a failure to fulfill the performance criteria in the standby agreement, the second Fund disbursement was not made until the summer of 1982. A rescheduling of Romanian debt could not be avoided.

A stabilization program with the Fund preceded the disbursement of the second tranche in the amount of $500 million. This program was aimed at a massive domestic adjustment to improve the balance of payments. In contrast to the program for Hungary, the Fund arrangement with Romania relied primarily on external quantitative criteria – apparently, balance-of-trade and balance-of-payments targets – rather than on policies to promote structural adjustment and market-oriented economic mechanisms. Some Western observers, however, criticized the Fund as not being tough enough in encouraging Romania to implement radical reforms in its highly centralized economic system (Marer 1984, p. 20).

During 1982–5 Romania made a large and painful adjustment, and its creditworthiness improved; nevertheless, it failed again to fulfill all of the conditions in the standby arrangement with the Fund. The last installment of 285 million SDRs was therefore not disbursed and the agreement was prematurely canceled in January 1984.[16] During 1985 and in early 1986 Romania diminished by repurchases its outstanding use of Fund credit.

Bank for International Settlements

Since 1945 the Bank for International Settlements (BIS) has functioned as a bank for central banks. Twenty-nine countries particpate in this international financial institution: the major Western European countries, the CMEA countries (without the Soviet Union and the GDR),[17] the United States, Canada, Japan, and Australia. The main objective of the BIS is to promote the cooperation of central banks and to provide additional facilities for international financial operations. Involvement in the BIS seems favorable for the Eastern European members.

Since the beginning of the 1980s, the BIS has played a major role in attempts to respond to the debt crisis. It has been a vehicle in conjunction with and through which Western central banks are channeling urgent, short-term financial assistance to debtor coun-

---

[16] Romania did not accept recommended further increases in domestic prices (and particularly energy prices), further devaluation of the leu, and an abolition of some subsidies to enterprises (Pissulla 1985, p. 6).
[17] In spite of the fact that the Soviet Union is not a BIS member, it used BIS assistance in the 1960s to finance its gold sales to the West (Campbell and Herzstein 1984, p. 33).

tries.[18] Its emergency credits are of short maturity (6–9 mo) and have been generally secured with some sort of collateral (e.g., reserves, usually gold). The credits have often been linked to some kind of automatic repayment following disbursement by the IMF, the World Bank, or banks.

In 1982 the BIS was actively involved in resolving the debt problems of Hungary, one of the first debtor countries to turn to it for assistance. The withdrawal of Western short-term deposits from this Eastern European country in the spring of 1982 resulted in a liquidity crisis. Hungary received both short-term BIS credit in the amount of $100 million and, in the second quarter of that year, a new $110 million "bridge" loan. Central banks from thirteen BIS members participated in these two credits arranged by the BIS (with strong support from the Bank of England). In September 1982, Hungary received a further six-month BIS credit in the amount of $300 million, having been refused a short-term credit from the BIS in July. The third bridge loan was granted on the basis of Hungary's membership in the IMF as of May 1982 and the understanding that Hungary would become eligible to draw on IMF facilities shortly after joining the Fund.

One can speculate about whether the membership of Poland in the IMF and the World Bank will increase its access to short-term BIS credits. Fritz Leutwiler, the former chairman of the BIS, stated that BIS loans are provided on the understanding that the debtor countries will repay promptly when IMF credits are available. This indicates that access to BIS credits in the case of Poland will depend mainly on its good standing with the Fund. Leutwiler stressed also that the BIS has no intention of becoming involved in rolling over credits for an unspecified period of time (Campbell and Herzstein, 1984, p. 31); in other words, the BIS does not intend to remain permanently involved in the process of resolving a country's debt problems over the medium term. However, taking into account the high level of Polish debt and the necessity of rolling it over at least until the end of this decade, the involvement of Western (primarily Western European) central banks in this process probably cannot be avoided. One may speculate, therefore, whether the BIS, as a bank for Western central banks, will continue to be involved in the pro-

[18] The BIS provided short-term credits also to nonmember debtor countries (Mexico and Brazil) in 1982.

cess. As regards the other Eastern European countries, their access to BIS short-term credits will depend primarily on the status of their hard-currency debt and their relations with Western commercial banks and governments.

World Bank

The World Bank is an international financial institution whose basic function is to deal with the economic development needs of developing member countries. Its main objective (as formulated by its former president A. W. Clausen) is to assist a particular developing country member "both to accelerate its economic growth and enhance the economic opportunities of its people" (Clausen 1982, p. 68).

The World Bank's primary objectives in the international financial community are the following:

to transfer resources to developing countries;
to influence policies for development;
to extent credits (on a sound banking basis) for economically viable projects;
to provide technical assistance to developing countries; and
to supply information about developing countries to the private international capital market.

Two questions arise: What are the main motives that led the Eastern European member countries to participate in the World Bank? What concrete benefits did Hungary and Romania gain from their membership in the early 1980s?

The main motives leading Hungary, Poland, and Romania to participate in the World Bank are economic, as in the case of their membership in the IMF. (The quotas of these countries are given in Table 4.2.) In addition to getting the Bank's "seal of approval," the following two motives also are pertinent: first, if designated as a less developed country,[19] access to advantageously priced Bank loans

[19] Romania, Poland, and Hungary are regarded in the World Bank as less developed countries, with per capita national income below $2,600. However, some estimates of the per capita national income of these countries, based not on their commercial exchange rates but on "adjusted purchasing-power parity," are higher: $2,680 for Romania, $3,120 for Poland, and $4,390 for Hungary (Marer 1984, p. 17).

Table 4.2. Selected World Bank quotas
(in millions of SDR and in percentages)

	Quotas in millions of SDR	Quotas in percentages
United States	13,809.8	20.9
United Kingdom	3,894.7	5.9
Germany	3,434.7	5.2
Japan	4,083.0	6.2
France	3,660.4	5.6
Canada	2,178.2	3.3
Yugoslavia	150.9	0.23
Romania	200.1	0.30
Hungary	420.3	0.64
Poland	24.9	0.04
Other countries	33,979.4	51.6
Total	65,836.4	100.0

Source: World Bank Annual Report (1986, pp. 174–7).

for project financing;[20] second, opportunity as a member of the World Bank to bid on Bank-financed projects in every country in the world.

The Hungarian economist Csikos-Nagy, in discussing the motives of Hungary in joining the World Bank, stressed that in the early 1980s his country wanted to be a member of the Bank not only to have access to new credits on favorable conditions, but, "first of all, to create the possibility of exporting capital goods to developing countries" (Csikos-Nagy 1984, p. 13). Winning contracts to supply World Bank–financed projects in developing countries can help improve a country's balance of payments because the Bank pays the suppliers promptly. Hungary and the other Eastern European countries are particularly interested in expanding their trade with the developing countries. Participation in the World Bank in the

[20] Project financing is designed to finance specified investment activities. Since the early 1980s projects have been funded not only in the public utility sector (including irrigation and rural electrification and transport) but also in education, population control, agricultural credit, livestock, and rural area development (Krueger 1983, p. 293).

case of Hungary, Romania, and Poland could create a favorable climate for expanding their exports to the Third World.

The Bank assisted Hungary and Romania in the early 1980s by financing their development projects. In addition, the Bank's loans helped directly and indirectly (through the "seal of approval") to improve the standing of these countries (especially of Hungary) in the private capital markets. In the case of Poland, potential access to the Bank's project loans (probably in agriculture, energy, and transportation) appears to be a very important incentive for joining the Bank; however, it will be unable to receive loans from the Bank before mid-1987 because of the lag in appraising projects after membership is approved. Its membership in the Bank (and the Fund) certainly would contribute to the gradual normalization of its relations with the commercial banks as well.

The concrete benefits for Hungary and Romania from their membership in the Bank include the projects already financed. During 1982–5 Hungary received seven loans in the amount of $629 million.[21] The first two project loans were approved and dibursed in 1983. (Hungary did not have U.S. support in the Bank for project loans in 1982 and the beginning of 1983. The United States supported Hungary's admission to the IMF and the World Bank, but then tried to block its access to the Bank loans.) In June 1983, Hungary received two loans totaling $239 million: The first credit of $130 million was provided to modernize grain production; the second credit of $109 million financed energy diversification, conservation, and technology development. The World Bank participated in cofinancing with private banks (syndicates led by the Arab Banking Corporation and the Industrial Bank of Japan) for both credits, which were estimated at $623 million.

In 1984, Hungary received two further Bank loans. The first credit ($110 million) was provided for industrial restructuring and export expansion (promotion). The second loan ($90 million) financed an oil and gas production program aimed at arresting the decline in local oil and gas production through a series of priority investments in exploration, field development, and rehabilitation and enhanced oil recovery. The World Bank participated again in

---

[21] The data on World Bank loans are from *World Bank Annual Report*, various issues.

cofinancing with private banks (syndicates led by the Arab Banking Corporation, the Industrial Bank of Japan, Manufacturers Hanover Trust, and others) for these two credits, estimated at $777 million. The Bank accepts the longer maturities; the commercial banks take the shorter ones.

Two further projects were cofinanced by the Bank during 1985: a road construction and an agroindustrial project for which the Bank's share of financing was $110 million. (The Bank's cofinancing activities in the case of Hungary were very successful.) A further loan for agriculture and rural development in the amount of $80 million also was provided in 1985. A vice-president of the World Bank, W. Wapenhans, said in a 1984 interview that Hungary had a good chance for Bank cofinancing and loans in the annual amount of $200 million in the future (Friedlaender 1985, p. 582). This would be an important factor in improving the country's credit-worthiness, since the direct loans and cofinancings would contribute substantially to financing the balance-of-payments deficits. However, it appears that the improved relations of Hungary with the Western banks will return the need for the involvement of the World Bank in cofinancing activities in the future.

Romania received three project loans totaling about $321 million in 1982. The first credit amounted to $95 million and was for an agricultural development project in the Moldova region. The second loan in the amount of $101 million was for oil recovery. The third loan ($125 million) financed a transportation project (railways and road). During 1983–5 (financial years) Romania did not receive further World Bank credits. A contributing factor may have been Romanian reluctance to borrow new funds, which reflects its policy, following the payments crisis of 1982, to reduce its debt.

Summary

The IMF and the World Bank were actively involved in resolving the debt difficulties of Romania and particularly of Hungary in the early 1980s. The BIS assisted by providing short-term credit lines to Hungary. However, the IMF's and the World Bank's involvement has not radically changed the adjustment strategy of either country. The Fund and the Bank helped the policymakers in these countries to implement economic measures that they were either ready or inclined to introduce independently. The Fund and the Bank supported this adjustment mainly by providing access to foreign credits.

The membership of Poland in the IMF and the World Bank could provide it with access to these organizations' funds, contributing to a gradual normalization of its relations with Western commercial banks. However, it would be too optimistic to expect that Poland will receive new credits soon after joining both international financial institutions.

5

Eastern European debt and the "prisoners' dilemma"

> If you owe your bank a hundred pounds
> you have a problem. But if you owe your
> bank a million pounds, it has . . .
>
> – John Maynard Keynes

The debt crisis of Eastern Europe in the late seventies and early eighties was the result both of policy mistakes by CMEA borrowers and of misjudgments by Western commercial banks and governments. As CMEA indebtedness rose to high levels the Western creditors and CMEA debtors increasingly became mutually dependent. A Swiss banker noted: "Make a small loan, and you have created a debtor; make a large loan and you have created a partner" (Janssen 1977, p. 13). The analysis of the debt problems of Eastern European countries in the previous chapters showed that the dangers of the debt crisis are many-sided, with major risks borne both by creditors and debtors. If lenders' behavior determined the timing of the crisis, the borrowers' behavior contributed to their own vulnerability.

Many interesting questions remain to be answered in the relationship between the CMEA debtors and their Western creditors. What strategies will the Western creditors and the Eastern European borrowers follow if debt problems revive? Will they cooperate or not? What would be the consequences of a Western credit embargo toward the CMEA countries? Does a moral-hazard problem exist in lending to Eastern Europe? An analytical framework for answering these questions is the concern of this chapter.

Creditor–debtor policy strategies

The position of Western creditors and Eastern European borrowers in a debt crisis resembles a two-person, non-zero-sum game. The payoffs to the players are not symmetric: The borrowers' gain is not necessarily a creditors' loss and vice versa. There is often a "prisoners' dilemma" aspect to the credit relations between East and West. The salient feature of the prisoners' dilemma is that each player, *A* or *B,* has two strategies: a cooperative one and a non-cooperative one. Cooperation implies that players in optimizing their self-interest take account of their actions' effects on the objectives of the other player. Noncooperation implies that creditors and debtors unilaterally try to maximize their returns, not taking into account the objectives of the other player. A *single* player gains most by being uncooperative in the face of cooperative strategies by all other players; for *all* players considered as a group, however, the maximum payoff is obtained from the cooperative strategy.

Using a game-theoretic approach such as this, the basic strategies of Western creditors and Eastern European borrowers in a debt crisis are either cooperative or noncooperative. What will determine the main strategies of Western creditors and CMEA borrowers in a debt crisis? The creditors (Western banks, governments, international institutions) might choose among the following alternatives:

reduce lending;
maintain lending; or
increase lending.

The CMEA borrowers might pursue one or both of the following two strategies:

dampen domestic aggregate demand;
suspend payments.

An illustration of the national costs and benefits for both sides from applying simultaneously these strategies in the short and medium term is presented in the payoff matrix shown as Table 5.1 (the first figure in each cell is the creditor payoff). The matrix is a construct to illustrate that the creditor benefits by being uncooperative when debtor behavior is cooperative, however, the debtor loses. Likewise, the debtor who is uncooperative benefits from cooperative creditor

Table 5.1. *Creditor–debtor strategies*

| | Debtor strategy | |
Creditor strategy	Dampen domestic aggregate demand	Suspend payments
Reduce credits	3, −1	−2, 1
Maintain or increase credits	4, 5	−5, 4

behavior, but the creditor loses. If they both behave cooperatively, however, both can benefit.

A jointly noncooperative strategy by the Western creditors and the Eastern European borrowers results in reducing credit flows and default. The payoff to the creditor and debtor, respectively, might be −2 and 1. This strategy is clearly dominated by the assumed payoff from a cooperative policy of increased (or maintained) credits and dampened domestic aggregate demand (4, 5). Jointly reducing credits and dampening demand favors creditors but results in a negative (unsatisfactory) payoff for the Eastern European debtor. Suspending payments leads to negative payoffs for the Western creditors, but might favor the debtor (at least initially) and return positive payoffs for the Eastern European borrowers.

What would be the actual costs and benefits for a CMEA country in dampening demand or suspending payments? The costs and benefits of dampening demand were analyzed in Chapter 2. The benefits from a policy of suspending payments are that the Eastern European country would save the real value of the outstanding debt. The costs are far more problematic, and they stem mainly from three sources. First, the debtor country would risk isolating itself economically from the Western world. That would result in partial or complete inability to borrow new credits in the Western capital markets, at least for some time after suspending payments. The Polish and Romanian cases in 1981 and 1982 showed this clearly. Second, the CMEA country's assets in the West – including bank accounts, aircraft, ships, and shipments of commodities – might be seized. Third, the ability of the country to trade with the West would be reduced even if no new net borrowing were involved. Suspending payments would surely lead to difficulties in obtaining short-term trade credits, making it impossible for the debtor to conduct trade with the West at normal levels. East–West trade has been built on a system of revolving trade credits since the late sixties. The denial of short-term revolving trade credits would mean that the Eastern European country would have to pay for its imports on a cash basis. To do this it might have to maintain reserves worth approximately six months of imports. Among the CMEA countries only the Soviet Union has large enough reserves to contemplate continued trade on a cash basis. Ironically, the Soviet Union is not likely to have serious debt-servicing difficulties.

Suspending payments by an Eastern European country is an act that cannot be regarded only from the economic point of view. Such a default would have implications for the whole system of East–West relations and is determined also by political and strategic considerations. Default by one Eastern European country might have a "domino effect," leading to a suspension of payments by other Eastern bloc countries with convertible-currency debt problems. Recent years showed that the Soviet Union is not willing to "share the burden" of a debt crisis with its allies; thus, a default by a particular CMEA country might lead to a "freezing" of the economic and political relations between East and West.

A freeze in East–West relations might result also if the Western countries respond to the debt crisis of a single CMEA country by reducing credit flows to the whole region. In the extreme, they might apply a credit embargo toward Eastern Europe. The main instruments of such an embargo might be the introduction of a license system or a direct prohibition of capital transfer, reduction or suspension of the national export credit guarantee systems, or a compulsory declaration of default.

What would be the consequences of such an embargo on the Soviet Union and the Eastern European Six? The Soviet Union probably would respond to the embargo by reducing its imports from the West (primarily Western machinery and equipment) and increasing exports of gold, weapons, oil, gas, and other raw materials. In addition it might reduce its assets in Western banks in order to service its debt. The great reserves of the Soviet Union would allow it to cope with the external disturbances while maintaining policies designed to achieve its long-run economic objectives (Twentieth Century Fund 1983, p. 49).

The burden of a credit embargo on Eastern Europe would fall on the CMEA Six because they are more vulnerable; however, their policy responses probably would be the same as those of the Soviet Union. In addition, because of their limited resources, one could expect requests for rescheduling of their debts. Outright default would also be a possible reaction. The Eastern European Six would be forced to cut back trade with the West drastically and to rely primarily on economic relations within the CMEA and on the assistance of the Soviet Union. Consequently those trying to liberalize their economic systems and introduce market-oriented reforms would probably abandon their reforms and reemphasize a highly centralized planned economy.

All Eastern European countries and particularly the "reform countries" – Hungary, Poland, and the GDR – need East–West trade because of the unavailability of many "hard" goods and modern technology in the CMEA. East–West trade plays an important role in the modernization of their industries through the importation of such technology and equipment. For their part, Western countries, and particularly the major Western European countries (West Germany, France, Italy, and Great Britain), seem unwilling to lose their market shares in CMEA trade, which would be the logical consequence of a "freezing" of the economic and political relations between East and West. They know as well that eventual Eastern bloc defaults could result in great losses for Western European (particularly West German) banks, which hold the biggest share of credits to the CMEA.[1] The Western governments also would have obligations on the suspended CMEA debts they had guaranteed, which would increase their budgetary deficits. The recent debt-servicing problems of Poland and Romania have demonstrated this fact very clearly.

This brief discussion of the main strategies and interests of the parties involved in East–West trade indicates that, from the economic viewpoint at least, a noncooperative strategy by the par-

[1] When Poland declared martial law in December 1981, several members of the Reagan Administration called for the United States to get tough with the Comecon countries and declare Poland's credits in default. However, the U.S. Treasury Department, the State Department, and the Western European countries opposed this course of action. They argued that the only practical accomplishment of a Polish default would be to relieve Poland of its debt obligations, causing at the same time serious harm to Western European financial interests.

ticipants in a future CMEA debt crisis is not a likely scenario. Scenarios involving mutually cooperative creditor–debtor actions are more likely; strategies would tend therefore to emphasize maintaining or increasing credits and dampening domestic aggregate demand. Particularly for Hungary, Poland, and Romania, participation in the IMF and the World Bank would be an important factor facilitating a cooperative creditor–debtor approach.

The debt problems of the Eastern European countries in the early 1980s showed that these countries are, in principle, anxious to avoid debt-servicing difficulties. Faced with liquidity shortages, all of them introduced deflationary economic policies in order to generate additional hard-currency earnings (through import compression and export promotion). This response to their debt problems was greatly influenced, however, by the restrictive credit policy of the Western countries; the reduction of credit flows and the withdrawal of short-term deposits exacerbated the debt-servicing difficulties of some of the Eastern European countries (i.e., Poland, Hungary, GDR, and Romania). This situation could have been avoided had the Western governments and commercial banks adopted a more cooperative strategy in 1981. Unfortunately, at that time the atmosphere of uncertainty both in the political arena and in the financial markets brought Western lenders close to panic. The application of a more cooperative strategy (allowing credit to continue to expand) in the case of Hungary a year later permitted it to maintain debt services. For Poland and Romania, reschedulings were the only feasible option that admitted a strategy allowing for creditor–debtor cooperation.

Moral hazard in lending to Eastern Europe

Could the willingness of Western creditors to adopt a cooperative strategy toward Eastern European debt problems create a moral hazard in lending to these countries, particularly in the case of Poland, Hungary, Romania, and the GDR?

Wilson Schmidt wrote in the midsixties that "in principle, countries always have the ability to pay debt service . . . If the creditor adopts a policy of offering new aid whenever a debtor threatens to default, debtors are likely to increase their threats of default in order to gain more assistance" (cited in Vaubel 1983, p. 65). The recent reschedulings of the Polish and Romanian debts, and the "bridging actions" in the case of Hungary and the GDR (credits from West Germany), showed unambiguously that the Western commercial banks, governments, and the international financial institutions committed themselves to providing debt relief motivated at least partly by the implicit threat of de facto unilateral default by these countries. One cannot exclude the possibility that this cooperative Western attitude could weaken the incentive to avoid mistakes in the future borrowing policies of the four Eastern European countries. This is particularly relevant in the case of Hungary and the GDR. One can expect also that Poland, as a member of the IMF, might rely heavily on the prospect of Fund resources to ease its difficult balance-of-payments problems. Poland would probably rely on debt rollover actions by the Western commercial banks and governments as well. The possibility of multiyear debt reschedulings could weaken further the incentive to avoid mistakes in debt management, since Poland would not be obliged to return for annual negotiations.

It is difficult to distinguish between a country's inability to service its debts and its refusal to do so in order to win concessions from creditors. The only reliable indicator of a country's firm intention not to service is outright debt repudiation. However, between debt repudiation and timely debt repayment, there is a range of possible outcomes that may result from various degrees of both inability and unwillingness to meet debt-servicing obligations. As mentioned, the recent debt problems of Poland, Hungary, Romania, and also the GDR have shown these countries' willingness to take policy actions to avoid debt-servicing difficulties. It is not clear, however, particularly in the case of Poland, how far those policy actions will be pushed to mobilize domestic capacity to service hard-currency debt; but there can be no doubt that Poland, Hungary, Romania, and the GDR rely first and foremost on achieving cooperative solutions to debt problems with their Western creditors. This suggests that, by adopting a cooperative attitude, Western creditors do create an element of "moral hazard" in their lending to Eastern Europe.

6

Lending to Eastern Europe: problems of country risk analysis

Country risk analysis is an integral part of any international portfolio management process. The debt problems of the developing and the Eastern European countries during the 1970s and 1980s have greatly increased interest by financial institutions in evaluating country risk. No single risk-evaluation system optimally fulfills the requirements of all financial organizations. In addition, no single system is optimal for evaluating country risk in both Eastern Europe and developing countries.

This chapter provides general discussion of approaches for evaluating country risk and the problems in assessing credit risk to Eastern Europe. Some of the indicators of the external debt burden discussed below appeared in the analysis in Chapter 2 and contribute to the projections in Chapter 7.

Methodologies of country risk evaluation

Assessment of a country's creditworthiness is based on its present, past, and future repayment capabilities; credit risk arises from future events, but most of them are not predictable with any degree of certainty. For many countries, country risk is indistinguishable from sovereign risk: Lending to any borrower in the country is equivalent (or actually the same) as lending to the government.[1] If risk can be defined as exposure to a peril, then, from a bank's point

---

[1] The distinctions among sovereign risk, country risk, and credit (or project) risk in international lending are unclear. Credit risk is associated with the ability of an individual borrower to repay its debts. In the case of the Eastern European countries, where lending is to governments and central banks, the sovereign, country, and credit (project) risks tend to be viewed as one and the same.

of view, risk is exposure to a loss. In this sense, country risk is exposure to a loss in cross-border lending, caused by events in a particular country. Lending across national borders involves both economic risks (balance-of-payments difficulties, general problems in economic management, etc.) and political risks (sociopolitical upheavals, willingness of the authorities to meet foreign debt obligations, etc.). These risks are not easy to assess. Even if the risks of any given economic policy or political decision could be gauged accurately, there would still be uncertainty over which policies would be adopted. Avromovic's (1964) appraisal of the uncertainty of creditworthiness and country risk evaluations is still valid today:

The appraisal of creditworthiness of anybody – be it an individual, a business firm, or a country – is a mixture of facts and judgments. Even if we had the theory of debt servicing capacity and could satisfactorily explain the likely behavior of major variables and their time path, we would still be facing the uncertainties arising from current economic and financial policies which the decision makers in the borrowing countries may choose to adopt, be it at their own initiative or in response to all sorts of pressures. (pp. 7–8)

At present, most country risk evaluations rely on a number of quantitative indicators, such as the ratio of debt service to exports (the debt service ratio), the level of reserves to imports, and others. Analysis of these indicators is meant to detect trends in the country's repayment capability over time. The indicators are also used to compare lending risk across countries.[2]

The analysis of an Eastern European country's creditworthiness requires an answer to two fundamental questions:

1. Are the country's liquid assets sufficient to cover its immediate needs (i.e., can debt service interruptions be avoided)?
2. Is the economy sound, well managed, and capable of generating adequate external revenue for debt service in the future?

---

[2] The World Bank publishes eight debt-burden indicators in its *World Debt Tables:* (1) debt outstanding and disbursed to exports of goods and all services; (2) debt outstanding and disbursed to gross national product; (3) total debt service to exports of goods and all services (the debt service ratio); (4) interest payments to gross national product; (5) interest payments to exports of goods and all services (the interest–service ratio); (6) total debt service to gross national product; (7) international reserves to debt outstanding and disbursed; and (8) international reserves to imports of goods and all services. These indicators are among those used also by most major financial institutions for evaluating country risk.

The first question relates to the country's immediate liquidity (foreign exchange) position, and the second to the country's ability to continue to solve its structural problems.

Liquidity index

Debt-servicing problems of a given Eastern European country result from a deteriorating trade balance and an inability to borrow enough new funds. These lead to a decline in reserves (gold, easily marketable securities, and liquid assets in Western banks) and then, if severe enough, to arrears on debt payments and possibly to debt reschedulings. Potential debt service difficulties in the near term can be analyzed by a *liquidity index,* which might be based on developments in some, many, or all of the following basic indicators of the hard-currency debt burden:[3]

total debt service relative to exports of goods and all services;
international reserves (or Western bank assets) relative to imports
    of goods and all services;
short-term trade related debt to three months of hard-currency
    imports (debt–trade ratio);
gross or net debt relative to exports of goods and all services;
interest payments relative to exports of goods and all services;
interest earned on international assets as a percentage of interest
    due on external debt;
current-account deficit relative to export of goods and all services;
the country's net compressible import capacity (imports other than
    raw materials, fuels, capital equipment, and food);
international reserves to total debt;
international reserves to short-term debt;
large reserve losses;
spreads over LIBOR;
access to the international financial markets and ability to roll
    over debts;
delayed payments and arrears; and
use of IMF/BIS credit lines for balance-of-payments support.

---

[3] A typical index is a weighted average of scores (varying on a scale of, say, 0 to 100) of the specific indicators. Usually an index value of 30–50 points is considered a gray area; 50 points and above suggests liquidity difficulties may occur.

Supplementing an evaluation of the country's liquidity position with an analysis of its structural problems, which might indicate the likelihood of future payments problems as well as the ability to solve existing ones, is particularly important in the case of Eastern Europe, where convertible-currency debt difficulties stem mainly from their structural problems. Most of these countries have not adjusted adequately to external disturbances experienced during the late seventies and the early eighties; thus the likelihood of potential future payments problems is great. Only Hungary and the GDR are pursuing structural adjustment policies, which if successful will have an important impact on their future creditworthiness.

Structural index

A broader index, one that takes account of those economic variables (external debt, GDP, GNP, etc.) that are most closely correlated with payments difficulties in the Eastern European countries, could help in evaluating the soundness of their economies. Such a *structural index* could include the following indicators:[4]

rate of growth of GNP or GDP;
growth of real per capita GNP or GDP (most recent 3–5 yr);
hard-currency exports relative to GNP or GDP;
the ratio of the percentage change in exports relative to the percentage change in GNP or GDP;
hard-currency imports relative to GNP or GDP;
gross or net debt relative to exports of goods and all services;
gross or net debt relative to GNP or GDP;
growth of total exports and of hard-currency exports (most recent year and 3-yr average);
percentage change in consumer prices (most recent year and 5-yr average);
lending by the World Bank for structural adjustment purposes; and
composition of intra-CMEA trade in clearing currency (transferable ruble).

---

[4] A typical index is a weighted average of scores of the specific indicators. On a scale similar to that in note 3, 50 points and above is the area indicating that debt repayment difficulties may occur.

Political risk assessment

An evaluation of distinct liquidity and structural indices normally would be accompanied by a political risk assessment. The significance of political risk in lending to Eastern Europe has been underestimated in Western financial circles. Eastern Europe has tended to be regarded as a region without domestic political tensions in which the "Soviet umbrella" guarantees assistance in case of economic difficulties. The recent CMEA debt problems (especially those of Poland and Romania) have shown this to be false. Thus, a political risk assessment also is important in lending to the Eastern European countries. A key element of such an assessment is an evaluation of a country's *leadership*: The chief of state and the politburo leadership. What are the professional skills of the leadership? Does it understand economics? Does it support technocrats or not? The answers to these questions may illuminate the prospects for the success of the country's economic and borrowing policies and its economic management. For example, an increase in the number of technocrats in the leadership may be regarded as a positive indicator that future policies will be oriented to economic reforms and debt management will be more effective.

Political risk assessment also requires an analysis of the *social conditions* in a given Eastern European country. The main question to be asked is this: Does strong social support exist for the government in the implementation of its economic policies? The events in Poland at the beginning of the 1970s and during 1980–1 showed how social tensions can precipitate political crisis and change the leadership. Social tensions can also lead to lower economic growth and labor productivity, creating difficulties in implementing economic reforms. An analysis of social conditions is thus a critical part of country risk evaluation for Eastern Europe, particularly for countries like Poland and Hungary.

Indicators of the debt burden and creditworthiness

The liquidity and structural indices are useful for comparative country risk analysis. The indicators they include show different aspects of the country's debt situation, but no one indicator is sufficient: Careful analysts will review developments in many indicators before coming to conclusions. Among the indicators that have been applied to country risk analysis in LDCs and Western industrialized countries, the following list has strong appeal as being important for similar analysis of Eastern European borrowers.

The traditional *debt service ratio,* developed by the World Bank economist D. Avramovic (1958, p. 63), is one of the key indicators used to assess a country's creditworthiness over short- and medium-term periods. Avramovic emphasized that:

a higher ratio of fixed service commitments to external earnings implies a considerable short-term rigidity in the debtor country's balance-of-payments. When export receipts fall, either due to a recession in external demand, or because of a breakdown in the country's supply of a principal export commodity, the entire impact of the fall must be borne by imports or the country must run a large deficit in the current balance-of-payments. (p. 102)

He noted, however, that "the significance of the debt service ratio for long-run analysis of debt servicing capacity is virtually nil . . . The size of the debt service, and thus of the debt service ratio, is heavily influenced by maturities" (1964, p. 42). Other experts suggest in turn that the debt service ratio provides a rough measure of an economy's long-run financial burden. If this ratio is high, a large proportion of export earnings must be devoted to debt servicing; thus expanding imports, or even maintaining real imports as prices rise, may increasingly depend on uninterrupted flows of new loans (D. Roberts, cited in Balassa 1984, pp. 20–1).

What constitutes a "critical" level of the debt service ratio: 10%, 20%, or more? The history of defaults of developing countries provides little direction as to what level is "critical." The same may be said for the recent debt problems of Eastern Europe. Some financial experts stress that even a 10% ratio can create difficulties. According to other experts, a debt service ratio below 10% is acceptable, whereas a ratio above 20% is potentially dangerous (Sofia 1981, p. 53). Avramovic points out that the "the degree of tolerance varies considerably from country to country with the breaking point in most countries during the 1930s at 25 to 30 percent" (1964, p. 40). Whether or not countries have reached a "critical" debt service ratio depends on the structure of their economies and the confidence of their creditors; however, the general rule at present is that a debt service ratio of 25% or more usually causes concern among bankers.

A good indicator of the short-term sustainability of a country's debt situation is the level of *international reserves* (or Western bank assets) *relative to hard-currency imports* of goods and all services. The size of reserves reflects the magnitude of the international cash flows of a given Eastern European country. When reserves are high (say, over 40% of a year's import requirements) shortfalls in exports can generally be compensated by drawdowns of reserves, thus reducing the likelihood of severe liquidity crises.

Another important indicator is the ratio of gross or *net debt relative to exports* of goods and all services. It is a long-term measure, indicating the soundness of the country's overall economy and policies. The net debt relative to hard-currency exports is essentially an alternative to the debt service ratio as an indicator of the debt burden. In addition, the rate of growth of export earnings, the rate of growth of new borrowing, the rate of interest, and the ratio of the current-account deficit to exports of goods and services should also be considered in the analysis of the country's liquidity position.

Some studies of developing economies' debt situations note that a fundamental longer-term indicator of debt-servicing capacity is the relationship between the *growth rate of export earnings and the interest rate*. If export growth exceeds the interest rate, the country is reasonably creditworthy assuming that credits are rolled over (M. H. Simonsen, cited in Balassa 1984, p. 21). This indicator shows the ability of a country to generate sufficient foreign exchange in order to service its external debt obligations. When it is applied to Eastern European country risk analysis, it appears particularly useful for an evaluation of the debt standing of those countries that have rescheduled their debt (Poland, Romania) or have experienced liquidity difficulties (Hungary, GDR). The *ratio of the current account deficit to export* of goods and services also is an indicator of the sustainability of the debt situation.

The ratio of *interest payments to exports* of goods and all services is a good measure of the liquidity position of a given Eastern European country. A high ratio (>15%–20%) indicates that debt-servicing difficulties and reschedulings are likely. The evaluation of this ratio should be considered jointly with the ratio of interest earned on international assets to interest due on convertible-currency debt. The latter obviously depends on whether a country has substantial international assets that may be available in case of "emergency."

The recent debt problems of the Eastern European countries suggest that country risk analysis should consider a ratio (Heller 1984, pp. 20–1) of *short-term, trade-connected debt relative to the value of imports.*

The main question to be answered by this debt–trade ratio is this: What amount of short-term debt should arise in the normal course of trade-related financing? Most trade financing is on a ninety-day basis; thus, the country's debt situation might be regarded as more likely to be sustainable if the short-term, trade-related debt at any given period of time is not much greater than the value of ninety days worth of imports. This ratio allows one to recognize an excessive reliance on short-term debt financing. The recent experience with the Eastern European debt showed that countries' liquidity problems became acute when short-term credit lines were no longer rolled over. The debt–trade ratio has an advantage compared to the traditional debt service ratio in that it might indicate debt-payment difficulties before the debt service ratio reaches alarmingly high levels.

Another important indicator of the sustainability of the country's debt situation is its *net compressible import capacity*. Avramovic defines this as export earnings plus new external resources obtained by the country minus interest payments, amortization, noncompressible imports, and losses in reserves. Noncompressible imports are many food products, raw materials, fuels, and capital equipment (1964, p. 27). Some analyses suggest that any given country can reduce its nonessential imports by 25% (Sofia 1981, p. 57). Using the noncompressible imports indicator permits one to evaluate the extent to which imports have been compressed (probably because of a shortage of foreign exchange) and the possibility for compressing them further without disrupting production or reducing consumption to an unacceptable level. In addition, the introduction of international reserves and new external resources through this indicator enhances its use in assessing the country's debt-servicing capacity. The country's debt situation is assumed to be sustainable when net compressible import capacity is substantially positive. When applied to the analysis of the Eastern European hard-currency debt, it appears desirable to evaluate both the total and the hard-currency net compressible import capacities, in order to take into account the country's economic relations both with the other CMEA countries and with the market economies.

The use of the ratios of gross or net *debt relative to GNP or GDP* is common in country risk analysis. These indicators, however, do not take into account the ability of an economy to transform domestic into hard-currency resources, a very important problem for the Eastern European countries. For this reason they should always be used jointly in analysis with the traditional debt service ratio, which includes hard-currency exports.

The soundness of the structure of an Eastern European economy might be evaluated by the rate of growth of GNP or GDP, the ratio of (hard-currency) exports relative to GNP or GDP, the ratio of percentage change in exports to percentage change in GNP or GDP, or the ratio of (hard-currency) imports relative to GNP/GDP. The higher the *growth of GNP or GDP* and the *ratio of exports relative to GNP or GDP,* the greater the surplus of exportables is likely to be and the lower the demand for foreign borrowing to cover the trade deficit. The ratio of the *percentage change in exports to the percentage change in GNP or GDP* indicates the level of structural adjustment to external disturbances and the country's ability to expand its exports by increasing economic growth and not by reducing domestic investments, consumption, or a combination of both. The ratio of *hard-currency imports relative to GNP or GDP* is a good measure of the country's dependence on imports and indicates the potential demand for financing the deficits in the balance of trade.

Recent experience with the Eastern European and the developing countries' debt has showed that high and rising debt service and debt/GNP(GDP) ratios are positively correlated with the interest rate premium or spread, expressed as a *margin over LIBOR.* This can be another indicator of risk in lending. Sachs argues that when the risk for the creditors increases they will make loans only so long as the interest rate premium compensates for the risk (1982, p. 33). The positive correlation between the interest rate premium and the increased risk for the creditors expressed in high borrower's debt service and debt/GNP(GDP) ratios have been confirmed in a model applying data for nineteen countries in the period 1976–80 (Balassa 1984, p. 21).

The composition of *intra-CMEA trade in the clearing currency* (transferable ruble) is an important indicator for the country's vulnerability to external shocks and for its ability to shift from Western to CMEA markets. In the case of a rising price of oil, for example, a country that is less dependent on energy deliveries in return for convertible currency (e.g., Bulgaria, Czechoslovakia) and relies on Soviet energy deliveries would not experience severe convertible-currency, balance-of-payments difficulties, in contrast to a country that imports a greater part of its energy requirements from countries outside the CMEA (e.g., Romania).

This list of indicators of the sustainability of the debt situation in the CMEA countries is lengthy, but by no means exhaustive. The recent Eastern European hard-currency debt problems have shown that analysis of a country's creditworthiness must involve the evaluation of such indicators as its ability to borrow in the international financial markets to roll over its debts; whether there have been large losses of reserves or deposits; its recent record of export growth, and so on. For the Eastern European countries that are members of the IMF and the World Bank (Hungary, Romania, and Poland), the evaluation of their credit standing with these organizations is also very important.

Problems in evaluating country risk in Eastern Europe

The nature of the centrally planned economies creates some problems in assessing credit risk by analyzing indicators of the debt burden and creditworthiness.[5] These problems are connected primarily with the interpretation of the following two basic economic variables included in the ratios: the levels (and rates of growth) of GNP or GDP, and those of hard-currency exports. There are problems also with the data on Eastern European international reserves.

The first problem results from the centrally planned economies' computation of the GNP or GDP. The Eastern European countries measure their domestic economic activity by the so-called *net material product* (NMP), which includes the production of physical goods but excludes the production of services (transportation, internal trade, etc.) – which *are* accounted for in a market economy's GNP (GDP). The rate of growth of the NMP in the official CMEA statistics is overstated because the exclusion of the heavily consumer-oriented production of services, with its below-average

---

[5] The main sources for data on Eastern European external debt and debt indicators are: BIS (*International Banking Developments*); OECD/BIS (*Statistics on External Indebtedness*); Morgan Guaranty Trust Company (*World Financial Markets* with tables on "Publicly Announced Eurocurrency Bank Credits" and "New International Bond Issues"); Euromoney Publications London (monthly tables of borrowing), IMF (*International Financial Statistics,* for information on Hungary, Poland, and Romania); World Bank (*World Debt Tables*); reports of the Western central banks and of some Eastern European central banks (Hungary, Poland); and estimates of the OECD Secretariat and consulting firms (PlanEcon, Wharton Econometric Forecasting Associates, and others).

rates of growth, inflates the trend growth in domestic output (S. Cohn, cited in Goldstein and Vanous 1983, p. 11). This leads to a problem when Eastern European countries are compared world-wide: The higher rates of economic growth make centrally planned economies look better. Country risk analysts have to take account of these deviations from "real" values.

Another problem in estimating the hard-currency debt ratios, including NMP (GNP or GDP), is the conversion of the NMP in national currency into convertible-currency values, usually U.S. dollars. What are the appropriate exchange rates for conversion? Recent studies[6] suggest as the most appropriate U.S. dollar conversion rates for ranking Eastern European national income those based on purchasing-power parity calculations. The problem is that there are no regularly published estimates for all of the Eastern European countries.[7] For practical reasons, therefore, the most appropriate conversion rate appears to be Eastern European commercial exchange rates to the convertible currencies. To avoid deviations from the real value of the Eastern European national income when converting it from national currencies into hard currencies, some experts suggest that the official commercial exchange rate be discounted by 25%–50% (Goldstein and Vanous 1983, p. 12).

The economic relations among the CMEA countries also require some consideration in assessing their hard-currency exports. Usually, country risk analysis takes into account only hard-currency exports to market economies. The dollar-denominated imports from other Eastern European countries of so-called hard-currency goods, which are potential exports to the Western countries, are disregarded. The recent debt problems of Eastern Europe showed that most of these countries (particularly Bulgaria, Czechoslovakia, and GDR) reexported energy imports (oil, gas) from the Soviet Union to the Western markets in order to improve their trade and payments balance. The value of these imports should be considered in assessing the creditworthiness of the Eastern European countries.

---

[6] See P. Marer (1985a).
[7] There are data available from UN publications for the Eastern European countries; from the IMF and the World Bank for its members (Hungary, Romania, and Poland; from International Financial Research, Inc. (Thad Alton and associates), for the Eastern Europe Six (estimates) and from publications of the U.S. government for the Soviet Union.

The Eastern European countries have expanded their interbloc trade in convertible currencies during the past decade. As mentioned in Chapter 2, Hungary and Romania in particular benefited from their convertible-currency exports to the Soviet Union. The inclusion of a portion of these dollar-denominated exports in the total hard-currency exports of a given Eastern European country may provide better information for analyzing the country's creditworthiness. (The Soviet Union now appears unwilling to expand the imports for which it pays in hard currencies from its allies.)

Another problem in assessing the level of the convertible-currency exports is the reexportation of raw materials from Arab countries. Most of the Eastern European countries (GDR, Romania, Bulgaria, Hungary) reexport considerable quantities of oil from the Middle East. The inclusion of these exports in the total hard-currency exports inflates the export base. Logic suggests that, in estimating debt ratios (debt service ratio, etc.), these reexports should be discounted by 75%–80% (i.e., "net" value excluding the value of the original imports).

Problems also arise in assessing Eastern European short-term liquidity positions. Among CMEA countries, only Hungary publishes comprehensive data on its national reserves. Debt ratios based on national reserves usually take into account only Eastern European hard-currency deposits in Western commercial banks: Excluded are short-term deposits held in Third World countries (mainly Arab countries) and in the West (other than hard-currency deposits in commercial banks), gold and precious metals, strategic commodity reserves (refined oil products, etc.), and other assets. These exclusions tend to lower the ratios and to make CMEA countries seen less liquid than they are. Research to determine the rough proportion of these reserves in the total national reserves data could improve the predictive value of reserve-based indicators.

7

Eastern European debt prospects

Western financial observers considered CMEA countries (again, except Poland) to be reasonably creditworthy in 1986. By then, all except Poland had generated surpluses on their hard-currency current accounts. Is the improved creditworthiness of these countries sustainable in the medium run? Can one look to further abatement of debt problems, or to a renewal of debt-servicing difficulties? An analysis of likely development in the individual Eastern European countries' balances of payments and external debts is a prerequisite to providing answers to those important questions.

This chapter[1] conducts such an analysis using a computer-based projection model of Eastern European indebtedness through 1988. The model incorporates likely developments in global economic conditions both in Eastern Europe and in Western industrial countries.

Projection model

The future level of the Eastern European hard-currency debt will be determined by a combination of changing economic and political factors that prohibit precise projections. In the model developed in this chapter, the influence of uncertain political factors on the debt level has not been considered. The analysis concentrates only on likely developments in the main economic variables.

A major limitation of the analysis is the lack of detailed information on the Eastern European countries' hard-currency debts and their balances of payments; use must be made of Western estimates.

---

[1] The materials for this chapter were prepared in early 1986. Since that time some of the assumptions and data have been shown to differ from events as they occurred. The general conclusions, however, still stand.

Most of the CMEA countries (Soviet Union, Bulgaria, Czechoslovakia, GDR) do not publish data on their hard-currency debt. The available statistics on the debt of Poland and Romania are often inadequate. There is also a lack of precise information on the composition of the convertible-currency debt, on the one hand between official/guaranteed and commercial bank credits, and on the other hand between short- and long-term debt. Few data are available also on the division of debt between major Western currencies (U.S. dollars, Deutsche marks, Swiss francs, etc.). Information on invisible transactions (transport, travel, and other services) are particularly inadequate.

The approach taken here is to calculate the nonsocialist hard-currency trade balance, the current-account balance, and the gross and net hard-currency debt for the Eastern European Six and the Soviet Union for each year through 1988 under alternative assumptions. These assumptions deal with the rates of economic growth in the developed market economies, international interest rates, the average exchange rate of the U.S. dollar relative to other major Western currencies, the weighted average of inflation rates in the OECD countries, and the economic growth, export/import possibilities, and the supply and demand constraints on new credits to the Eastern European countries.

Exports

The main specification and assumptions of the projection model, presented in Table 7.1, are as follows. Eastern European hard-currency exports are determined by exports to developing countries, to other centrally planned economies, and to the OECD area. The projections of exports to the developing countries and the CMEA area are based on the estimates of Wharton Econometric Forecasting Associates (1986). Exports to the OECD area depend on the rate of growth in the OECD countries. Empirical analysis indicates that the elasticity of OECD import growth with respect to OECD economic growth is $g_m = -4.6 + 3g_r$, where g_m is the percentage growth of total OECD imports and g_r is the OECD growth rate (Cline 1983, p. 47). A 3.0% rate of OECD growth is assumed in 1986, and 3.3% in 1987–8. These assumptions for OECD economic growth are based on World Bank estimates.[2]

[2] These assumptions conform to the central case projections in World Bank (1986).

Table 7.1. *Basic assumptions on global economic parameters, 1985–8*

	1985	1986	1987	1988
OECD economic growth (%)	2.8	3.0	3.3	3.3
U.S. dollar depreciation (%)	1.0	8.3	5.3	5.4
Inflation (%)	4.0	5.0	5.5	5.5
Economic growth in Eastern Europe (%)	3.0	3.0	3.5	3.5
Average interest rates (%)[a] on external debt				
Bulgaria	8.4	7.0	7.0	7.2
Czechoslovakia	8.7	7.4	7.4	7.5
GDR	8.3	6.8	6.8	7.0
Hungary	9.1	7.4	7.5	7.7
Poland	9.7	7.8	7.8	7.8
Romania	8.1	6.8	6.9	7.1
Soviet Union	8.4	7.1	7.1	7.3

[a]The assumptions on the average interest rates are from WEFA, CPE Service (April 1986).
Source: World Bank (1986).

In addition the projections consider the response of real export prices to OECD economic growth. Experience in recent years has shown that the export prices of commodites from the Eastern European and the developing countries tend to increase faster than average world inflation when OECD economic growth accelerates. In the model, the export values rise by 2.5% for each percentage point rise in the OECD economic growth. The export value is influenced also by inflation rates in the OECD countries: The assumption is that export value increases along with the average rate of inflation in the year in question. The model assumes inflation of 5.0% in 1986 and 5.5% in the period 1987–8.

Another element that affects export values is U.S. dollar depreciation/appreciation. Changes in the value of the U.S. dollar relative to other major Western currencies influences the dollar prices of Eastern European exports in the industrial countries. Analysis based on the experience of the late 1970s and early 1980s shows that when the U.S. dollar appreciates/depreciates, the dollar price of exports from OECD countries tends to decline/rise by that percentage adjusted for the underlying inflation rate. The change in dollar export prices thus equals inflation plus dollar depreciation (minus dollar appreciation). Also, since approximately 50% of the Eastern European hard-currency debt is denominated in U.S. dollars and the rest in Duetsche marks, Swiss francs, and other currencies, dollar depreciation affects the dollar value of debt servicing obligations on past borrowings. It is assumed in the projections that the average dollar depreciation in real terms is 8.3% in 1986, 5.3% in 1987, and 5.4% in 1988 (Table 7.1).[3]

To sum up: The value of hard-currency exports of Eastern Europe to the developed market economies are determined by real OECD growth, inflation, and developments in the U.S. dollar exchange rate.

Imports

The hard-currency imports of the individual CMEA countries are determined by imports from developing market economies, from other centrally planned economies, and from the OECD area. As for projections of exports, the import values from developing countries and the CMEA area are based on Wharton Econometric Forecasting Associates (1986) estimates. The imports of the Eastern European countries from the OECD depend mainly on the import requirements of economic growth and the constraints imposed by their hard-currency balances of payments. In the years to come, one can expect that import-stimulated growth, financed by borrowing from the West for capital goods imports, can only become more attractive for the Eastern European Six and the Soviet Union as they ease their present policies of import restriction. There is little evidence that the ambitious targets for increasing the productivity of capital over the 1986-90 plan period could be achieved relying only on domestic resources to accelerate technical progress. In addition, the low-quality CMEA-produced capital goods will contribute little to the implementation of policies oriented to modernize and reequip the Eastern European economies.

The CMEA countries as a group reduced considerably their hard-currency debt during 1982-4. Thus, the constraints on their hard-currency balance of payments in 1981-3 will not impose (except for Poland) the same pressure on imports as in 1981-3. In the projec-

---

[3] These assumption conforms to the midrange of projections shown for the high and low case in World Bank (1986).

tion model, it is assumed that the real NMP grows 3% in 1986 and 3.5% in 1987–8.[4] Further it is assumed that, if the planners' strategy is to "soften" their hard-currency import restrictions, an increase of real NMP by one percentage point leads to a rise in the hard-currency imports of the East European Six by two points and of the Soviet Union by 1.5 points. (The import elasticity with respect to Eastern European economic growth in the past fifteen years has not been stable. The relatively high elasticity assumed for the six CMEA countries is based on the expectation that they will have to boost their hard-currency imports rapidly after almost five years of austerity.) The other component in calculating import values is price changes: Hard-currency import prices rise in response to inflation, and, as with exports, dollar appreciation/depreciation also affects import values.

The trade balance is the difference between total hard-currency exports and imports. The other elements of the balance of payments – exports and imports of services (transport, travel, and others) – are calculated as constant proportions of merchandise exports and imports. Interest payments, fees, and so on are calculated on a net basis by considering the average interest rate in percentage and the average level of net debt in the preceding year.

Capital account and indicators of creditworthiness

The main specifications of the construction of the capital account are the following. The total amount of gross annual lending required to finance the balance of payments equals the current-account deficit/surplus plus repayments due on all debt. Total gross debt at the end of the year equals the previous year's debt plus net borrowing. Net debt is determined by the difference between gross debt and reserves (hard-currency assets held by Eastern European countries in BIS-area banks and gold reserves). In the projections, another (and quite significant, particularly for the Soviet Union) item is the change in net hard-currency lending to other CMEA countries and the LDCs. The projections on net lending to the CMEA and LDCs are based on estimates of Wharton Econometric Forecasting Associates (1986).

---

[4] These assumptions are based on IMF estimates (*World Economic Outlook*, April 1986, pp. 166–7).

Debt retirement is based on estimated levels of debt in various categories. Repayments of medium- and long-term debt equals one-sixth of long-term debt in the preceding year. (The recent borrowing of the Eastern European countries on the international financial markets have shown a tendency toward longer credit maturities: 5–7 yr.) Estimates of the repayments of medium- and long-term debt due from Poland and Romania are based on their rescheduling agreements in 1981–6. Principal repayments include payments on short- and long-term debt. It is assumed that short-term debt repayments equal the short-term debt levels in the previous year.

On the basis of the Eastern European maturity structure in 1985, short-term debt is estimated as a certain proportion of gross debt in the year in question. The estimates are as follows: for Bulgaria, 40%; Czechoslovakia, 30%; GDR, 35%; Hungary, 20%; Romania, 10%; and the Soviet Union, 35%. The assumption about Polish short-term debt is that it equals 50% of imports from the OECD countries. Hard-currency assets in 1986–8 are estimated as proportions of the value of Western hard-currency imports in the year in question: for Bulgaria, 45%; Czechoslovakia, 30%; GDR, 50% in 1986 and 40% in 1987–8; Hungary, 30%, Poland, 25%; Romania, 25%; and the Soviet Union, 30%.

Five ratios are calculated in order to evaluate the trends in the countries' creditworthiness:

1. total debt service (repayment of long-term debt plus interest) to exports of goods and all services (the debt service ratio);
2. gross debt to exports of goods and all services;
3. net debt to exports of goods and all services;
4. interest payments to exports of goods and all services (interest-service ratio); and
5. hard-currency assets to imports of goods and all services (liquidity ratio).

Scenarios

Four scenarios of the projection model are estimated. The main questions asked in the scenairos are as follows:

1. What would the Eastern European debt level be if its countries continue to pursue their economic policy of the first half of the 1980s?

2. What would their debt level be if they increase their imports from the West?
3. What would their indebtedness be if, while increasing economic growth and Western imports, Eastern Europe pursues a policy aimed at controlling its net debt level?

The scenarios are estimated based on the assumption that there will be no constraints from the leaders' side in providing credits to Eastern Europe (except for Poland and Romania) in the next few years, and on the basis of different assumptions about the Eastern European hard-currency imports and economic growth. The constraints assumed on credits to Poland imply that Western commercial banks will lend no more than $150 million in 1986, $250 million in 1987, and (optimistically) $500 million in 1988. For Romania it is assumed that Western credits will be limited to $150 million in 1986 and $250 million in 1987–8.

Scenario 1 estimates the developments in hard-currency indebtedness under the assumption that Eastern European countries will continue to pursue a policy of restricted imports; therefore imports will remain the same in real terms. This scenario is not applied to Poland because it is not realistic to expect that this country will continue to compress the imports below the level in 1981.

Scenario 2 provides similar estimates for the six Eastern European countries and the Soviet Union under the assumption that they will ease their policy of import restriction and increase their borrowing from the West. Further it is assumed that there will be no constraints on external borrowing from the lenders' side (except for Poland and Romania).

Scenario 3 shows the East European countries easing the import restriction policy and increasing external borrowing, but controlling the net debt level. It is assumed that if the net debt in year 2 is greater than the net debt in a year 1, then the planners will restrict hard-currency imports from OECD countries to the same real level.

Scenario 4 assumes that the Eastern European countries will increase external borrowing but control the net debt level to grow no faster than the growth of the economy. If the net debt grows faster than economic growth, then (as in Scenario 3) imports from OECD countries remain the same in real terms.

Two subvariants of the scenarios are calculated for Poland under assumptions about anticipated access to IMF and World Bank credits in the years to come. It is assumed that Poland might have the chance to borrow up to $700 million from the IMF and the World Bank in 1988.

Results and implications

The projections[5] lead to fairly optimistic conclusions because they assume that, in the medium-term, the economies can contain imports as they grow and get acccess to foreign borrowing without problems (except for Poland and Romania). Tables 7.2–7.6 present some of the results of the simulations. They point to three main conclusions:

1. Under scenario 1, with the growth of imports from Western countries fixed in real terms, Eastern European debt problems recede considerably.
2. Under scenarios 2–4, with growth of Western imports increasing strongly, the external payments situation would deteriorate rapidly for some countries. Debt servicing would create no difficulties in Bulgaria, Czechoslovakia, Romania, GDR, and the Soviet Union, but there could be severe problems in Poland and Hungary.
3. Finally, with the actual outcome likely to be a mix of the scenarios, there seems little likelihood of a new debt crisis in Eastern Europe considered *as a region*. Eastern European debt should be manageable in the medium term.

However, there is no evidence that Poland can overcome its debt-servicing difficulties easily in the years to come, and there is even an underlying risk of "insolvency," a situation requiring extraordinary measures to cope with debt-servicing problems. Under the best circumstances, Poland's problems could last into the early 1990s. Of the other countries, Hungary might encounter renewed liquidity problems if it adopts an import-oriented economic growth policy in the late 1980s.

---

[5] Some of the projected time series take unrealistic values (e.g., import growth rates that seem implausibly high), but they are not adjusted in order to preserve the same assumptions across all countries. That means that the projections show scenarios rather than best guesses of likely outcomes.

Eastern European Six

Bulgaria. Bulgaria is considered by the Western financial observers to be reasonably creditworthy at present. It reached its peak level of hard-currency debt to the Western countries in the late 1970s, which resulted in a short-term liquidity crisis. Since the beginning of the 1980s, Bulgaria's hard-currency debt obligations have decreased steadily. The net debt is estimated at $635 million in 1985. Bulgaria borrowed in 1985–6 on very favorable terms.

For Bulgaria, the discussion centers on the first two scenarios. The results of scenarios 3 and 4 are similar to those of scenario 2 since projected net debt does not increase. The simulations (Tables 7.2 and 7.3) show that Bulgaria should be able to manage its debt confortably in the next few years. Illiquidity is not a likely outcome; debt ratios all are at a reasonable level. The debt declines considerably in scenario 1, and Bulgaria would eliminate its debt in 1988. Even under a strategy of increasing Western imports (Table 7.3) the current account does not deteriorate, the gross debt remains at a relatively low level, and Bulgaria still would eliminate net debt by 1988.

Czechoslovakia. Czechoslovakia's Western debt is not a cause for serious concern. Czechoslovakia's rates of economic growth were negative in 1981–2, with only a slight improvement in 1983–5, but the planning authorities have followed a cautious borrowing policy. As mentioned earlier, gross and net debt were at reasonable levels during 1980–5. The projections (Tables 7.2 and 7.3) show that the current-account balance stays positive through 1988. (The results of scenarios 3 and 4 are similar to those of scenario 2 because net debt steadily decreases.) Net debt declines considerably if the authorities sustain the existing import restrictions policy, and Czechoslovakia would eliminate its net debt and become a net creditor in 1988. Import-oriented economic growth (a probable scenario considering the 1986–90 five-year plan) will lead to increased borrowing, but the gross debt remains relatively low – $1.8 billion in the late 1980s. The net debt profile remains sound. The debt ratios are at reasonable levels, indicating that debt servicing will be manageable.

GDR. The GDR's large debt obligations would probably cause

Table 7.2. *Scenario 1: projections of hard-currency balance of payments and debt, 1986–8 (in millions of U.S. dollars)*

	1986	1987	1988
Bulgaria			
TB	116	292	513
CA	306	572	910
D_g	1,246	951	—
DSR (%)	8	4	2
NDX (%)	10	—	—
Czechoslovakia			
TB	655	1,008	1,324
CA	661	1,081	1,486
D_g	2,508	1,545	
DSR (%)	10	7	8
NDX (%)	28	4	3
GDR			
TB	1,600	2,612	3,620
CA	1,843	3,117	4,527
D_g	9,923	6,671	2,323
DSR(%)	19	11	6
NDX (%)	52	19	—

	1986	1987	1988
Hungary			
TB	293	641	1,063
CA	−253	76	507
D_g	11,546	11,659	11,460
DSR (%)	45	38	33
NDX (%)	189	162	132
Romania			
TB	1,792	2,536	3,196
CA	−408	1,566	2,596
D_g	6,292	4,774	2,181
DSR (%)	37	18	12
NDX (%)	88	56	20
Soviet Union			
TB	446	4,213	7,111
CA	−1,196	2,487	5,654
D_g	27,848	25,244	20,576
DSR (%)	11	10	8
NDX (%)	47	33	16

Note: TB, trade balance; CA, current account; D_g, gross debt; DSR, debt service ratio; NDX, net debt relative to exports of goods and services; —, nil or negligible.
Source: Author's calculations.

Table 7.3. *Scenario 2: projections of hard-currency balance of payments and debt, 1986–8 (in millions of U.S. dollars)*

	1986	1987	1988
Bulgaria			
TB	−8	−15	−28
CA	183	257	338
D_g	1,425	1,527	1,232
DSR (%)	8	5	4
NDX (%)	14	5	—
Czechoslovakia			
TB	465	539	496
CA	471	598	608
D_g	2,754	2,359	1,808
DSR (%)	10	8	6
NDX (%)	32	16	4
GDR			
TB	1,121	1,425	1,525
CA	1,364	1,898	2,313
D_g	10,642	8,844	7,075
DSR (%)	19	12	8
NDX (%)	56	32	12

	1986	1987	1988
Hungary			
TB	75	101	110
CA	−471	−480	−505
D_g	11,829	12,594	13,531
DSR (%)	45	39	36
NDX (%)	193	175	158
Romania			
TB	1,685	2,2273	2,730
CA	−514	1,275	2,032
D_g	6,425	5,237	3,260
DSR (%)	37	18	13
NDX (%)	193	175	158
Soviet Union			
TB	−1,179	186	337
CA	−2,820	−1,655	1,874
D_g	29,960	32,219	36,004
DSR (%)	11	11	11
NDX (%)	52	48	45

Note: Abbreviations same as for Table 7.2.
Source: Author's calculations.

more concern among the Western creditors if its citizens were not Germans. The debt service ratios were between 36% and 60% during 1980–4 (see Table 2.16); but, as discussed in chapter 2, the special relationship with West Germany ("West German umbrella") has many economic advantages: "bridge" loans, interest-free swing-credit facility for intra-German trade, and so on. Moreover, the country's reputation in the West for sobriety and production-mindedness is in fact not unjustified.

The projected current account and debt (Tables 7.2 and 7.3) show no deterioration in the debt situation in coming years. Even if the GDR allows an expansion of its Western imports to modernize the economy to expand productive capacity, the current-account will be reduced but the net debt will not rise. The GDR probably will be able to achieve a considerable surplus in its hard-currency balance of trade.

The GDR built up considerable assets in the BIS banks during 1983–5 and has other reserves outside the BIS area that are disregarded in the projections because of lack of information; thus the level of net debt (in both scenarios 1 and 2) might be lower. The debt ratios are at reasonable levels. In scenario 1 net debt might be eliminated in 1988. The buildup of reserves in recent years would give considerable flexibility to the GDR to meet its convertible-currency import requirements and would reduce its vulnerability to changes in the Western capital markets' perception of its creditworthiness.

A limitation of the projections is that they do not consider the ruble debt of the GDR. The GDR probably will have to reduce its ruble deficits with the Soviet Union in the next few years (as will all other Eastern European countries). The Soviet Union considers GDR as the main supplier of high-quality machinery and equipment in the CMEA market. Although declining (or stabilizing) oil prices will improve its terms of trade, the GDR will have to export increasing volumes of capital goods in return for Soviet raw materials and energy resources. This will leave less room to maneuver to reduce hard-currency debt, suggesting that the debt levels might well be higher than those shown in the projections.

Hungary. The projections of Hungary's currency account and debt (Tables 7.2–7.5) show that the gross and net debt will remain at high levels in the late 1980s. The current account deteriorates under a

Table 7.4. *Scenario 3: projections of*
hard-currency balance of payments and debt,
1986–8 (in millions of U.S. dollars)

	1986	1987	1988
Hungary			
TB	174	455	799
CA	−373	−119	218
D_g	11,731	12,135	12,347
DSR (%)	45	39	35
NDX (%)	191	167	141
Romania			
TB	1,868	2,153	2,730
CA	−514	1,155	2,001
D_g	6,425	5,387	3,410
DSR (%)	37	18	13
NDX (%)	90	63	32
Soviet Union			
TB	−937	1,499	3,594
CA	−2,579	−326	1,830
D_g	29,719	30,648	30,728
DSR (%)	11	11	10
NDX (%)	51	44	34

Note: Abbreviations same as for Table 7.2.
Source: Author's calculations.

strategy of increasing Western imports. The gross and net debt
might reach roughly $13 and $10 billion, respectively, in 1988. The
projected deficits are large in scenarios 2–4. The debt ratios are
high, indicating the possibility of liquidity problems. The efforts to
control the levels of net debt may not be very successful.

It will be difficult for Hungary to achieve a meaningful surplus in
its balance of trade in the late 1980s under the assumptions of
scenarios 2–4. Some of the reasons are diminishing earnings from
reexport of Soviet and Arab oil, losses of markets in the LDCs, and
difficulties for exports of agricultural products to most Western
European countries (because of the barriers erected by the Euro-

Table 7.5. Scenario 4: projections of
hard-currency balance of payments and debt,
1986-8 (in millions of U.S. dollars)

Hungary			
TB	174	455	110
CA	−373	−119	−470
D_g	11,731	12,135	13,036
DSR (%)	45	39	35
NDX (%)	191	167	151
Soviet Union			
TB	−937	1,499	337
CA	−2,579	−326	−1,759
D_g	29,719	30,648	34,318
DSR (%)	11	11	10
NDX (%)	51	44	42

Note: Abbreviations same as for Table 7.2.
Source: Author's calculations.

pean Community's agricultural policy). In addition, Hungary has always had great difficulty in exporting manufactured products to the West. There is little evidence that the present structural adjustment policy and economic reform will lead to a substantial increase in the production of exportables in the medium run. The secretary of the Hungarian Communist Central Committee, F. Havasi, noted in 1986 that structural changes in industry could not solve the problems (Financial Times, June 26, 1986, p. 2).

The debt situation deteriorates particularly rapidly in the scenario 2; but taking into account the flexibility of Hungarian debt management, the buildup of considerable reserves in 1984-5,[6] access to IMF and World Bank funds, and the "seal of approval" associated with them for raising credits from comercial banks, it might be expected that Hungary will be able to manage liquidity problems encountered during the projection period and to avoid

---

[6] It has to be noted that the level of Hungarian net debt (in all scenarios) might be lower because reserves held outside BIS-area banks are disregarded in the projections.

rescheduling of its debt. However, external debt will present a serious problem to the Hungarian economy in the late 1980s.

Poland. Poland, of course, is a cause for serious concern in the projection period. The projections (Table 7.6) show a relatively slow increase of debt but the absolute debt levels remain very high. The assumption in the model is that Poland will be able to improve gradually its relations with Western banks and gain access to the IMF's and World Bank's credits in the late 1980s, which would enable it to increase its hard-currency imports. Such an increase in the next few years would contribute to an increase of the gross debt that would reach more than $34 billion in 1988. The tension in external payments could be eased by access to the IMF's and World Bank's funds, the implementation of IMF- and IBRD-supported policies to improve the export position and generate an increase in the current account, and an effort to control the growth of net debt; still, the debt level would remain high – between $31 and $33 billion. The debt ratios are very high in all scenarios. New reschedulings of Poland's debt will be necessary in the next few years.

The solution to the debt crisis lies in the hands of the Polish leadership. Their commitment (and ability) to pursue a course of economic reform is very important in this connection. Policies for structural adjustment, to eliminate excess demand and to improve supply elasticities, export performance, and price structure, are urgently needed. Their adoption and successful implementation could ease debt problems by the early 1990s. However, taking into consideration the inflexible Polish centrally planned structure and the lack of social support for economic reform, optimistic expectations are unlikely to be justified in the medium term.

The only viable strategy for recovery in the present situation appears to lie in the expansion of economic relations with the OECD countries; but the Polish manufactured goods have a declining quality – in part as a consequence of shortages of high-quality imported inputs – and they compete poorly on the OECD market. The prospects for revenues from Polish coal exports are also not very buoyant because of falling coal prices in line with further weaking of oil prices on the world market.

One might expect that Poland after its admission to the World Bank and IMF will improve its relations with its Western creditors in the years to come. Still, the Western commercial banks will prob-

Table 7.6. *Projections of hard-currency balance of payments and debt of*

	1986				
	TB	CA	D_g	DSR (%)	NDX (%)
Scenario 1					
Increasing hard-currency imports					
a. without access to IMF and					
World Bank funds	924	−1,779	31,686	53	455
b. with access to IMF and					
World Bank funds					
Scenario 2					
Increasing hard-currency imports					
and sustaining the net debt level					
a. without access to IMF and					
World Bank funds	1,064	−1,639	31,510	53	453
b. with access to IMF and					
World Bank funds					
Scenario 3					
Increasing hard-currency imports					
and controlling the net debt not to					
grow faster than the economic growth					
a. without access to IMF and					
World Bank funds	1,064	1,064	31,510	53	453
b. with access to IMF and					
World Bank funds					

Note: Abbreviations same as for Table 7.2.
Source: Author's calculations.

ably provide new loans under the following main conditions: an IMF standby program must be successfully negotiated; Paris Club members must agree to lend new money; new commercial bank loans must be collateralized; and new loans must be for projects proven capable of producing net export revenue streams. However, if Western capital markets do not react flexibly, Poland might become more indebted to the Soviet Union and even more tied to the Eastern European countries. The abatement of the Polish

Poland, 1986-8 (in millions of U.S. dollars)

	1987					1988			
TB	CA	D_g	DSR (%)	NDX (%)	TB	CA	D_g	DSR (%)	NDX (%)
1,074	−1,462	33,290	48	409	1,276	−961	34,480	40	360
					1,276	24	33,558	40	349
1,575	−920	32,483	48	400	2,227	177	32,422	36	340
					2,227	1,162	31,450	38	330
1,575	−921	32,483	48	400	1,277	−773	33,611	38	350
					1,277	212	32,688	38	340

debt crisis seems to depend heavily on political considerations.

Romania. Romania considerably reduced its hard-currency debt during 1983-5. The projections (Tables 7.2-7.4) of the current account and debt show the trade and current-account balances pointing toward optimistic improvement because of the assumptions that exports will expand and that relations with the Western financial community (commercial banks, the Paris Club, and international organizations) will improve in the next few years. The debt ratios are at reasonable levels. In all scenarios Romania will be able to reduce net debt in the years to come, and debt levels will be between $2.2 and $3.4 billion in 1988. These conclusions are based on the assumption that the economy could contain imports as they grow and get access to foreign borrowing. However, if Romania adopts a strategy for increased Western imports after several years of austerity (not an improbable scenario) and does not improve its relations with the Western financial markets, liquidity difficulties might arise, leading to new reschedulings of its debt.

Soviet Union

The Soviet Union's debt is now considerable, but so are Soviet oil, gas, and raw material resources, gold production, and reserves. The projections of its current account, under the assumption that imports remain the same in real terms,[7] show steadily increasing surpluses in the period 1987–8 (Table 7.2). The estimated hard-currency debt declines to $20 billion in 1988. If the Soviet Union accepts a strategy to increase Western imports, the current account deteriorates rapidly (Table 7.3) and the gross debt might reach about $36 billion in 1988. The debt rises less rapidly if the planners control the net debt levels (Table 7.4 and 7.5); but the gross debt levels would remain high in 1988 – about $30 and $34 billion, respectively, for scenarios 3 and 4.

In all scenarios the debt ratios remain at reasonably low levels, indicating that debt-servicing difficulties are not likely. The Soviet Union will continue to borrow (as long as the terms of borrowing are acceptable and there are no constraints from the creditors side) to finance Western imports of machinery, equipment, technology, and particularly agricultural products (grain).

In the years to come, the Soviets will face declining earnings from oil exports (more than 50% of export revenues in recent years) because of the falling (or stabilizing) world prices for oil, the de-

---

[7] Import-oriented economic growth based on borrowing in the West does not appear plausible for the Soviet Union in the medium term. The efforts of the Gorbachev leadership will probably be to increase labor discipline and make more efficient use of domestic resources. However, the plans to double industrial production by the year 2000 (*Ekonomiceskaja gazeta*, Moscow, No. 11, March 1986) indicate that imports of high-quality Western machinery and equipment might increase substantially by the end of the 1980s.

preciation of the U.S. dollar, and lower quantities of oil available for export. An effort to increase exports of manufactured goods is unlikely to compensate fully for declining oil revenues. A rapid expansion of natural gas production and of gas deliveries to Western Europe will be crucial. There are also uncertainties concerning "invisibles" income. Revenues from gold sales could change considerably, depending not only on the Soviet sales strategy, but also developments in South Africa and their effects on gold prices. Arms sales may remain high, but are not immediate income producers if the sales (as usual) are financed on long-term credits. All of this indicates that the Soviet Union will probably lose some flexibility with respect to its hard-currency trade and debt policies.

The Soviet imports from the West seem (despite the above forcast on the oil-export earnings) unlikely to be seriously restricted by hard-currency shortages in the near future. The Soviets will probably borrow significant, additional credits if their balance of payments deteriorates, and their debt might rise much higher than the $36 billion projected scenario 2.[8] One might expect that they will be active on the international securities market and will try to raise funds in the form of direct investment through joint ventures with Western firms.

Some of the factors that could constrain Soviet import expansion in the medium term are as follows:

anticipation of a coming hard-currency shortage stemming from a decline of oil, gold, and arms sales;
inability to absorb increased imports of capital goods from the West efficiently;
increased imports of machinery and equipment from the CMEA countries; and
political and economic prestige associated with a stable or declining debt levels.

To sum up: The Soviet Union has various options in its approach to trade with the Western countries in the medium term and could increase its imports substantially without risking unmanageable problems with its hard-currency debt.

---

[8] Official Soviet statement on borrowing policy is usually that the Soviet Union does not want to borrow in the West.

8

Conclusion

To conclude, the analysis of Eastern European debt in the 1970s and 1980s conducted in this study sheds light on two major issues:

1. how the problems arising from indebtedness have affected the financing of East-West trade; and
2. the current prospects for ease in debt-servicing problems and the outlook for the economies of Eastern Europe.

This final chapter draws together some important observations and implications for the analysis of these two issues.

Eastern European debt and its impact on financing East-West trade

The debt problems of the Eastern European countries were the most important economic factor leading to the stagnation of East-West trade at the beginning of the 1980s. They have also considerably influenced the forms of financing East-West trade. The CMEA debt-servicing difficulties have diminished the role of some of the traditional financing mechanisms for East-West trade: Euromarket credits, switch, transit, and à forfait deals. Since the 1980s began, project financing and particularly countertrade deals have increased in importance. In 1985, approximately 15% of East-West trade was conducted under countertrade provisions,[1] where servicing flows are wholly or partially made in the form of commodities.

CMEA countries advocated and pioneered the use of countertrade in international business. The increased significance of the countertrade deals in the mid-1980s is an outgrowth of two key fac-

[1] OECD (1985a, p. 11).

tors related to the hard-currency debt difficulties of Eastern Europe: first, the need to secure convertible-currency balance-of-payments adjustment; second, the need to circumvent liquidity constraints, which arise because borrowing in the Western financial markets is either infeasible (at least in the case of Poland) or unaffordable. The main countertrade deals applied in East–West trade are barter, compensation (counterpurchase, precompensation), and product buy-back. After 1980, CMEA countries insisted on up to 100% compensation to meet financing needs. The level of compensation in countertrade agreements usually is no higher than 90%. The highest compensation levels are typically found in agreements with Poland (60%–90%) and Romania (60%–80%).

The trend toward the expanded use of countertrade probably will continue, with these deals being used by the Eastern European countries as a tool to ease pressure on their hard-currency trade and payments balances. Western countries, and particularly Western European countries, probably will accept these CMEA requirements in order to retain market shares in this region.

Another impact of Eastern European debt problems on financing East–West trade is the increased significance of IMF and World Bank credits. As discussed in Chapter 4, the debt difficulties of the CMEA countries were the main reason that some of them (Hungary and Poland) applied to join the IMF and the World Bank at the beginning of the 1980s. Hungary and Romania, as members of these international organizations, received credits, which were also used for financing their purchases in the Western markets. The significance of IMF and World Bank credits for financing East–West trade could increase further with the membership of Poland in the institutions.

Debt and economic prospects

The Eastern European debt problems in the 1970s and early 1980s, like those of the heavily indebted developing countries (Brazil, Mexico, Argentina, and others), resulted mainly from economic mismanagement in the borrowing countries, the oil-price "shocks," and weaknesses in the international lending system. The CMEA countries considerably increased their borrowing in the West in the early 1970s in order to modernize their economies and to improve the competitiveness of their goods in Western markets.

It was expected that the resulting debt would be repaid through increased exports in the late 1970s and the 1980s. The degree of liberalization of convertible-currency imports and borrowing in Eastern Europe was different in the individual countries, depending on their internal political choices. Some of them (Poland, Hungary, GDR, Romania) borrowed heavily, whereas others (Bulgaria, Czechoslovakia, Soviet Union) were relatively cautious in raising funds in the international financial markets. The Eastern European countries were regarded as reliable borrowers and their access to Western credits was unconstrained. The systemic inability of the CMEA centrally planned economies to assimilate Western technology efficiently and their marketing inexperience in the Western markets were the main internal factors contributing to their failure to repay the accumulated debt through increased convertible currency exports. In the late 1970s the borrowing in the West was for general balance-of-payments purposes and to finance net imports. Some of the Eastern European countries (Poland, Hungary, GDR, Romania) entered the 1980s with external convertible-currency debt, which presents a serious burden for their national economies. The consequences of the economic mismanagement and inefficient use of borrowed funds in these countries are that they are at present worse off than if they had borrowed significantly less during the 1970s.

The protracted recession in the West and accompanying high interest rates help explain the CMEA debt crisis in 1981 and 1982. Poland, Romania, GDR, and Hungary faced severe debt-servicing difficulties. The "West German umbrella" for the GDR and the "bridging" actions of the international financial community in the case of Hungary helped to overcome the liquidity crisis in both countries, but Poland and Romania had to reschedule their debts. The success of debt reschedulings for both countries resulted from the generally cooperative strategy adopted by Western lenders and Eastern European borrowers in resolving debt problems. Active participants in the rescue packages for Hungary have included the international financial institutions: the IMF, the BIS, and the World Bank.

The Eastern European countries, like the Latin American countries and Yugoslavia, have had to accept deflationary economic policies to adjust to the external disturbances to the balance of payments, at the expense of slowing the pace of their economic development. The main tool of this CMEA policy has been the typical, centrally planned, direct control of the components of domestic absorption. There is little evidence that these countries (with the partial exception of Hungary and the GDR) will implement effective structural adjustment to their economies in the near future. There is also little evidence that Eastern Europe will try to follow an outward development strategy (like many East Asian countries) that would allow it to cope with external convertible-currency debt in the long term. The direct planning control in Eastern Europe has proven itself to be poorly designed for the promotion of the efficient use of resources and for export expansion. The widening technological gap between East and West will also present a serious problem for the convertible-currency exports of the CMEA countries. All of this makes Eastern Europe potentially vulnerable to new external disturbances.

CMEA debt fell considerably during 1983-4, a result mainly of cutting imports and increasing exports to the West. Debt began to rise again in 1985-6. However, a significant portion of the borrowed funds was used by Hungary, the GDR, and the Soviet Union to increase convertible-currency assets in BIS-area banks. The effect of the U.S. dollar devaluation on the non-dollar-denominated liabilities also raised the dollar value of the debt level, as earlier dollar appreciation in the early 1980 had reduced it.

The characteristic of CMEA borrowing policy in 1985-6 was relative caution in raising funds on the international financial markets (except for Hungary and the Soviet Union). Western banks and governments, and particularly the American banks and government, were not willing to increase considerably their loan exposure to Eastern Europe. It has to be noted, however, that Japanese banks have increased their lending to CMEA. These borrower-creditor policy strategies are likely to be sustained for some years to come.

There is no regionwide debt crisis in Eastern Europe. However, Poland continues to have very serious debt-servicing difficulties – both to Western commercial banks and to governments. New reschedulings of the Polish debt will be essential for several years. Polish prospects will be influenced heavily by the future role played in Poland by the international financial institutions (IMF, World Bank) and depend on the continued willingness of Western commercial banks and governments to roll over maturing obligations.

The possibility that Poland will *base* its borrowing strategy on the presumption of such willingness creates a moral hazard problem in lending to this country. Crucial for the improved export performance of Poland and for the abatement of its debt crisis is a substantial de facto modification of the economic system and the introduction of policies for structural adjustment. However, the inflexible Polish centrally planned structure and the lack of social support for economic reform leave little room for optimistic expectations in this regard.

Romania significantly reduced its debts in 1983–5 and fulfilled all the obligations from the rescheduling agreements with the Western official and commercial creditors; but debt-servicing difficulties arose in 1986, leading to new commercial bank rescheduling. If this country does not improve its relations with the Western financial community, rescheduling of this debt may become again necessary in the future.

The other Eastern European countries and the Soviet Union seem quite creditworthy in 1986. Bulgaria and Czechoslovakia have a relatively low hard-currency debt. The Soviet Union's debt is quite high but so are Soviet oil, gas, and raw material resources, gold production, and international reserves. The GDR and Hungary still have high levels of hard-currency debt but have avoided serious debt-servicing difficulties. The "West German umbrella" for the GDR, and the IMF and the World Bank's "seal of approval" for Hungary, do contribute to the good credit standing of these countries on the international financial markets. However, Hungary's heavy borrowing in 1985–6 could result again in liquidity difficulties in the late 1980s.

There is little evidence that the Eastern European countries will pursue a policy oriented inward toward the CMEA market in the future. All these countries need Western technology and the high-quality goods available in East–West trade. The ambitious five-year plans for the period 1986–90 for modernization and increased efficiency of resource utilization would hardly be realized by further compression of such Western imports. The Soviet Union and the Eastern European Six realize that economic and political isolation from the West (as in the 1950s and 1960s) would have an adverse impact on their development. However, these countries will continue their efforts to implement joint investment projects within CMEA. This might lead to decreased pressure on the convertible-currency imports for investment purposes in the individual CMEA countries. In the case of the Eastern European Six, if oil prices continue to fall or stabilize, they may be able to reduce their ruble debt to the Soviet Union; this would leave them more resources to be mobilized for convertible-currency exports in the late 1980s. All of this would consequently decrease the debt burden on their economies.

Analysis of the Eastern European debt problems leads to the following main economic conditions for an avoidance of future debt difficulties:

Recovery in the Western countries, particularly the West European countries, is essential.

New protectionist barriers in the developed market economies (particularly the European community) against the exports of Eastern Europe have to be avoided.

Commercial banks must resume lending at modest rates (especially, to Poland) in return for structural adjustment efforts.

The World Bank should lend to facilitate structural adjustment in Hungary, Romania, and Poland and raise project financing to these countries.

If Western capital markets do not react flexibly, these countries will be in danger of becoming more indebted to the Soviet Union and thus even more tied to the Eastern bloc.

The debt situation in Eastern Europe (except for Poland and Romania) has been manageable. There is little evidence to expect a new debt crisis by the end of this decade. Overborrowing similar to that of the 1970s appears unlikely considering the self-imposed constraints of Eastern European countries and Western lenders; but Eastern Europe will feel the effects of the debt "shock" of 1981–2 through 1990.

Debt-servicing difficulties, however, could intensify if short-term credits are not rolled over. The recent CMEA debt problems have unambiguously shown that the credit standing of these countries depends as much on the confidence of Western lenders as on objective criteria of debt capacity. One lesson to be learned from the liquidity crises in Hungary, Romania, and Poland in the early 1980s is that careful appraisal of individual country risk gives banks little protection when short-term credit withdrawals hit Eastern European borrowers.

More serious CMEA debt problems might arise, particularly in deeply indebted countries such as Poland, Hungary, Romania, and the GDR, if these countries ease restraints on imports of Western high technology and equipment. If increased Western imports are not accompanied by increased hard-currency export earnings (always a possible outcome because of the many structural problems in Eastern Europe, low demand in the West, and competition from the developing countries), the CMEA countries may again find themselves trying to finance their convertible-currency balance-of-payments deficits by unsustainable levels of external borrowing.

Appendix

Table A.1. *Eastern European debt to Western commercial banks between December 31, 1980 and December 31, 1985: quarterly and semiannual data (millions of U.S. dollars)*

Date	Gross debt (liabilities)		Deposits (assets)		Net debt (net liabilities)	
	Q'ly	Semiann.	Q'ly	Semiann.	Q'ly	Semiann.
Soviet Union and CMEA banks						
Dec. 31, 80	13,388	13,438	8,568	8,572	4,820	4,866
June 30, 81	14,143	14,479	3,617	3,679	10,526	10,800
Dec. 31, 81	15,882	16,278	8,451	8,680	7,431	7,598
June 30, 82	14,589	14,917	6,695	6,885	7,894	8,032
Dec. 31, 82	14,211	14,596	10,027	10,354	4,184	4,242
June 30, 83	14,462	14,966	9,477	9,770	4,985	5,196
Dec. 31, 83	14,871	15,582	9,652	9,967	5,219	5,615
June 30, 84	16,263	15,713	11,499	n.a.	4,764	n.a.
Dec. 31, 84	16,640	15,787	11,343	n.a.	5,297	n.a.
Mar. 31, 85	16,029		8,779		7,250	
June 30, 85	18,875	18,094	9,569	n.a.	9,306	n.a.
Sept 30, 85	21,150		11,106		10,044	
Dec. 31, 85	22,627		13,061		9,566	
Eastern European Six						
Dec. 31, 80	46,374	46,301	7,044	6,513	39,330	39,788
June 30, 81	43,015	43,094	5,656	5,525	37,359	37,569
Dec. 31, 81	44,806	44,428	6,598	6,156	38,208	38,272
June 30, 82	39,472	39,052	5,024	4,691	34,448	34,361

Dec. 31, 82	39,067	38,684	6,275	5,905	32,792	32,779
June 30, 83	35,903	35,436	7,149	6,687	28,754	28,749
Dec. 31, 83	34,058	34,707	8,805	8,410	25,253	26,297
June 30, 84	33,403	32,478	9,654	n.a.	23,749	n.a.
Dec. 31, 84	31,566	30,878	10,769	n.a.	20,797	n.a.
Mar. 31, 85	31,359		10,393		20,966	
June 30, 85	32,299	31,918	12,008	n.a.	20,291	n.a.
Sept 30, 85	35,566		13,345		22,221	
Dec. 31, 85	37,647		13,916		23,731	
Bulgaria						
Dec. 31, 80	2,614	2,876	777	779	1,837	2,097
June 30, 81	2,139	2,324	759	787	1,380	1,537
Dec. 31, 81	2,123	2,371	806	830	1,317	1,541
June 30, 82	1,950	2,103	784	797	1,166	1,306
Dec. 31, 82	2,006	2,067	957	1,014	1,049	1,053
June 30, 83	1,693	1,779	1,022	1,071	671	708
Dec. 31, 83	1,608	1,716	1,026	1,109	582	607
June 30, 84	1,684	1,653	1,233	n.a.	451	n.a.
Dec. 31, 84	1,577	1,530	1,429	n.a.	148	n.a.
Mar. 31, 85	1,672		1,233		439	
June 30, 85	1,733	1,757	1,595	n.a.	138	n.a.
Sept. 30, 85	2,379		1,884		495	
Dec. 31, 85	2,847		2,091		756	
Czechoslovakia						
Dec. 31, 80	3,413	3,545	1,257	1,256	2,156	2,289
June 30, 81	3,173	3,264	808	827	2,365	2,437
Dec. 31, 81	3,174	3,319	1,065	1,097	2,109	2,222

Table A.1. (*cont.*)

Date	Gross debt (liabilities)		Deposits (assets)		Net debt (net liabilities)	
	Q'ly	Semiann.	Q'ly	Semiann.	Q'ly	Semiann.
June 30, 82	2,740	2,914	638	676	2,102	2,238
Dec. 31, 82	2,688	2,848	728	742	1,960	2,106
June 30, 83	2,644	2,742	932	1,002	1,712	1,740
Dec. 31, 83	2,448	2,748	914	931	1,534	1,817
June 30, 84	2,680	2,684	1,238	n.a.	1,442	n.a.
Dec. 31, 84	2,418	2,390	1,006	n.a.	1,412	n.a.
Mar. 31, 85	2,395		959		1,436	
June 30, 85	2,419	2,476	958	n.a.	1,461	
Sept. 30, 85	2,525		1,031		1,494	
Dec. 31, 85	2,675		1,011		1,664	
GDR[a]						
Dec. 31, 80	9,462	9,928	2,038	2,146	7,424	7,782
June 30, 81	9,626	10,388	1,816	1,885	7,810	8,503
Dec. 31, 81	10,092	10,729	2,154	2,180	7,938	8,549
June 30, 82	8,747	9,351	1,506	1,541	7,241	7,810
Dec. 31, 82	8,516	8,859	1,878	1,986	6,638	6,873
June 30, 83	7,889	8,263	2,404	2,470	5,485	5,793
Dec. 31, 83	7,828	8,449	3,230	3,349	4,598	5,100
June 30, 84	8,569	8,538	4,192	n.a.	4,377	n.a.
Dec. 31, 84	8,309	8,434	4,546	n.a.	3,773	n.a.
Mar. 31, 85	8,206		4,490		3,716	
June 30, 85	8,692	8,776	5,261	n.a.	3,431	n.a.

Sept. 30, 85	9,378		5,892		3,486	
Dec. 31, 85	10,232		6,494		3,738	
Hungary						
Dec. 31, 80	7,447	8,002	1,376	1,392	6,071	6,610
June 30, 81	6,626	6,991	978	1,050	5,645	5,941
Dec. 31, 81	7,487	7,714	903	917	6,584	6,797
June 30, 82	6,499	6,418	402	417	6,097	6,001
Dec. 31, 82	6,407	6,757	730	747	5,677	6,010
June 30, 83	6,163	6,424	736	759	5,427	5,665
Dec. 31, 83	6,490	7,003	1,271	1,290	5,219	5,713
June 30, 84	6,710	6,383	919	n.a.	5,791	n.a.
Dec. 31, 84	6,932	6,763	1,543	n.a.	5,389	n.a.
Mar. 31, 85	6,934		1,667		5,267	
June 30, 85	7,426		1,866		5,560	
Sept. 30, 85	8,505	7,296	2,455	n.a.	6,050	n.a.
Dec. 31, 85	8,631		2,273		6,358	
Poland						
Dec. 31, 80	15,137	16,173	660	646	14,477	15,527
June 30, 81	14,109	14,699	546	634	13,563	14,065
Dec. 31, 81	14,674	15,288	757	797	13,917	14,431
June 30, 82	13,205	13,797	732	842	12,473	12,955
Dec. 31, 82	13,394	13,910	965	1,045	12,429	12,865
June 30, 83	11,662	12,158	1,021	1,134	10,641	11,024
Dec. 31, 83	10,430	10,934	1,078	1,216	9,352	9,718
June 30, 84	9,868	9,611	1,369	n.a.	8,499	n.a.
Dec. 31, 84	8,922	8,687	1,547	n.a.	7,375	n.a.
Mar. 31, 85	8,813		1,598		7,215	

Table A.1. *(cont.)*

Date	Gross debt (liabilities)		Deposits (assets)		Net debt (net liabilities)	
	Q'ly	Semiann.	Q'ly	Semiann.	Q'ly	Semiann.
June 30, 85	8,782	8,639	1,774	n.a.	7,008	
Sept. 30, 85	9,398		1,672		7,726	
Dec. 31, 85	9,972		1,594		8,378	
Romania						
Dec. 31, 80	5,297	5,776	263	292	5,034	5,484
June 30, 81	5,108	5,428	319	342	4,789	5,086
Dec. 31, 81	4,763	5,067	300	335	4,463	4,732
June 30, 82	4,154	4,469	361	418	3,793	4,051
Dec. 31, 82	4,042	4,243	297	371	3,745	3,872
June 30, 83	3,806	4,070	208	251	3,598	3,819
Dec. 31, 83	3,474	3,857	445	515	3,029	3,342
June 20, 84	3,618	3,609	676	n.a.	2,942	n.a.
Dec. 31, 84	3,190	3,074	647	n.a.	2,543	n.a.
Mar. 31, 85	3,103		386		2,717	
June 30, 85	2,987	2,974	486	n.a.	2,501	n.a.
Sept. 30, 85	3,100		323		2,777	
Dec. 31, 85	3,033		364		2,669	
Residual[b] Eastern Europe						
Dec. 31, 80	3,004	1	673	2	2,331	−1
June 30, 81	2,234	0	430	0	1,880	0
Dec. 31, 81	2,493	0	613	0	1,804	0

June 30, 82	2,177	0	601	0	1,576	0
Dec. 31, 82	2,043	0	720	0	1,323	0
June 30, 83	2,046	0	826	0	1,220	0
Dec. 31, 83	1,780	0	841	0	939	0
June 30, 84	274		27	0	247	0
Dec. 31, 84	218		61		157	0
Mar. 31, 85	236		60		176	
June 30, 85	260	0	68	0	192	0
Sept. 30, 85	281		88		193	
Dec. 31, 85	257		89		168	

[a]Excluding GDR debt to and deposits with West German commercial banks.

[b]Based on returns from Swiss banks, which do not identify their assets and liabilities by country. This residual may include some Soviet liabilities and assets.

Sources: WEFA, *CPE Current Analysis*, No. 63-4:7-9 (1984), No. 59-60:7-10 (1985); PlanEcon, *Report*, No. 17-18:9-12 (May 1986).

Table A.2. *Eastern European indebtedness to Western commercial banks, 1981–June 1985 (millions of U.S. dollars)*

Date	Assets	Liabilities	Net	Maturity of liabilities (percentages given in parentheses)				Undisbursed credit
				Up to 1 yr	1–2 yr	Over 2 yr	Unalloc'd.	
Soviet Union								
June 81	3,679	14,479	−10,800	6,755 (46.7)	1,016 (7.0)	4,261 (29.4)	2,447 (16.9)	2,006
Dec. 81	8,680	16,278	−7,598	8,166 (50.2)	869 (5.3)	4,736 (29.1)	2,507 (15.4)	1,976
June 82	6,885	14,917	−8,032	7,226 (48.4)	740 (5.0)	4,379 (29.4)	2,572 (17.2)	2,447
Dec. 82	10,354	14,596	−4,242	6,622 (45.4)	1,010 (6.9)	4,342 (29.7)	2,622 (18.0)	3,859
June 83	9,770	14,966	−5,196	6,888 (46.0)	1,268 (8.5)	4,206 (28.1)	2,604 (17.4)	3,466
Dec. 83	9,967	15,582	−5,615	6,960 (44.7)	1,402 (9.0)	4,899 (31.4)	2,321 (14.9)	4,758
June 84	n.a.	15,713	n.a.	6,589 (41.9)	1,273 (8.1)	5,282 (33.6)	2,569 (16.4)	2.986
Dec. 84	n.a.	15,787	n.a.	6,582 (41.7)	1,241 (7.8)	5,412 (34.3)	2,552 (16.2)	1,892
June 85	n.a.	18,094	n.a.	8,157 (45.1)	1,472 (8.1)	5,863 (32.4)	2,602 (14.4)	2,442
Eastern Europe Six								
June 81	5,525	43,094	−37,569	15,915 (36.9)	5,753 (13.4)	15,125 (35.1)	6,301 (14.6)	5,695

Dec. 81	6,156	44,428	−38,272	17,359 (39.1)	5,232 (11.8)	15,204 (34.2)	6,633 (14.9)	5,170
June 82	4,691	39,052	−34,361	14,218 (36.4)	4,622 (11.8)	14,351 (36.8)	5,861 (15.0)	3,816
Dec. 82	5,905	38,684	−32,779	13,880 (35.9)	4,436 (11.5)	14,626 (37.8)	5,742 (14.8)	3,360
June 83	6,687	35,436	−28,749	12,245 (34.6)	3,853 (10.9)	14,157 (39.9)	5,181 (14.6)	2,753
Dec. 83	8,410	34,707	−26,697	11,962 (34.5)	3,982 (11.5)	14,325 (41.3)	4,431 (12.7)	2,184
June 84	n.a.	32,478	n.a.	11,279 (34.7)	4,480 (13.8)	12,378 (38.1)	4,341 (13.4)	2,641
Dec. 84	n.a.	30,878	n.a.	10,897 (35.3)	4,317 (14.0)	11,662 (37.8)	4,002 (12.9)	3,264
June 85	n.a.	31,918	n.a.	11,200 (35.1)	3,976 (12.5)	12,832 (40.2)	3,910 (12.2)	5,962
Bulgaria								
June 81	787	2,324	−1,537	904 (38.9)	468 (20.1)	709 (30.5)	243 (10.5)	317
Dec. 81	830	2,371	−1,541	1,137 (48.0)	342 (14.4)	613 (25.8)	279 (11.8)	585
June 82	797	2,103	−1,306	1,043 (49.6)	331 (15.8)	476 (22.6)	253 (12.0)	358
Dec. 82	1,014	2,067	−1,053	1,069 (51.7)	363 (17.6)	406 (19.6)	229 (11.1)	321
June 83	1,071	1,779	−708	940 (52.8)	272 (15.3)	377 (21.2)	190 (10.7)	325
Dec. 83	1,109	1,716	−607	1,011 (58.9)	196 (11.4)	383 (22.3)	126 (7.4)	375

Table A.2. (*cont.*)

Date	Assets	Liabilities	Net	Maturity of liabilities				Undisbursed credit
				Up to 1 yr	1–2 yr	Over 2 yr	Unalloc'd.	
June 84	n.a.	1,653	n.a.	932 (56.4)	222 (13.4)	362 (21.9)	137 (8.3)	534
Dec. 84	n.a.	1,530	n.a.	858 (56.1)	253 (16.5)	288 (18.8)	131 (8.6)	611
June 85	n.a.	1,757	n.a.	960 (54.6)	287 (16.3)	321 (18.3)	189 (10.8)	622
Czechoslovakia								
June 81	827	3,264	−2,437	1,215 (37.2)	186 (5.7)	1,635 (50.1)	228 (7.0)	209
Dec. 81	1,097	3,319	−2,222	1,250 (37.7)	264 (7.9)	1,540 (46.4)	265 (8.0)	223
June 82	676	2,914	−2,238	872 (29.9)	229 (7.9)	1,551 (53.2)	262 (9.0)	274
Dec. 82	742	2,848	−2,106	888 (31.2)	235 (8.3)	1,480 (51.9)	245 (8.6)	284
June 83	1,002	2,742	−1,740	885 (32.3)	257 (9.4)	1,344 (49.0)	256 (9.3)	266
Dec. 83	931	2,748	−1,817	867 (31.6)	300 (10.9)	1,371 (49.9)	210 (7.6)	216
June 84	n.a.	2,684	n.a.	919 (34.2)	302 (11.5)	1,249 (46.5)	214 (8.0)	312
Dec. 84	n.a.	2,390	n.a.	828 (34.7)	316 (13.2)	1,035 (43.3)	211 (8.8)	394

June 85	n.a.	2,476	n.a.	939 (37.9)	356 (14.4)	971 (39.2)	210 (8.5)	417
GDR								
June 81	1,885	10,388	−8,503	4,201 (40.4)	1,816 (17.5)	2,774 (26.7)	1,597 (15.4)	1,512
Dec. 81	2,180	10,729	−8,549	4,572 (42.6)	1,642 (15.3)	2,900 (27.0)	1,615 (15.1)	1,745
June 82	1,541	9,351	−7,810	3,645 (39.0)	1,519 (16.2)	2,723 (29.1)	1,464 (15.7)	1,258
Dec. 82	1,986	8,859	−6,873	3,457 (39.0)	1,203 (13.6)	2,748 (31.0)	1,451 (16.4)	1,176
June 83	2,470	8,263	−5,793	3,203 (38.8)	1,192 (14.4)	2,588 (31.3)	1,280 (15.5)	916
Dec. 83	3,349	8,449	−5,100	3,266 (38.7)	1,326 (15.7)	2,774 (32.8)	1,083 (12.8)	823
June 84	n.a.	8,538	n.a.	3,658 (42.8)	1,594 (18.7)	2,214 (25.9)	1,072 (12.6)	902
Dec. 84	n.a.	8,434	n.a.	3,723 (44.1)	1,589 (18.8)	2,122 (25.2)	1,000 (11.9)	1,132
June 85	n.a.	8,776	n.a.	3,953 (45.1)	1,298 (14.8)	2,513 (28.6)	1,012 (11.5)	1,378
Hungary								
June 81	1,050	6,991	−5,941	2,509 (35.9)	571 (8.2)	3,393 (48.5)	518 (7.4)	625
Dec. 81	917	7,714	−6,797	3,114 (40.4)	556 (7.2)	3,473 (45.0)	571 (7.4)	354
June 82	417	6,418	−6,001	2,128 (33.2)	553 (8.6)	3,165 (49.3)	572 (8.9)	333

Table A.2. (cont.)

Date	Assets	Liabilities	Net	Maturity of liabilities				Undisbursed credit
				Up to 1 yr	1–2 yr	Over 2 yr	Unalloc'd.	
Dec. 82	747	6,757	−6,010	2,246 (33.2)	960 (14.2)	2,955 (43.8)	596 (8.8)	489
June 83	759	6,424	−5,665	2,315 (36.0)	907 (14.1)	2,627 (40.9)	575 (9.0)	356
Dec. 83	1,290	7,003	−5,713	3,205 (45.8)	943 (13.5)	2,315 (33.1)	540 (7.7)	320
June 84	n.a.	6,383	n.a.	2,866 (44.9)	1,046 (16.4)	1,930 (30.2)	541 (8.5)	471
Dec. 84	n.a.	6,763	n.a.	2,712 (40.1)	1,009 (14.9)	2,484 (36.7)	558 (8.3)	573
June 85	n.a.	7,296	n.a.	2,833 (38.8)	916 (12.6)	2,956 (40.5)	591 (8.1)	1,492
Poland								
June 81	634	14,699	−14,065	4,745 (32.3)	2,252 (15.3)	5,256 (35.8)	2,446 (16.6)	2,285
Dec. 81	797	15,228	−14,431	5,499 (36.1)	1,895 (12.4)	5,284 (34.7)	2,550 (16.8)	1,786
June 82	842	13,797	−12,955	4,728 (34.3)	1,617 (11.7)	5,149 (37.3)	2,303 (16.7)	1,124
Dec. 82	1,045	13,910	−12,865	4,569 (32.8)	1,375 (9.9)	5,783 (41.6)	2,183 (15.7)	674
June 83	1,134	12,158	−11,024	3,568 (29.3)	908 (7.5)	5,856 (48.2)	1,826 (15.0)	522

Dec. 83	1,216	10,934	−9,718	2,735 (25.0)	911 (8.3)	5,818 (53.2)	1,470 (13.5)	290
June 84	n.a.	9,611	n.a.	2,051 (21.4)	1,000 (10.4)	5,134 (53.4)	1,426 (14.8)	296
Dec. 84	n.a.	8,687	n.a.	2,103 (24.2)	888 (10.2)	4,413 (50.8)	1,283 (14.8)	347
June 85	n.a.	8,639	n.a.	1,762 (20.4)	827 (9.6)	4,870 (56.4)	1,180 (13.6)	351
Romania								
June 81	342	5,428	−5,086	2,341 (43.1)	460 (8.5)	1,358 (25.0)	1,269 (23.4)	747
Dec. 81	335	5,067	−4,732	1,787 (35.3)	533 (10.5)	1,394 (27.5)	1,353 (26.7)	477
June 82	418	4,469	−4,051	1,802 (40.3)	373 (8.4)	1,287 (28.8)	1,007 (22.5)	469
Dec. 82	371	4,243	−3,872	1,651 (38.9)	300 (7.1)	1,254 (29.5)	1,038 (24.5)	416
June 83	251	4,070	−3,819	1,334 (32.8)	317 (7.8)	1,365 (33.5)	1,054 (25.9)	368
Dec. 83	515	3,857	878	313 (22.8)	1,664 (8.1)	1,002 (43.1)	160 (26.0)	
June 84	n.a.	3,609	n.a.	853 (23.6)	316 (8.8)	1,489 (41.3)	951 (26.3)	126
Dec. 84	n.a.	3,074	n.a.	673 (21.9)	262 (8.5)	1,320 (42.9)	819 (26.7)	207
June 85	n.a.	2,974	n.a.	753 (25.3)	292 (9.8)	1,201 (40.4)	728 (24.5)	207

Sources: WEFA, *CPE Current Analysis*, No. 63–4:11–12 (1984), No. 59–60:11–13 (1985); PlanEcon, *Report* No. 17–18:13–15 (1986).

Table A.3. *Eastern European borrowing sources, 1975–83 (in percent of total in*

	Euromarket			Arab banks		IMF, World Bank, and EIB		
	1975	1982	1983	1982	1983	1975	1982	1983
Bulgaria	11	1	—	4	3	—	—	—
Czechoslovakia	2	21	13	—	—	—	—	—
GDR	9	8	8	—	—	—	—	—
Hungary	18	28	25	2	5	—	10	12
Poland	40	19	17	—	1	—	1	1
Romania	0.2	16	16	4	1	14	31	36
Soviet Union	21	2	2	—	—	—	—	—
CMEA Banks	n.a.	19	11	—	—	—	—	—

Sources: Portes (1977, p. 39); *Business Eastern Europe,* April 20, 1984, p. 125.

end-1975, end-1982, and end-1983)

Supplier credits			Buyer credits			Factoring, forfeiting, and switch		
1975	1982	1983	1975	1982	1983	1975	1982	1983
3	70	65	n.a.	22	28	n.a.	3	4
19	64	67	n.a.	11	17	n.a.	4	3
—	84	83	n.a.	3	5	n.a.	5	4
—	22	19	n.a.	38	39	n.a.	—	—
18	50	48	n.a.	29	33	n.a.	—	—
4	34	33	n.a.	15	14	n.a.	1	1
56	95	92	n.a.	2	5	n.a.	1	1
n.a.	48	58	n.a.	33	31	n.a.	—	—

Table A.4. *Hard-currency exports and imports, 1981-5 (millions of U.S. dollars;*

	Exports					Growth rates				
	1981	1982	1983	1984	1985	1981	1982	1983	1984	1985
Bulgaria										
Total	3308	3263	3053	3307	3142	9.1	−1.4	−6.4	8.3	−5.0
To or from DMEs	1439	1298	1266	1163	1167	−12.4	−9.8	−2.5	−8.1	0.4
Czechoslovakia										
Total	4300	4081	4177	4102	4028	−5.0	−5.1	2.4	−1.8	−1.8
To or from DMEs	2923	2774	2702	2773	2748	−9.8	−5.1	−2.6	2.6	−0.9
GDR										
Total	6714	7875	8543	8717	9119	27.2	17.3	8.5	2.0	4.6
To or from DMEs	5446	6296	7102	7417	7732	30.5	15.6	12.8	4.4	4.2
Hungary										
Total	4877	4973	4983	4931	4448	−1.3	2.0	0.2	−1.0	−9.8
To or from DMEs	2625	2640	2876	2967	3065	−13.7	0.6	8.9	3.2	3.3
Poland										
Total	5772	5741	5890	6257	6032	−27.6	−0.5	2.6	6.2	−3.6
To or from DMEs	3908	3661	3756	3996	4040	−33.2	−6.3	2.6	6.4	1.1
Romania										
Total	7281	6235	6246	6898	6850	10.8	−14.4	0.2	10.4	−0.7
To or from DMEs	3783	3408	3675	4159	4150	−4.8	−10.0	7.8	13.2	−0.2
Soviet Union										
Total	31997	35515	36136	35259	31163	1.9	11.0	1.7	−2.4	−11.6
To or from DMEs	23942	25948	26479	26733	23300	−1.9	8.4	2.0	1.0	−12.8

Source: Calculated from WEFA, CPE Service, April 1986.

growth rates in percentages)

Imports					Growth rates				
1981	1982	1983	1984	1985	1981	1982	1983	1984	1985
2656	2623	2646	2733	3471	30.1	−1.2	0.9	3.3	27.0
2157	1917	1710	1736	1818	29.6	−11.1	−10.8	1.5	4.7
3983	3598	3402	3327	3388	−11.9	−9.7	−5.4	−2.2	1.8
3244	2919	2732	2590	2786	−12.1	−10.0	−6.4	−5.2	7.6
6654	6366	7218	7659	8193	−4.0	−4.3	13.4	6.1	7.0
5952	5508	6218	6559	7047	2.3	−7.5	12.9	5.5	7.4
4960	4514	4450	4323	4334	−1.6	−9.0	−1.4	−2.9	0.3
3670	3213	2921	2809	3203	−1.1	−12.5	−9.1	−3.8	14.0
5868	4309	4451	4771	4994	−34.6	−26.6	3.3	7.2	4.7
4475	3167	3056	3270	3452	−33.1	−29.2	−3.5	7.0	5.6
7065	4710	4558	4617	4800	−12.7	−33.3	−3.2	1.3	4.0
3525	1933	1448	1493	1600	−11.0	−45.2	−25.1	3.1	7.2
33396	32954	32692	31088	30482	11.3	−1.3	−0.8	−4.9	−1.9
25143	26007	25220	23960	23901	3.9	3.4	−3.0	−5.0	−0.2

Table A.5. *Industrial production*[a] *index in the CMEA countries, 1975–85*

| | 1975–80 (1975 = 100) | | | | | | Annual growth rates, 1981–5 | | | | |
	1975	1976	1977	1978	1979	1980	1981	1982	1983	1984	1985
Bulgaria	100.0	102.9	106.9	110.7	114.6	117.6	4.9	4.6	3.9	4.2	4.0
Czechoslovakia	100.0	103.9	107.4	110.2	112.0	114.1	2.1	1.1	2.8	4.0	3.4
GDR	100.0	103.9	106.1	109.0	112.6	115.7	7.0	5.6	7.1	8.3	9.0
Hungary	100.0	103.3	108.1	112.0	113.1	111.6	2.8	2.4	0.8	2.7	0.8
Poland	100.0	101.7	103.5	105.5	104.4	102.9	−13.6	−1.7	6.4	5.3	3.8
Romania	100.0	106.2	111.5	116.5	120.2	124.2	2.6	1.1	4.7	6.7	4.9
Soviet Union	100.0	105.0	111.0	116.0	120.0	124.0	3.4	2.9	4.2	4.1	3.9

[a]Gross output.
Sources: Alton et al. (1984), pp. 15–19; PlanEcon Report, *Developments in the Economies of the Soviet Union and Eastern Europe*, No. 7–11, 15–16 (1986); PlanEcon, *Review and Outlook*, December 1985; the 1976–80 data for the Soviet Union are from *Narodnoe hozjaistvo USSR*, Moscow (1980, 1983).

Table A.6. *Change in the terms of trade by region, 1979–84*
(percentage change from the previous year)

	1979	1980	1981	1982	1983	Jan.–June 1984
Developed market economies	−0.9	−6.5	−2.0	2.0	1.0	−1.0
Developing market economies	12.1	14.8	1.2	−2.1	−3.5	0.1
CMEA countries	2.3	2.8	1.6	−1.1	−0.1	0.1
Eastern European Six	−0.6	−2.4	−2.2	−3.9	−1.5	−1.6
Soviet Union	5.8	9.1	5.7	1.6	1.8	1.6

Source: United Nations, *Economic Bulletin for Europe* 36:34 (1984).

Table A.7. *CMEA countries' terms of trade with the world, 1971–7*
(1970 = 100)

	1971	1972	1973	1974	1975	1976	1977
Bulgaria	98.4	98.9	99.3	97.5	96.0	91.7	—
Czechoslovakia	99.7	99.1	95.8	96.3	90.4	87.9	—
GDR	100.4	99.1	94.5	90.0	87.2	85.5	—
Hungary	99.0	98.1	96.8	89.1	83.1	85.6	82.5
Poland	105.1	106.1	104.4	102.4	102.8	103.5	102.1
Romania	105.8	100.3	94.5	—	—	—	—
Soviet Union	104.4	102.6	109.1	108.3	111.9	108.8	—

Source: Portes (1980a, p. 30).

Table A.8. *CMEA countries' terms of trade with developed market ecomomies, 1971-7 (1970 = 100)*

	1971	1972	1973	1974	1975	1976	1977
Bulgaria	98.2	99.6	99.6	115.0	108.2	112.2	—
Czechoslovakia	99.1	97.7	88.7	87.4	86.0	84.2	—
GDR	105.1	105.6	95.0	87.0	82.7	93.8	—
Hungary	99.2	101.0	97.1	85.4	81.2	86.6	—
Poland	110.7	113.0	107.9	116.6	122.4	119.8	—
Romania	107.0	104.0	103.0	114.0	106.0	111.0	—
Soviet Union DMEs only	144.2	120.6	115.0	213.7	189.2	250.4	203.8
+ most developing countries	108.5	101.1	117.9	118.1	115.7	103.6	112.8
CMEA	102.8	96.9	94.7	118.2	109.6	125.2	126.6

Source: Portes (1980a), p. 28.

Table A.9. *Agricultural production[a] index in the CMEA countries, 1970–83*

	1970	1975	1976	1977	1978	1979	1980	1981	1982	1983
Bulgaria	89.9	100.0	102.3	91.9	92.6	191.2	84.1	88.3	93.3	86.6
Czechoslovakia	89.0	100.0	95.0	107.6	104.0	101.2	107.4	96.3	104.5	107.7
GDR	87.0	100.0	91.2	100.8	98.5	103.4	103.7	106.7	105.1	108.4
Hungary	82.4	100.0	93.5	106.1	105.0	101.9	108.1	107.2	113.4	110.2
Poland	94.8	100.0	101.7	102.2	110.8	104.4	95.1	99.2	103.7	107.6
Romania	77.2	100.0	125.2	122.8	128.5	131.7	117.2	117.6	127.0	126.6
Soviet Union	97.0	100.0	106.0	111.0	114.0	110.0	108.0	107.0	113.0	120.0

[a]Gross output.
Source: Alton et al. (1984, p. 20); the data for the Soviet Union are from *Narodnoe Hozajistvo USSR,* Moscow (1980, 1983).

Table A.10. *Industrial and agricultural output[a] in the Soviet Union,*
1978–85, (average annual and annual growth rates, percentages)

	1971–9	1979–82	1980	1981	1982	1983	1984	1985
Industrial	6.6	3.3	3.6	3.4	2.9	4.0	4.1	3.9
Agricultural	1.6[b]	0.4[b]	−1.9	−1.0	5.5	5.0	−0.1	0.0

[a]Gross output.
[b]Annualized change in production levels.
Sources: United Nations, *Economic Bulletin for Europe* 36:42 (1984); WEFA, *CPE Current Analysis,* No. 25–6:6 (1985); PlanEcon *Report,* No. 7:12–16 (1986).

Table A.11. *Inventory investment in the CMEA countries, 1981–5*
(average annual growth in real terms, percentage)

	1981	1982	1983	1984	1985
Bulgaria	12.2	−13.7	−21.8	n.a.	n.a.
Czechoslovakia	−55.3	47.2	−18.6	n.a.	n.a.
GDR	−28.1	−87.8	640.0	n.a.	n.a.
Hungary	57.4	−6.9	30.4	n.a.	n.a.
Poland	−69.5	400.0	30.3	8.0	n.a.
Romania	−77.7	105.1	n.a.	n.a.	n.a.
Soviet Union	−7.4	61.7	7.6	−5.3	3.3[a]

[a]Estimation.
Sources: WEFA, *CPE Current Analysis,* No. 26–7:11 (1984), No. 61–2:3 (1985), No. 63–4:12 (1985).

Table A.12. *Eastern European Six and Soviet Union: total export and import volumes, 1971–June 1984 (annual growth rates, percentages)*

	1971–9	1979–82	1980	1981	1982	1983	June 1984
Eastern European Six							
Export volume	8.4	4.2	2.6	1.1	5.5	7.1	8.6
Import volume	8.0	−2.2	0.7	−6.4	−4.7	3.5	6.1
Soviet Union							
Export volume	5.9	2.2	1.6	1.9	4.6	3.3	2.9
Import volume	9.2	6.1	7.5	6.4	9.8	4.0	4.0

Source: United Nations, *Economic Bulletin for Europe,* 36:42 (1984).

Bibliography

Adam, Jan (1985) "The Hungarian Economic Reform," unpublished Ms.

Allen, Mark (1982) "Adjustment in Planned Economies," *IMF Staff Papers* 29(3).

Allen, Richard A. (1982) *The Evolution of the External Debt and Balance of Payments of Eastern Europe and the USSR since 1970.* BIS Working Papers No. 7, Basle.

Alton, Thad P., et al. (1984) *Research Project on National Income in East Central Europe*, New York, L. W. International Financial Research.

Avramovic, Dragoslav (assisted by Ravi Gulhati) (1958) *Debt Servicing Capacity and Postwar Growth in International Indebtedness*, Baltimore, Johns Hopkins.

   (1964) *Economic Growth and External Debt*, Baltimore, Johns Hopkins.

   (1984) "Bretton Woods II: An Agenda," *Journal of Development Planning* 14:111-16.

Balassa, Akos (1975) "Central Development Programs in Hungary," *Acta Oeconomica* 14(1):91-108.

Balassa, Béla (1984) *The Problem of the Debt in Developing Countries*, World Bank Discussion Paper DRD 88, Washington, DC.

Balassa, Béla, and Laura Tyson (1983) *Adjustment to External Shocks in Socialist and Private Market Economies*, Washington, DC, World Bank Discussion Paper DRD 61.

   (1985) "Policy Responses to External Shocks in Hungary and Yugoslavia: 1974-76 and 1979-81," in U.S. Joint Economic Committee Congress, JEC (1985, pp. 57-80).

Baneth, Jean (1983) "A Comment on the Krueger Paper," in Brunner and Meltzer (1983, pp. 313-23).

Bauer, Tamas (1978) "Investment Cycles in Planned Economics, "Acta Oeconomica* 21(3):243-60.

   (1983) "The Hungarian Alternative to Soviet Type Planning," *Journal of Comparative Economics* 7(3):304-16.

Bergson, Abram, and Hans Heymann, Jr. (1954) *Soviet National Income and Product 1940-48*, New York, Columbia University Press.

Bergson, Abram (1961) *The Real National Income of Soviet Russia since 1928*, Cambridge, MA, Harvard University Press.

Bergson, Abram, and Simon Kuznets (1963) *Economic Trends in the Soviet Union*, Cambridge, MA, Harvard University Press.

Bergson, Abram, and Herbert S. Levine, (eds.) (1983) *The Soviet Economy toward the Year 2000*, London, Allen & Urwin.

BIS, *International Banking and Financial Market Developments*, Basle, various years.

Borchard, Edwin (1951) *State Insolvency and Foreign Bondholders*, Vol. 1, New Haven, Yale University Press.

Brada, Josef C., and John M. Montias (1985) "Industrial Policy in Eastern Europe: A Comparison, of Poland, Czechoslovakia, and Hungary," in U.S. Congress, JEC (1985, pp. 194–225).

Brainard, Lawrence J. (1981) "Bankers Trust's Approach to International Risk Assessment," in Ensor (1981, pp. 93–98).

(1984) "Trade and payments in Eastern Europe: The Debt Crisis Forces Policy Chages," unpublished Ms.

Brainard, Lawrence J., and Thomas J. Trebat (1981) "The Role of Commercial Banks in Balance of Payments Crises: The Cases of Peru and Poland," unpublished Ms.

Brau, E., R.C. Williams, et al. (1983) *Recent Multilateral Debt Restructurings*, Washington, DC, International Monetary Fund Occasional Paper, No. 25.

Brown, Alan A., and Egon Neuberger (eds.) (1968) *International Trade and Central Planning: An Analysis of Economic Interactions*, Berkeley and Los Angeles, University of California Press.

Brunner, Karl, and Allan H. Meltzer (eds.) (1983) *Money, Monetary Policy and Financial Institutions*, Amsterdam, North-Holland.

Brus, Wlodzimierz (1973) *The Economics and Politics of Socialism*, London, Routledge & Kegan Paul.

(1982) "Aims, methods and political determinants of the economic policy of Poland 1970–80," in Nove et al. (1982, pp. 91–138).

Burghardt, Anton M., and Csaba Kortvelyessy (1984) "The Prospects of Comecon Foreign Trade and Hard-Currency Debt," in *Wirtschaftsanalysen*, Vienna, Die Erste Oesterreichische Spar-Casse-Bank, pp. 28–43.

Business Eastern Europe (1984) Vienna, Business International, April 20.

Campbell, Barry R. (1984a) "The Bank for International Settlements – out of the Shadows and into the Fray?" in Campbell and Herzstein (1984, pp. 25–33).

(1984b) The Scope of the International Liquidity Problem," in Campbell and Herzstein (1984, pp. 9–21).

Campbell, Barry R., and Robert E. Herzstein (1984) *The International Debt Problem and Its Impact on Finance and Trade*, New York, Practising Law Institute.

Caves, Richard E., and Ronald W. Jones (1981) *World Trade and Payments*, Boston, Brown and Company.

Clausen, A. W. (1982) "A Concluding Perspective," in Fried and Owen (1982, pp. 67–81).

(1983) *Third World Debt and Global Recovery*, 1983 Jodidi Lecture at the Center for International Affairs, Boston, MA, Harvard University.

Cline, William R. (1983) *International Debt and the Stability of the World Economy*, Washington, DC, Institute for International Economics.

(1984) *International Debt: Systematic Risk and Policy Response*, Washington, DC, Institute for International Economics.

Crane, Keith (1985) *The Creditworthiness of Eastern Europe in the 1980s*, Rand Corporation.

Csikos-Nagy, Bela (1984) "Significance of the Hungarian Reform Movement," unpublished Ms.

Dale, Richard S., and Richard P. Mattione (1983) *Managing Global Debt,* Washington, DC, Brookings Institution.

Davies, R.T. (1985) "The Political Economy of Reform in Poland: International Aspects," unpublished Ms.

Delamaide, Darrell (1984) *Debt Shock,* New York, Doubleday.

de Larosierre, J. (1984a) *The World Economy in 1984: Problems, Policies, and Prospects,* Washington, DC, IMF.

(1984b) *Adjustment Programs Supported by the Fund: Their Logic, Objectives, and Results in the Light of Recent Experience,* Washington, DC, IMF.

Deutsches Institut für Wirtschaftsforschung, *Wochenbericht,* Berlin (West), various issues.

Dillon, Burke K., Maxwell C. Watson, Russell G. Kincaid, and Chanpen Puckahtikom (1985) *Recent Developments in External Debt Restructuring,* Occasional Paper 40, Washington, DC, IMF.

Economist, London, various issues.

Eichler, Gabriel (1986) "The Debt Crisis: A Schematic View of Rescheduling in Eastern Europe," in U.S. Congress, JEC (1986, pp. 192–209).

Ekonomiceskaja gazeta, Moscow, various issues.

Enders, Thomas O., and Richard P. Mattione (1983) *Latin America: The Crisis of Debt and Growth,* Brookings Discussion Papers in International Economics, Washington, DC, Brookings Institution.

Ensor, Richard, (ed.) (1981) *Assessing Country Risk,* London, Euromoney.

Fallenbuchl, Zbigniew M. (1984) "Polish Foreign Trade in the 1980s," unpublished Ms.

(1985a) "The Balance of Payments Problems and the Economic Crisis in Poland," Carl Beck Papers in Russian and East European Studies, edited by William Chase and Ronald Linden, Pittsburgh, University of Pittsburgh, Paper no. 406.

(1985b) "The Present State of Economic Reform in Poland," unpublished Ms.

Fekete, Janos (1982) *Back to the Realities: Reflections of a Hungarian Banker,* Budapest, Akademiai Kiado.

(1986) *Financing of East–West Trade and Cooperation 1986–1990,* paper presented at the conference "New Horizons in East–West Trade and Cooperation," Vienna, June 16–19, 1986.

Financial Times, various issues.

Fink, Gerhard (1984) "Verrechunungssystem and Hartwaehrungshandel im RGW," *Suedosteuropa* 29(6):341–51.

Fink, Gerhard, and Kurt Mauler (1984) *Die Verschuldung der RGW-Laender und die Perspektiven des Ost–West-Handels,* Vienna, Vienna Institute for Comparative Economic Studies.

Fried, Edward R., and Henry D. Owen (eds.) (1982) *The Future Role of the World Bank,* Washington, DC, Brookings Institution, pp. 67–81.

Friedlaender, Michael (1985) *Ungarns Aussenhandel, Beziehungen zum GATT, dem IWF und der Weltbank,* Vienna Institute for Comparative Economic Studies.

Fundenberg, D., and E. Maskin (1985) *Moral Hazard in Repeated, Principal-*

Agent Games, discussion paper, Department of Economics, Cambridge, MA, Harvard University.

Gilberg, Trond (1975) *Modernization in Romania since World War II,* New York, Praeger.

Gold, Joseph (1982) *Order in International Finance: The Promotion of IMF Standby Arrangements, and the Drafting of Private Loan Agreements,* Washington, DC, IMF.

Goldmann, Joseph, and Karel Kouba (1969) *Economic Growth in Czechoslovakia,* New York, White Plains.

Goldstein, Elizabeth, and Jan Vanous (1983) "Country Risk Analysis: Pitfalls of Comparing Eastern Bloc Countries with the Rest of the World," *Columbia Journal of World Business* 18(4):10–16.

Gomulka, Stanislaw, and Alec Nove (1984) *East-West Technology Transfer,* Paris, OECD.

Gregory, P.R. (1981) *Soviet Economic Structure and Performance,* New York, Harper & Row.

Grossmann, Gregory, and Ronald L. Solberg (1983) *The Soviet Union's Hard Currency Balance of Payments and Creditworthiness in 1985,* Rand Corporation, R-2956-USDP.

Guitian, Manuel (1981) *Fund Conditionality: Evolution of Principles and Practices,* Washington, DC, IMF.

Gumpel, Werner (1983) *Sozialistische Wirtschaftssysteme,* München, Günter Olzog Verlag.

Hanson, Philip (1982) "The End of Import-Led Growth? Some Observations in Soviet, Polish and Hungarian Experience in the 1970s," *Journal of Comparative Economics* 6:130–47.

Hardt, John P. (ed.) (1975) *Tariff, Legal and Credit Constraints on East-West Commercial Relations,* Ottawa, Carleton University Press.

Hardy, Chandra S. (1982) *Rescheduling Developing Country Debts, 1956–1981: Lessons and Recommendations,* Washington, DC, Overseas Development Council.

Heller, Robert H. (1984) "The Debt Crisis," *Managing International Development* 1(4):7–27.

(1985) "A Banker's Perception of Country Risk," unpublished Ms.

Heller, Robert H., and Emmanuel Frankel (1982) "Determinants of LDC Indebtedness: A Statistical Analysis of Five Factors Involved in Determining a Country's Indebtedness," *Columbia Journal of World Business* 17(1):28–33.

Hewett, Ed. A. (1983a) "Foreign Economic Relations," in Bergson and Levine (1983, pp. 269–310).

(1983b) "Hungary's Adjustment to External Economic Shocks," unpublished Ms.

(1983c) "Response to External Shocks: USSR and Hungary," unpublished Ms, November.

(ed.) (1983d) *Journal of Comparative Economics* 7, special issue devoted to Hungary.

(1984) "Soviet Central Planning: Probing the Limits of the Traditional Model," unpublished Ms.

Holzman, Franklyn D. (1974) *Foreign Trade under Central Planning,* Cambridge, MA, Harvard University Press.

(1978) "CMEA's Hard Currency Deficits and Ruble Convertibility," in Watts (1978, pp. 144–63).

(1979) "Some Theories of the Hard Currency Shortages of Centrally Planned Economies," in U.S. Congress, JEC (1979, pp. 297–316).

(1981) "Creditworthiness and Balance of Payments Adjustment Mechanism of Centrally Planned Economies," in Rosefield (1981, pp. 163–84).

(1982) *The Soviet Economy Past, Present and Future,* Washington, DC, Foreign Policy Association.

(1983) "Systematic Bases of the Unconventional International Trade Practices of Centrally-Planned Economies," *Columbia Journal of World Business* 18(4):4–8.

Hope, Nicholas C. (1981) *Developments in and Prospects for the External Debt of the Developing Countries: 1970–80 and Beyond,* Washington, DC, World Bank Staff Working Paper No. 488.

Hough, Jerry F. (1982) *The Polish Crisis: American Policy Options,* Washington, DC, Brookings Institution.

IMF (1984) *The International Monetary Fund: Its Evolution, Organization, and Activities* (4th ed.), Washington, DC.

Annual Report, Washington, DC, various issues.

IMF Press Release, Washington, DC, various issues.

IMF Survey, Washington, DC, various issues.

World Economic Outlook, various issues.

International Herald Tribune, various issues.

Janssen, Richard F. (1977) "Soviet Bloc Borrowings from the West Surge, amid Mystery and Fears," in U.S. Senate, Committee on Governmental Affairs (1977, pp. 11–16).

Jedrychowski, Stefan (1982) *Zadluzenie Polski w krajach kapitalistycznych,* Warsaw, Ksiazka i Wiedza.

Kalecki, Michal (1969) *Introduction to the Theory of Growth in a Socialist Economy,* Oxford, Basil Blackwell. English translation of *Zarys teorii vzrostu gospodarki socjalistyczne,* Warsaw, 1963.

(1972) *Selected Essays on the Economic Growth of the Socialist and the Mixed Economy,* Cambridge, Cambridge University Press.

(1976) *Essays on Developing Economies,* Hassocks, Sussex, Harvester Press.

Kaminski, Bartlomiej (1985) "Balance of Payments Adjustment Policies," unpublished Ms.

Kenen, Peter B. (1984) "Prospects for Reform of the International Monetary System," *Journal of Development Planning* 14:103–10.

Khan, Mohsin S., and Malcolm D. Knight (1985) "Fund-Supported Adjustment Programs and Economic Growth," Occasional Paper 41, Washington, DC. IMF.

Kharas, Homi. (1984) "The Long-Run Creditworthiness of Developing Countries: Theory and Practice," *Quarterly Journal of Economics* 99(3):415–39.

Killick, Tony (ed.) (1982) *Adjustment and Financing in the Developing World: The Role of the International Monetary Fund,* Washington, DC, IMF.

Killick, Tony, and Mary Sutton (1982) "Disequilibria, Financing, and Adjustment in Developing Countries," in Killick (1982, pp. 13–16, 48–72).

Kindleberger, Charles P. (1968) *International Economics* (4th ed.), Homewood, IL, Richard D. Irwin.

Kindleberger, Charles P., and Jean-Pierre Laffargue (1982) *Financial Crises: Theory, History, and Policy,* Cambridge, Cambridge University Press.

Kornai, Janos. (1959) *Overcentralization in Economic Administration,* London, Oxford University Press.

(1972) *Rush versus Harmonious Growth,* Amsterdam, North-Holland.

(1980) *Economics of Shortage,* Amsterdam, North-Holland.

(1982) *Growth, Shortage and Efficiency,* Berkeley, University of California Press.

(1983) "Comments on the Present State and Prospects of the Hungarian Economic Reform," *Journal of Comparative Economics* 7(3):225–52.

(1984) "Comments on the Papers Prepared in the World Bank about Socialist Countries, unpublished Ms.

(1985) "Some Lessons of the Hungarian Experience for Chinese Reformers," unpublished Ms.

Krueger, Anne O. (1983) "The Role of the World Bank as an International Institution," in Brunner and Meltzer (1983, pp. 281–311).

Kyn, Oldrich, and Wolfram Schrettl (ed.) (1979) *On the Stability of Contemporary Economic Systems: Proceedings of the Third Reisensburg Symposium,* Göttingen, Vandenhoeck and Ruprecht.

Kyn, O., W. Schrettl, and J. Slama (1979) "Growth Cycles in Centrally Planned Economies," in Kyn and Schrettl (1979, pp. 109–132).

Lacko, Maria (1980) "Cumulating and Easing of Tensions," *Acta Oeconomica* 24(3–4):357–77.

Lange, Oscar (1961) *Teoria reprodukcji i akumulacji,* Warsaw, Panstwowe wydawnictwo naukowe.

Lavigne, Marie (1985) *Economie Internationale des Pays Socialistes,* Paris, Armand Colin.

Lenz, Allen, and Robert Teal (1980) *Projected CMEA Hard Currency Debt Levels under Selected Trade Growth Assumptions,* Washington, DC, U.S. Department of Commerce.

Machlup, Fritz (1976) *International Payments, Debts, and Gold* (2nd ed.), New York, New York University Press.

Majda, P. (1982). "L'importance du Funds Monetaire International pour la Pologne et les autres pays d'Europe Orientale," *Revue d'études comparatives Est–Ouest Revue de l'Est* 13(4):79–100.

Marer, Paul (1984) "Issues on the Participation of Centrally Planned Economies in the International Monetary Fund and the World Bank," unpublished Ms.

(1985a) *Dollar GNPs of the USSR and Eastern Europe,* Baltimore, Johns Hopkins University Press.

(1985b) "Centrally Planned Economies in the I.M.F., the World Bank and GATT, unpublished Ms.

(1985c) "Centrally Planned Economies in the International Monetary Fund and World Bank," unpublished Ms.

(1985d) "On the Hungarian Economic Reform," unpublished Ms.

Marer, Paul, and John M. Montias (eds.) (1980) *East European Integration and East-West Trade,* Bloomington, IN, Indiana University Press.

Marrese, Michael (1981) "The Bureaucratic Response to Economic Fluctuation: An Econometric Investigation of Hungarian Investment Policies," *Journal of Policy Modeling* 3(2):221-43.

(1985) "The Economic Burden on the Soviet Union," unpublished Ms.

Meltzer, Allan H. (ed.) (1983) *International Lending and the IMF: A Conference in Memory of Wilson E. Schmidt,* Washington, DC, Heritage Foundation.

Mendelsohn, M.S. (1983) *Commercial Banks and the Restructuring of Cross-Border Debt,* New York, Group of Thirty.

Nagy, Pancras J. (1981) *Country Risk: How to Assess, Quantify and Monitor It,* London, Euromoney.

Narodnoe hozjaistvo USSR, Moscow, Finansi i Statistika, various issues.

National Foreign Assessment Center (1980) *Estimating Soviet and East European Hard Currrency Debt,* Research Paper ER 80-10327, Washington, DC.

Neuberger, Egon, and Larua D' Andrea Tyson (eds.) (1980) *The Impact of International Economic Disturbances on the Soviet Union and Eastern Europe: Transmission and Response,* New York, Pergamon Press.

New York Times, various issues.

Nove, Alec (1977) *The Soviet Economic System,* London, Allen & Unwin.

Nove, Alec, Hanns-Hermann Hoehmann, and Gertrand Seidenstecher (eds.) (1982) *The East European Economies in the 1970s,* London, Butterworths.

OECD (1981) "Relationships between Comecon Countries and Western Financial Markets," *Finanacial Market Trends* 18:1-26.

(1982) *External Debt of Developing Countries 1982 Survey,* Paris.

(1984) *External Debt of Developing Countries 1983 Survey,* Paris.

(1985a) *Countertrade: Developing Country Practices,* Paris.

(1985b) "Recent Trends in the International Financial Situation of Eastern Europe," *Financial Market Trends* 30:15-45.

(1986) "East-West Financial Relations: Developments in 1985 and Future Prospects," *Financial Market Trends* 33:14-52.

OECD/BIS, *Statistics on External Indebtedness: Bank and Trade Related Non-Bank External Claims on Individual Borrowing Countries and Territories,* Paris and Basle, various issues.

Pissulla, Petra (1985) "Experiences of Hungary and Romania in the IMF and Implications for Poland," unpublished Ms.

PlanEcon (1985) *Review and Outlook,* Washington, DC, December.

PlanEcon Report, *Developments in the Economies of the Soviet Union and Eastern Europe,* Washington, DC, various issues.

Plowiec, Ursula (1984) "The Functioning of Poland's Foreign Trade: Experience and Prospects," unpublished Ms.

Portes, Richard, (1977) *West-East Capital Flows: Dependence, Interdependence, and Policy,* Stockholm, Institute for International Economics Studies, Seminar Paper No. 72.

(1980a) "Effects of the World Economic Crisis on the East European Economies," *World Economy* 3(1):13-52.

(1980b) "External Disturbances and Adjustment in Eastern Europe," in Neuberger and Tyson (1980, pp. 20-29).

(1981) *The Polish Crisis: Western Economic Policy Options,* London, Royal Institute of International Affairs.

(1983) *The Soviet Balance of Payments Constraint* (October 1982 Ms), in Twentieth Century Fund (1983, pp. 13-92).

(1984) "The Theory and Measurement of Macroeconomic Disequilibrium in Centrally Planned Economies," unpublished Ms.

Poznanski, Kazimierz (1986) "Economic Adjustment and Political Forces: Poland since 1970," *International Organization* 40(2):455-88.

Pravda, Moscow, various issues.

Rea, Graeme F. (1984) "The Role of the International Monetary Fund in Resolving the International Debt Crisis," in Campbell and Herztein (1984, pp. 35-55).

Richter, S. (1980) "Hungary's Foreign Trade with CMEA Partners in Convertible Currency," *Acta Oeconomica* 25:323-36.

Robinson, Sherman, Laura Tyson, and Leyla Woods (1984) "Conditionality and Adjustment in Socialist Economies: Hungary and Yugoslavia," unpublished Ms.

Rocznik statystyczny, Wasrsaw, various issues.

Rodriguez, Rita M., and Eugene E. Carter (1984) *International Financial Management* (3rd ed.), Englewood Cliffs, NJ, Prentice-Hall.

Romania (1983) *Economic Memorandum,* Romanian Government Document.

Rosefielde, Steven (ed.) (1981) *Romanian Welfare and the Economics of Soviet Socialism: Essays in Honor of Abram Bergson,* Cambridge, Cambridge University Press.

Sachs, Jeffrey (1982) *LDC Debt in the 1980s: Risk and Reforms,* Cambridge, MA, NBER Working Paper No. 861.

(1984) *Theoretical Issues in International Borrowing,* Princeton, NJ, Princeton University Press.

Sachs, Jeffrey, and Daniel Cohen (1982) *LDC Borrowing with Default Risk,* Cambridge, MA, NBER Working Paper No. 925.

Scaba, Laslo (1984) "The Role of CMEA in the World Economy," *ACES Bulletin* 2/3:1-29.

Schroeder, Klaus. (1983a) "Zur gegenwaertigen Problematik der Finanzbeziehungen zwischen Ost und West," *Osteuropa-Wirtschaft* 28(1):42-51.

(1983b) *Die Umschuldungen mit den Laendern des RGW, Ursachen, Ziele, Modalitaeten,* Ebenhausen (Germany), Stiftung Wissenschaft und Politik.

(1984) *Zu den Folgen eines Kreditembargos gegenueber Osteuropa,* Ebenhausen (Germany), Stiftung Wissenschaft und Politik.

Shmeljov, N. (1984) "Krediti i politika," *Mezdunarodnaja Zizn* (Moscow) 3:82–91.

Sofia, A Zuheir (1981) "Rationalizing Country Risk Ratios," in Ensor (1981, pp. 49–68).

Soldaczuk, Josef (1985) *Poland's Economic Development Strategy for the Second Half of Eigthies and Her Relations with Western Countries,* Warsaw, Institut Koniunktur i Cen Handlu Zagranicznego.

Stoilov, S. (1984) "Problema vneshneekonomicheskoi sbalansirovannosti v stranah SEV," *Serija Ekonomicheskaja, Izvestija Akademii Nauk SSSR,* 6:105–118.

Tiraspolsky, Anita (1984) "An Evaluation of Gains and Losses in Intra-CMEA Trade: Terms of Trade from 1970 to 1982," *Soviet and Eastern European Foreign Trade* 20(4):32–62.

Tokyo Financial Review 9(8), August 1984.

Twentieth Century Fund (1983) *Deficits and Détente: Report of an International Conference on the Balance of Trade in the Comecon Countries,* New York.

Tyson, Laura, D'Andrea, and Peter B. Kenen (1980), "The International Transmission of Disturbances: A Framework for Comparative Analysis," in Neuberger and Tyson (1980, pp. 33–62).

United Nations, ECE, *Economic Bulletin for Europe,* Geneva, various issues.

U.S. Congress, Joint Economic Committee (1979) *Soviet Economy in a Time of Change,* Vol. 2, Washington, DC, USGPO.

(1985) *East European Economies: Slow Growth in the 1980's,* Washington, DC, USGPO.

U.S. Senate, Committee on Governmental Affairs (1977) *The Rising Soviet and East European Debt to the West,* Washington, DC, USGPO.

van Brabant, Jozef M. (1973) *Bilateralism and Structural Bilateralism in Intra-CMEA Trade,* Rotterdam, Rotterdam University Press.

(1974) *Essays on Planning, Trade and Integration in Eastern Europe,* Rotterdam, Rotterdam University Press.

(1977) *East European Cooperation: The Role of Money and Finance,* New York, Praeger.

(1980) *Socialist Economic Integration: Aspects of Contemporary Economic Problems in Eastern Europe,* Cambridge, Cambridge University Press.

(1984) "CMEA Institutions and Policies versus Structural Adjustment: A Comment," unpublished Ms.

(1985) *Exchange Rates in Eastern Europe – Types, Derivation, Application,* Washington, DC, World Bank Staff Working Paper No. 778.

Vanous, Jan (1983) *Convertible Currency Indebtedness of the CMEA Countries, Its Implications and Outlook for 1983–87,* Brussels, NATO Economics Directorate.

Vanous, Jan, and Michael Marrese (1984) "Soviet–East European Trade Relations: Recent Patterns and Likely Future Developments," Washington, DC, unpublished Ms, prepared for the U.S. Department of State.

212   *Bibliography*

Vanous, Jan, and Charles Movit (1985) *Balance of Payments and Debt Forecast for Centrally Planned Economies,* Washington, DC, PlanEcon.

Vaubel, Roland (1983) "The Moral Hazard of IMF Lending," in Meltzer (1983, pp. 65–79).

Wall Street Journal, various issues.

Washington Post, various issues.

Watts, Nita G. (1978). *Economic Relations between East and West,* New York, MacMillan.

Weintraub, Robert E. (1983) *International Debt: Crisis and Challenge,* Fairfax, VA, George Mason University.

Weintraub, Sidney (ed.) (1977) *Modern Economic Thought,* Philadelphia, University of Pennsylvania Press.

Wiles, Peter J.D. (1962) *The Political Economy of Communism,* Cambridge, MA, Harvard University Press.

(1968a) *Communist International Economics,* Oxford, Basil Blackwell.

(1968b) "Foreign Trade of Eastern Europe: A Summary Appraisal," in Brown and Neuberger (1968, pp. 166–73).

Wharton Econometric Forecasting Associates (WEFA), *Centrally Planned Economies Current Analysis,* Washington, DC, various issues.

(1986) CPE Service, unpublished projections, April.

Wolf, Thomas, A. (1980) "On the Adjustment of Centrally Planned Economies to External Economic Disturbances," in Marer and Montias (1980, pp. 86–111).

(1984) "The Role of Exchange Rates in Economic Stabilization and Structural Adjustment in Four Planned Economies," Ms revised and published as Wolf (1985b).

(1985a) "Economic Stabilization in Planned Economies: Toward an Analytical Framework," *IMF Staff Papers* 32(1):78–128.

(1985b) "Exchange Rate Systems and Adjustment in Planned Economies," *IMF Staff Papers* 32(2):211–47.

World Bank, *World Bank Annual Report,* Washington, DC, various issues.

World Debt Tables, Washington, DC, various issues.

World Bank, Economic Analysis and Projections Department, *Central Case Projections for World Development Report 1986,* Washington, DC.

World Financial Markets, New York, Morgan Guaranty Trust Company, various issues.

Wynne, William H. (1951) *State Insolvency and Foreign Bondholders,* Vol. II, New Haven, Yale University Press.

Zloch, Iliana (1984) "Der Internationale Waehrungsfonds und die osteuropaeischen Staaten," *Wirtschaftspolitische Blaetter* (Vienna) 31(2):192–9.

(1986a) *Hard-Currency Debt Problems of Poland,* Washington, DC, World Bank, mimeo.

(1986b) *Hard-Currency Debt and the Growth of the Eastern European Economies,* Washington, DC, World Bank ED Staff Working Paper No. 12, December.

Zycie Gospodarcze, Warsaw, various issues.

Index

Page numbers followed by an "f" or "t" refer to Figures or Tables, respectively. An "n" refers to a footnote.

r